É

Memoirs of the Life and Times of the Famous Jonathan Wild

by

Captain Alexander Smith

with a new introduction
for the Garland Edition by
Malcolm J. Bosse

Garland Publishing, Inc., New York & London

1973

Bibliographical note:
*This facsimile has been made from a copy in the
British Museum
(615.a.28)*

Library of Congress Cataloging in Publication Data

Smith, Alexander, fl. 1714-1726.
   Memoirs of the life and times of the famous Jonathan
Wild.

   (Foundations of the novel)
   Facsim. reprint. Original t.p. has imprint: London,
Printed for S. Briscoe at the Bell-Savage, and sold by
J. Jackson, 1726.
   1. Wild, Jonathan, 1682?-1725.   I. Title.
II. Series.
HV6248.W48S54 1726a   364.1'092'4 [B]   76-1'/0567
ISBN 0-8240-0560-0

Introduction

Captain Alexander Smith, whose name is probably a pseudonym because his life is wholly unknown, wrote a number of collections of criminal narrative which combine journalism and legend, violence and exhortation, low life and moral purpose. The title page of Memoirs of Jonathan Wild *indicates that this record of famous thefts and murders, committed by Wild, the Hawkins brothers, Sawney Beane, Eleonor Sympson, Jack the Tinman, and others, was taken from Newgate documents by Captain Smith, whose apology for revealing such sensational accounts of crime depends upon their instructive value, "whereby those of an honest Disposition may be induc'd to imitate the Examples of the Vertuous" (p. 1).*

Smith followed the example of other popularizers of crime by naming Jonathan Wild in the title of his collection; in 1725, the year before it appeared, eight biographies of Wild had been published, among them Defoe's.[1] Smith's expedient manipulation of fact and legend is evident from the outset. Wild's face has "the very Features of a Baboon" (p. 2), and he commits incest with his mother; on the other hand, Smith wrongly reports him to have been a trunk-maker's apprentice and fails to add that Wild married before setting out for London. The real Wild abandoned his

5

INTRODUCTION

wife in the city and struck up a liaison with Mary Milliner, with whom he operated a brothel. Thereafter he organized a network of thieves, much like a corporation, and became a well-known broker of stolen goods, using his own home as an office for the recovery of lost property whose theft he himself planned. Among his more infamous exploits was his management of the arrest and execution of Joseph Blake, known as Blueskin, a companion of the celebrated Jack Sheppard, whose capture Wild also arranged. After a vain attempt at suicide in prison by an overdose of laudanum — an incident which Smith fails to record — Wild was hanged at Tyburn on 24 May 1725. Smith's account of Wild is distinguished by an unremitting portrayal of the criminal's deceitful nature and business acumen, which made him a vicious schemer rather than a glamorous highwayman of the kind so popular in crime literature of the period. Smith dispels the view of criminals as heroic, but replaces that distortion with one of his own — Wild and the others become monsters, who are scarcely credible as fictional characters.

Smith employs the same format in succeeding biographical portraits, each account beginning with the criminal's parentage. If Smith's report is essentially true, most of these eighteenth-century felons came from working-class backgrounds rather than from the desperate poor. No insight is offered, however, into the psychological basis of criminal careers. Smith implies that mere predisposition, coupled with a natural irreligiosity, forces certain individuals into a life of crime. In a plodding, relentless prose, which attends to place-names at the exclusion of motivation, the careers of highwaymen, thieves, and murderers, some of them associated with Wild and Jack Sheppard, are set forth in haphazard order, each account isolated from the rest, without an integrating summary for the collection. One sketch, reputedly written by William Hawkins about the life and capture of his highwayman brother, possesses a raw vigor and passion which, despite frequent grammatical lapses and unnecessary length, raises it above most of the other accounts. A Defoe-like attention to the telling detail lends it a tone of reality and truth:

> *So we rid off, and Robb'd the* Huntington *Coach ... taking from the Right Worshipful Sir* Edward Lawrence, *a Green Purse, in which was a Guinea and a Half, his Pocket-Book in which were Notes of great Value, his Cloak-Bag, in which were five* Holland *Shirts, two White Wastecoat, a Tye-Wig, a new Piece of Fustain, a Piece of new Blue Cloth, a Piece of new Shalloon, a Piece of new Muslin, several Neckcloths, and Turnovers, a Plad-Gown, lin'd with Red Calimanco, six Pounds of Chocolate, a Canister of Tea, and several other Things. (p. 93)*

At the end of this account Hawkins vehemently denies having informed on his brother and their companions, after which he humbly repents of his own misdeeds, for which he hopes a long confinement will sufficiently punish him, so that, "as soon as I obtain my Liberty, I will endeavour, thro' God's Grace, to procure,

INTRODUCTION

by living an honest sober Life, the Love, and Esteem, of all Mankind" (p. 98).

This traditional concept of penance and retribution threads its way through many of the accounts, but despite Smith's attempt to make repenters of some of these sinners, the impression which he leaves is of a callous, inventive, extraordinarily active and wholly treacherous group of rogues, who delighted in the sheer villainy of their escapades. Notwithstanding the crude blend of fact and fiction, these biographical sketches offer a vivid picture of the eighteenth-century underworld. If Smith's work lacks the art of Defoe's, at least it describes the slang, clothes, weaponry, and modus operandi *of English criminals, which is difficult to come by in official documents of the period.*

Malcolm J. Bosse

NOTE

[1] W. R. Irwin, The Making of Jonathan Wild *(New York, 1941), pp. 4-29.*

MEMOIRS
OF THE
LIFE and TIMES,
Of the Famous
JONATHAN WILD,
Together with the
HISTORY and LIVES,
OF
MODERN ROGUES,

Several of 'em his Acquaintance, that have been Executed before and since his Death, for the HIGH-WAY, PAD, SHOP-LIFTING, HOUSE-BREAKING, PICKING of POCKETS, and impudent ROBBING in the STREETS, and at COURT.

———— *little Villains must submit to Fate,*
While Great Ones do enjoy the World in State.

Garth's *Dispensary.*

Never before made Publick.

Writen by Capt. *Alexander Smith,* Author of the History of the High-Way-Men in Three Volumes. Royal Concubines and Gamesters.

Intermixt with strange Discoveries of several unheard of barbarous MURDERS; all taken out of the RECORDS of *NEWGATE,* continued down to the present TIMES.

Adorn'd with CUTS.

LONDON: Printed for *Sam. Briscoe,* at the *Bell-Savage* on *Ludgate-Hill.* and Sold By *J. Jackson,* in the *Pall Mall. J. Isted, J. Crokatt,* and *T. Wotton,* in *Fleet-Street.* 1726.

THE
INTRODUCTION.

Iography, or the Lives of Men, whether good, or bad, is (as I have taken Notice in One of my *Prefaces* to my former Volumes of Thieves) very profitable for diſplaying the Rewards of Vertue and Vice ; whereby thoſe of an honeſt Diſpoſition may be induc'd to imitate the Examples of the Vertuous ; and thoſe of an evil Temper may be diſpos'd not to tread in the deſtructive Steps of the Vicious, for fear Diſgrace and a ſhameful Death ſhould be the Fatal *Cataſtrophe* of ſuch preſumptive Folly.

A   This

This being the fourth biographical Piece of this Sort I have ever writ ; the firſt Deſign being purely to deteƈt the many unheard of and unparallell'd Villanies, which Rogues uſe to ruin honeſt People by; which Diſcovery may make them more cautious of preſerving their Money and Goods for the future. And to make this Work as compleat as poſſible, I have trac'd Theft from the Time that ever any Laws were made againſt it in this Kingdom; which, I think, is above Two Thouſand Years ago. Moreover, I have in this inſerted a Sort of Robberies, not taken Notice of in any of my other Three Pieces, and thoſe are Court-Robberies ; which are ſo ſtrangely ſurprizing, that the Readers will rather think it fiƈtitious than Matter of Faƈt, that ſo much ſucceſsful Theft and Villany ſhould be aƈted in the very Palaces of crowned Heads.

Now I ſhall take Notice of the chief Cauſes of ſo much private and publick Theft committed in *Great-Britain,* but moſtly in that Part of it call'd *England.*

The

The Multitude of unhappy Wretches, that every Year are put to Death for Trifles in our Great Metropolis, has long been afflicting to Men of Pity and Humanity ; and continues to give great Uneasiness to every Person, who has a Value for his Species. Many good Projects have been thought of to cure this Evil, by sapping the Foundation of it. A Society has been set up to reform our Manners ; and neither Work-Houses, or Discipline for small Crimes, have been wanting. An Act has been made against prophane Cursing and Swearing ; and many Charity Schools have been erected ; but the Event has not answer'd hitherto the good Design of those Endeavours. The City of *London* abounds as much with loose, lazy, and dishonest Poor : There is as much Mischief done by ordinary Felons ; and Executions for Theft and Burglary are as frequent as ever : Nay, it is believ'd, That *London* is more pester'd with low Villany than any other Place whatever, the Proportion of Bigness between them left unconsider'd. As there is no Effect without a Cause, so something must be the Reason of this Calamity. I have long and carefully examin'd into this Matter, and am forced to ascribe the Mischief

chief complain'd of to Two palpable Evils, diſtinct from thoſe we have in Common with other large overgrown Cities. One regards Proſecutions, the other the Treatment that is given to Malefactors after they are taken. I ſhall begin with the Firſt : I mean the Neglect of ſuch Proſecutions, occaſion'd by our ſhameful Negotations with Thieves, or their Agents, for the Recovery of *Stoln Goods*, by which, in Reality, we become Aiders and Abettors to them.

The Laws of *England* is ſo tender of Mens Lives, that whoever juſtly Proſecutes and Convicts a Perſon of a capital Crime, has nothing to anſwer for to his Conſcience, but, on the Contrary, has done a Service to his Country, without Offence to God, or the leaſt Breach of Charity to his Neighbour. But as every Body has not Strength of Mind, and Reſolution enough to perform Duties that are repugnant to his Nature, ſo, making allowances for human Frailties, I could excuſe the Backwardneſs of a meek home-bred Perſon, who ſhould complain, that to appear in open Court, and to ſpeak before a Judge, are terrible Things to him. But

But I think it unpardonable, that a Man should knowingly act against the Law, and by so doing powerfully contribute to the Increase, as well as Safety and Maintenance of Pilferers, and Robbers, from no other Principle, than a criminal Selfishness, accompany'd with an utter Disregard to the Publick ; yet, nothing is more common among us. As soon as any Thing is missing, suspected to be Stoln, the first Course we steer, is directly to the *Office* of a *Thief-Taker*. If what we want is a Trinket, either Enamell'd, or otherwise curiously Wrought if there is Painting about it, if it be a particular Ring, the Gift of a Friend ; or any Thing we esteem above the real Value, and offer more for it than Mr. *Thief* can make of it, we are look'd upon as good Chaps, and welcome to redeem it. But if it be plain Gold or Silver, we shall hardly see it again, unless we pay the full Worth of it.

Some Years ago, it is true, a Man might, for half a Piece, have fetch'd back a Snuff-Box that weigh'd twenty or thirty Shillings ; but this was in the Infancy of the Establishment. Now they are grown wiser, and calculate exactly what such a Thing

will

will melt down for ; to offer less is thought
unreasonable ; and unless Mr. *Thief-Catcher*
stands your Friend indeed, if you have it,
you will seldom save any Thing but the
Fashion. If in this Place you can hear no
Tidings of your Goods, it is counted a
Sign, that they are in the Hands of irregular Practitioners, that Steal without
Permission of the *Board*. In this Case we
immediately put an Advertisement in some
News-Paper or other, with a Promise,
that such a Reward will be given, and no
Questions ask'd. I own, that in the Printing these short Epistles, there is no manner of Harm, if we abstract the Act it
self from the Concern the Publick has in
it. The Tenor of them is rather benevo-
lent than injurious : And a Panegyrist on
the present Times, might justly say of
them, *That in no Performances the true Spirit*
of Christianity *was so conspicuous as in these :*
That they were not only free from Calumny and
ill Language, but likewise so void of Reproach,
that speaking to a Thief, we never call'd him
so in those Charitable Addresses : That in them
the very Catalogues of Injuries receiv'd, were
penn'd with as little Heat, or Resentment, as
ever Tradesman shew'd in a Bill of Parcels
directed to his best Customer : That here we
are

are so far from hating our Enemy, that we prof-
fer him a Recompence for his Trouble, if he
will condescend to let us have our own again;
and leaving all Revenge to God, to shew that we
are willing to forgive and forget; we consult,
in the most effectual Manner, the Safety of a
Person that deserves Hanging for the Wrong he
has done us. Yet, notwithstanding the kind
Constructions that may be put on these
civil Offers, they all tend to the Compounding of Felony, and are the Occasion
of a double Mischief : They invite the
Indigent and Lazy to pick Pockets, and
render the Negligent more careless than
probably they would be, was this Practice
abolish'd. A Pocket-Book, or Memoran-
dum, may be Stole from a Man that is of
vast Concern to him, and yet of no Use
but to the Owner ; if this be taken by a
regular *Thief*, a listed *Pilferer*, it is easily
recover'd for a small Reward.

I don't suppose any one so Silly, that he
would for that very Reason go to Places,
and in Companies, on Purpose to have his
Pocket pick'd ; but I can't help thinking,
that if those Things were never to be
heard of again, and the Loss irretrievable
many young Rakes, and other loose Re
probates

probates, would be under great Appre-
henfions, aud more upon their Guard, at
leaft, when they had fuch a Charge about
them, than the Generality of them now
are. And again, if nothing could be
made of Letters, Papers, and Things of
that Nature, fuch as have no known Worth,
and are not readily turn'd into Money,
the Numbers of Rogues, and Whores,
Young, and Old, that are employ'd in
the *Diving Trade*, would decreafe confider-
ably; many of them, from a Principle
of Prudence, refufing to meddle with any
Thing elfe. For as on moft of the Things
now fpoke of, no real Value can be fet,
the Punifhment would be inconfiderable,
if any, fhould the Things be found upon
them, or themfelves be taken in the Fact.
Moft Men will agree to all this, whilft un-
concern'd; but when private Intereft is
touch'd, it foon ftifles thefe Confiderations.
I fhould be a Fool, fays one, when a
Thing of Value is Stoln from me, not to
get it back, if I can for a Trifle. If I lofe
a Sword, or a Watch, I muft have another, and to fave the Fafhion of thefe
Things is confiderable; it is better to lofe
the Half than the Whole. I have nothing to do with the Thief, fays another,

if

if I have my own again, it is all I want;
what Good would it do me to have a poor
Fellow hang'd ? A third, more compaf-
fionate, will tell us, that if he knew the
Thief, he would not meddle with him,
and that he would lofe ten Times the
Value of what has been taken from him,
rather than be the Occafion of a Man's
Death. To thefe I reply, That the Legi-
flator, feem to have known, how the Generality of Men would Argue, and what
Excufes they would make; they had an
Eye on the Frailty of our Nature; confider'd that all Profecutions are trouble-
fome, and often very expenfive; that
moft Men preferr'd their own Intereft,
their Eafe, and Pleafure, to any Regard
of the Publick; and therefore they provided againft our Paffions with fo much
Severity. Compounding of Felony is not
prohibited, under a fmall Penalty, or at-
ton'd for by a little Fine; it is next to
Felony; and the moft creditable Citizen,
that is convicted of it, ceafes to be an
honeft Man.

This Rigour of the Legiflature is a full
Demonftration, that they thought it a
Crime of the moft pernicious Confequence

to

to Society; yet it is become Familiar to us; and our Remiſſneſs in ſeveral Matters, relating to Felons, is not to be parallell'd in any other civiliz'd Nation. That Rogues ſhould be induſtriouſly diſpers'd throughout the City, and Suburbs; that different Hours, and Stations, ſhould be obſerv'd among 'em; and regular Books kept of Stoln Goods; that the Superintendant in his hopeful OEconomy ſhould almoſt every Seſſions, for a Reward, Betray, Proſecute, and Hang, one or more, of theſe his Acquaintance, and at the ſame Time keep on his Correſpondence with the Survivors, whom, one after another, he ſends to their *Triangular Home*; that Magiſtrates ſhould not only know and ſee this, but likewiſe continue to make Uſe of ſuch a Perſon for an Evidence, and in a Manner own that they were beholden to him in the Adminiſtration of Juſtice; that, I ſay, all theſe Things ſhould be Facts, is ſomething very extraordinary, in the principal City, and the home Management of a Kingdom, ſo formidable Abroad, and of ſuch Moment in the Ballance of *Europe*, as that of *Great-Britain*.

The

The Mischief that one Man can do as a Thief, is a very Trifle to what he may be the Occasion of, as an Agent, or Concealer of Felons. The longer this Practice continues, the more the Number of Rogues must Daily increase; and therefore, it is high Time that regular Booking-keeping of *Stoln Goods* should cease, and that all Gangs and Knots of Thieves, should be broke and destroy'd, as much as is possible, at least, none of them suffer'd to form themselves into *Societies* that are under *Discipline*, and Act by Order of a *Superiour*. It is highly Criminal in any Man, for Lucre, to connive at a Piece of Felony, which he could have hinder'd: But a profess'd *Thief-Catcher* above all, ought to be severely punish'd, if it can be prov'd that he hath suffer'd a known Rogue to go on in his Villany, tho' but one Day, after it was in his Power to apprehend and convict him, more especially if it appears that he was a Sharer in the Profit.

Why indeed, such a one was *JONA-THAN WILD*, he has suffer'd many Rogues to go on in their Villany for
Snack

Snacks with 'em; and Hang'd feveral
who were not in his Intereft; but now
he is juftly fent out of the World for
his manifold Tranfgreffions, as you may
Read in the Hiftory of his Memoirs,
which begins this fourth Volume, and
will impartially bring to light fuch unparallell'd Pieces of Villany acted by this
Villain, that no Hiftory in any Age paft
can produce the like.

MEMOIRS

MEMOIRS
OF THE
LIFE and TIMES
Of the Famous
JONATHAN WILD, &c.

 S *Jonathan Wild*, exceeded all Mankind hitherto Born in all Manner of Villany, we give him the Preference of all other Vallains, in permitting him to lead the Van of 'em. He was Born in the Year 1682, of very mean Parents, in the Town of *Wolverhampton* in *Staffordshire.* They had several Children, but he was the

B   First

First Fruit of his Father and Mother's Nocturnal Labours, which made them very fond of him, tho' he had a Skin like a *Mulatto*, and in his Face the very Features of a *Baboon*, insomuch that some Men conjectur'd that his Mother permitted, for Change of Diet, such a Creature to make a Cuckold of his Father, who put this their first and eldest Child to a Free School, where he became so apt a Scholar, that in four or five Years Time he could make a shift to Read and Write his own Name.

Afterwards he was bound Apprentice for Seven Years, to learn the Art and Mystery of a *Trunk-Maker*, and not a *Buckle-Maker*, as some report, but he served not out his Time, according to the Tenor of his Indentures, by Two Years, when he ran away from his Master, and took a Tour to *London*, where falling into irregular Courses, and contracting Debts too large for his mean Circumstances to answer, he was in a short Time arrested, thrown into *Wood Street Compter*, and remain'd there many Months in very great Straits. Now as he was naturally addicted from the very Time of his wearing Hanging-Sleeve Coats to all Manner of Roguery, he would perpetrate any Villany to live handsomely in Idleness; and from this Propensity to Wickedness, he in the abovesaid Goal commenc'd a very strict Acquaintance with a Female Fellow-Prisoner, one *Jane Sprackling*, who had a thorough Knowledge of

of all the Ill People of the Town, and had
herself gone round the whole Circle of Vice;
and having at length both obtain'd their Enlargement, it was soon made Publick, that
they were become *One Flesh*; accordingly
they Cohabited together, and liv'd in private
Lodgings in a By-Alley in *Old-Street*, where
to support themselves by an honest Livelihood, they follow'd the Art of Coining Money, for which being closely follow'd by the
Master of the Mint, they luckily made their
Escape, but being struck with pannick Fear
at the Discovery of their Trade, they seemingly left it off, and went and kept a little
Bawdy-House in *Lutener's-Lane*, towards the
Upper-End of the East-Side of the Hundreds
of *Drury*, entertaining none but People of
the first Rank in that Neighbourhood.

The Gentlemen of the *Wipe-Lay*, *Kid-Lay*,
File-Lay, *Lob-Lay*, together with the *Locks*
and *Fences*, exercising their several Functions
with a sort of Impunity in this Part of the
Town, gave *Jonathan Wild* a very great Opportunity of detecting them, by his being so
conveniently Seated among 'em; after several
successful Adventures of that Nature, he became very terrible to the Inhabitants, who
threatned his Expulsion by Fire, and indeed
the Place soon grew too Hot to hold him, the
People being very Tenacious of their Antient
Rights and Privileges, and the Name of a
Thief-Catcher was not to be born with by
them.

Jonathan

Jonathan Wild found himfelf under a ne-
ceffity of quitting his Abode, a Piftol having
been fired at him, from a Window, as he
was coming Home late one Night, and with
his Houfhold he departed into *Water-Lane*
in *Black-Friers*. But foon after, a Quarrel
happening between him and the *Bone of his
Bone*, by whom he had Iffue feveral hopeful
Children, the Eldeft of whom is now about
Twenty Years of Age, and is at prefent with
his Grandmother at *Wolverhampton*, a promifing young Fellow as his lately deceas'd
Father, they parted very abruptly ; but *Jonathan*'s Circumftances being greatly mended,
and chiefly by her Advice and Management,
in Honour he could not but make fome Provifion for her, and not leave her entirely difti-
tute ; and tho' the Breach was irreconcileable,
he was yet prevail'd on to put her up in a
Vaulting School near *Moor-Fields*, himfelf
taking Care of the Children.

After many Intrigues, and fruitful Amours,
of the *Thief-Taker*, he became highly Enamour'd of One Mrs: *Mary Read*, a Gentlewoman of a very good Family and Account,
being one of the Daughters and Co-Heireffes
of *Jerry Read*, late of *Padington*, in the
County of *Middlefex*, Gent. deceas'd, and
who had an Acquirement in *America*, whether fhe was in all hafte going, but was prevented by her Marriage with *Jonathan Wild*.
They lived together as moft Married People
do, fometimes in Calms, and at others in
Storms,

Storms, and he was counted a midling Sort of a Husband, as she was a Wife.

He was now become very Eminent in his Profession of *Thief-Catching*, and other Rogueries, and made a confiderable Figure in the World, having a Silver mounted Sword, and a Footman at his Heels; and fcarce an Affize, or Seffions, paft but *Jonathan* flew his Man. This Succefs fet up many Rivals, and Pretenders to his Art, as *Dick Yeomans*, who Married *Mol Pines*, a notorious *Shoplifter*, and Hempen Widow: *Jewifh Moll*, a Ballad-Singer's Husband; But the moft Confiderable of his Rivals was Mr. *Hitchman*, formerly the City Marfhal, which occafion'd a Paper-War between them, Two very Satyrical Pamphlets having been Wrote againft each other; but *Jonathan* carrying all before him, he infolently caufed himfelf to be Proclaim'd in One of the *Weekly-Journals*, *THIEF-CATCHER-GENERAL* of *GREAT-BRITAIN* and *IRELAND*, as Acting by his Deputies in that Kingdom. About this Time an Accident happen'd, which gave him no fmall Reputation in his Bufinefs: The Countefs of *Godolphin* being to Vifit a Lady in *Piccadilly*, the Chairmen waiting at a neighbouring Ale-Houfe for her Ladyfhip's Return, had the Chair, with the Crimfon Velvet Seat, and Furniture of great Value ftoln, and entirely carry'd off: Application was immediately made to *Wild*, who after taking his Fee, told the Inquirers, he

would

would confider of it ; and when they came again, he infifted on a pretty handfome Donation, which being comply'd with, he order'd the Chairmen not to fail of attending the Prayers at *Lincoln's-Inn* Chapel the next Morning ; when to their no fmall Surprize, and Satisfaction , they found their Lady's Chair, exactly in the Manner as it was in when Sloln , under the Piazzas of the Chapel,

When Mrs. *Knapp*, a Widow Gentlewoman, was barbaroufly Murder'd in *Jockey-Fields*, near *Gray's-Inn*, by four Foot-Pads, as fhe was coming from *Sadler's-Wells*, in Company of her Son, and One Hundred Pounds being offer'd as a Reward for Difcovery of the Murderers, befides the Forty Pounds that is allow'd by Act of Parliament for apprehending and convicting a Highwayman, *Ifaac Ragg*, One of the bloody Gang, making himfelf an Evidence againft his Comrades *White*, *Thurland*, and *Chapman*, who were concern'd with him in this Fact, he was entituled to the faid Reward of One hundred and Sixty Pounds, but was chous'd out of it by *Jonathan Wild*, and Tranfported into the Bargain. Not long after this, complaint was made of one *Arnold Powell*, a notorious Houfe-Breaker, committing great Depredations in the Town : Being afterwards committed to *Newgate*, honeft *Jonathan* paid him a Vifit, and gave him to underftand he expected a Prefent from him by way of Hufh-Money ;

Money ; but *Powell* being deaf to his Hints, as thinking he could do him neither Good nor Harm : Mr. *Thief-Catcher* found out that he broke open the House of Mr. *Eaftlick* a Glafs-Maker at *Fleet-Ditch,* and robb'd him ; whereupon the next Seffions an Indict- ment was found for this Burglary and Felony, and the Profecution was left to *Wild* to manage : Now *Powell's* obdurate Heart began to relent, and he foon ftruck up a Peace with *Jonathan,* who had his own Terms. *Jonathan* finding he had already made a fad Havock and Wafte among his Brethren, and that *Powell* being a very ufeful Hand, it would be carrying the Jeft too far to cut him Off; he therefore retracted his Zeal, and thought of an Expedient to work his Deliverance, which he had almoft Effected, by villainoufly leading Mr. *Eaftlick* fo much in the Dark, that his Recognizances had like to have been eftreated, and the next Day there was to have been an Order of Court for the Prifo- ner's Enlargement : But in the mean Time, this dark Tranfaction coming to the Profecu- tor's Knowledge, he apply'd himfelf to Sir *William Thompfon,* the Recorder of *Lon- don,* who call'd upon *Wild* in Court, and after a fevere Reprimand for ftifling the Pro- fecution againft fo notorious an Offender, order'd him to ftand committed to *Newgate*; and *Arnold Powell* was decently Hang'd.

Two old Women once came to *Jonathan Wild's* House, which was at the Sign of King

Charles

Charles the Firſt's Head in the *Great Old-Baily*, telling him they were Lodgers in the Houſe of a wealthy Cane-Chair-Maker in *Worm-wood-Street*, near the *South-Sea* Houſe, which might be very eaſily robb'd by a good Hand, to whom they would give their beſt Aſſi-ſtance, provided they had a Moiety of the Booty : *Wild*, how well ſoever he might ap-prove of the Propoſal, thought it not advi-ſeable to be an Adventurer in ſuch an Enter-prize, the Application being ſo Odd, and the Women Strangers, without Recommenda-tions, or proper Credentials from any of the Buſineſs, he very diſcreetly made a Merit of the Matter, by Seizing them ; they were committed to *Newgate*, and at the enſuing Seſſions convicted of the Miſdemeanor, and for it Fined and Impriſon'd. Thus *Wild* went on ſucceſsfully in Diſcoveries, which drew ſuch a vaſt Reſort of People of all Ranks and Degrees to his Houſe, that it was become a Queſtion, and Matter of Diſpute in the Town, whether the Lord *High-Chancellor*, or the *Thief-Taker*, had the largeſt Levee.

About this Time *Mary Read*, his ſecond Wife, dying without Iſſue, he quickly was taken with the Charms of one Mrs. *Mary Dean*, the Relict of *Jack*, alias *Scul Dean*, the Son of a Cabinet-Maker by *Little Old-Baily*, who was executed at *Tybourn*, after he had one Child by her : Her Aunt Mrs. *Spurling*, who keeps the Tap-Houſe in *New-gate*, a Woman in very good Circumſtances, gave

gave all the Oppofition fhe was capable of to the
Match, but their Loves being reciprocal, in
fpite of all the Difturbance of the Aunt, the
Treaty went on, and upon the 13th Day
of *February*, 1718-19, the Day as *Prior*, *Vic-
kars*, and *Parquot*, fuffer'd at *Tybourn*, for
Robbing Mr. *Squire*, One of his Majefty's
Meffengers, on the Highway ; the Marriage
was Solemniz'd according to the Rites and
Ceremonies of the Church of *England*, at St.
Pancras Church, a little without *London.* The
Ordinary of *Newgate*, fo call'd from being an
ordinary Man indeed, and *Dick Arnold* the
Hangman, appearing at *Tybourn* with Gloves and
Favours, furpriz'd the Spectators, and it was
concluded among the Mob, that One of the
Malefactor was (according to the Tradition
of the Town) to be Married to fome tender
Hearted Virgin under the Gallows : But the
Vulgar continued not long under this Miftake,
for in the Afternoon, it was known all over
the Town, that *Wild* and Madam *Dean* had
that very Morning, enter'd into the State of
Matrimony together : Favours and Gloves,
were alfo plentifully diftributed to the Turn-
Keys, and their Affiftants, of the feveral Goals
in the Cities and Liberties of *London* and
Weftminfter, and Borough of *Southwark* ;
but the Bridegroom's Benevolence was extended in a very particular Manner to *Newgate*,
where divers Anchors of Brandy were given
to be made into Punch : The Wedding was
kept for feveral Days fucceffively, with the

utmoft

utmoſt Splender and Magnificence at *Wild*'s House, ſituated as above mentioned ; but ſeveral Months paſſing without affording the leaſt Proſpect of Iſſue by this Marriage, the *Phyſicians* who were acquainted with the *Fatigue* and *Breaches* his *Conſtitution* had undergone, gave him but little Encouragement to hope for any.

The Earl of *Burlington*, and the Lord *Bruce* being robb'd in *Richmond-Lane*, of a Gold Watch, and a Blue Saphyr Ring of great Value, beſides Money, *Wild*, whether by Divination, or what other Means we will not pretend to determine, knew the Rogues, and being inform'd of the Haunts of *James Wright*, One of the Perſons concern'd in the Fact, he apprehended him at the Queen's-Head Tavern on *Tower-Hill*, brought him to *Newgate*, and being convicted of other Robberies in *Middleſex*, he was executed at *Tybourn* ; which proved a beneficial Jobb to *Jonathan*, who beſides the Lord *Bruce*'s Gold Watch, that was found in *Wright*'s Pocket, had the whole Reward, as given by Act of Parliament, for the Apprehending and Convicting of a Highwayman.

A Warrant being once iſſued by the Lord *Chief-Juſtice* of the *King's-Bench*, for apprehending a Highwayman, who greatly infeſted the County of *Oxford*, this *Wild* was ſent down to execute it : The *Thief*, and *Thief-Catcher* met very odly on the Road, and exchang'd a Piſtol Ball, or Two, at each other ; the Former dropt
from

from his Horſe, and languiſh'd of his Wounds
'till next Morning, and then died ; his ſurviving Relations being People of Fortune and
Diſtinction, and who had been much Scanda-
liz'd by his evil Courſes, were glad to hear
that no worſe Miſchance had befallen him :
Wild gave Security to anſwer the Conſequence
at the Aſſizes ; but there being no Proſecu-
tion, he return'd to *London* in great Triumph,
loaden with the Glories of this Atchieve-
ment.

It is admirable to me, how *Jonathan Wild*
came to be ſo bold, as to fight a ſingle Man,
for I have often ſeen him Kikt, Buffeted, and
Pull'd by the Noſe, without reſenting it in
the leaſt ; and once one *Jack*, Nick Nam'd
the *Tinman*, from his having been an Apprentice to that Trade, being put into an Information for Robbing on the Highway, *Jonathan*
met him in *Fleet-Street*, and telling him the
News, they went into the Caſtle-Tavern,
and in a private Room up one Pair of Stairs,
Mr. *Thief-Taker* talks the Matter over to him,
with a great many *Items* of his wanting ſome
Gold to let him make his Eſcape : Quoth *Jack*,
I always took you for my Friend *Jonathan*,
and ſhould be very Ungrateful if I did not
Acknowledge your extraordinary Favours; here
Drawer, bring us t'other Bottle of *Champaigne*,
which was accordingly brought in. But replies *Jonathan*, I don't want to put you to
any Charges in Treating me, come, come
the ready Rhino, it is that I muſt live by, for

Money

Money is the Life of all Bufinefs. Qooth *Jack*,
I vow *Jonathan* you could not have met me
in a worfe Time, for if I have one Farthing
about me at prefent, I am the arranteft Rogue
that ever fpoke, therefore I doubt not but
your unknown Generofity will readily vouch-
fafe to condefcend, not only to pay the Reckoning, which is only Ten Shillings, but alfo
lend me a Guinea, for which I have a very
great Occafion at this Time: Says *Jonathan*,
of all the Rogues I have had to do with, I
never faw your Fellow before ; what pay the
Reckoning, and lend you Money out of my
Pocket too, at a Time when your Life lies in
my Hands ? No, no, this will never do, and
therefore Confcience obliges me to take you
Prifoner, in order to bring you to Juftice. *Jack*
then pulling a Brace of Piftols out of his
Pocket, and prefenting them to *Jonathan*'s
Head and Breaft, fwore by more Oaths than
were ever vented at one Time among the
lofing Gamefters at the *Groom-Porter's*, that
he would certainly Shoot him dead on the
Spot, if he was prefently Hang'd for it, unlefs
he paid the Reckoning, and lent him a Guinea
to boot ; cry not out for Affiftance, for before any can come I'll certainly Difpatch you :
Jonathan being here brought to a *Ne plus ultra*,
was obliged to capitulate upon *Jack*'s Articles,
who went ftrait about his Bufinefs, leaving
him fwearing, curfing, and vowing Revenge,
if ever he catch'd him again ; but he faved
him that Trouble, for he was taken by others,
who

who Profecuted and Hanged him, after he was cur'd of the Wounds he receiv'd, in making a vigorous Refiftance, when the Conftable and others went to apprehend him at his Lodgings in *Dirty-Lane* by *Long-Acre*.

Neverthelefs, *Jonathan* continued Bufinefs at his Office in Town, doing fome Good, but more Evil, driving a wonderful Trade in Pocket-Books, Watches, Plate, Linnen, and other Things; and Advertifements were daily cram'd into the Publick News-Papers, calling loudly out for all Sorts of ftray'd Valuables, to be brought into Mr. *Jonathan Wild's* in the *Old-Baily*, upon Promife of great Rewards, and no Queftions. Tho' a Claufe was inferted in a late Act of Parliament, for paying a Reward of forty Pounds, to any Perfon, or Perfons, who fhould Convict any One of taking Money, or Reward, of Perfons, under Pretence of helping them to ftoln Goods; yet *Wild* went ftill on in Defiance of all Laws, and fatal was it to one *John James*, who threatened to put the above-mentioned Act in Execution againft him. *John James* was a private Dealer on the Highway, always doing Bufinefs by himfelf; but *Wild* would fuffer him no longer, vows Revenge, and at laft Apprehending him, carried him before a Magiftrate, who committed him to *Newgate*, and at the Seffions enfuing, being Convicted upon feveral Indictments, fuffered Death at *Tybourn*.

It

It has been reported, that *Wild* had his Chaplain, Groom of the Chambers, Gentleman of the Horfe, Valets, and others to attend him, and lived after the Manner of the Nobility, his Table was very Splendid, he feldom Dining under five Difhes; the Reverfions whereof were generally beftow'd on the Common Side Felons in *Newgate*. *Quilt Arnold*, who was lately his Fellow-Prifoner, ferved him in Quality of Clerk of the Northern Roads, as *Abraham Mendez* a *Jew*, did in that of the Weftern Road, and had the Character of being fober and well behaved Men, as partly appears by the Depofition of their Mafter, in *October* Seffions 1723, when *Arnold* being Indicted for Entering the Houfe of Mr. *Bellamy*, and ftealing a Pair of Silver Buckles, then *Wild* teftified for his Man, that he had Command to fearch for a Perfon who had forg'd a Note of Nine Guineas in his, *Wild's* Name; and that he had been affifting with him in the Apprehending an hundred and fifty Perfons, the greater Number of which had been Profecuted according to Law; *Arnold* was acquitted, but *Wild* feverely reprimanded by the late Lord Chief Juftice *Prat*, for Countenancing Perfons to enter Houfes by no other Authority than his Orders.

One Mr. *Wafey*, a Surgeon, paffing through *Lincoln's Inn-Fields* at Midnight, was robb'd of a Gold Watch, a Twezer-Cafe, a Sword, and Money: The next Day *Wafey* waited on

Wild,

Wild, and acquainted him with his Misfortune, who after asking him sundry Questions, told him he should be glad to see him again in two or three Days, by which Time he hoped he should be able to give him some Account of the Robbers, who were *Peter Levee*, *Edward Frazier*, and *John Allen*; and shortly *Wasey* had his Watch brought him again by a Porter, he paying five Guineas as a Reward for the Care that had been taken of it; but the last of the abovesaid Persons was Hang'd for it, and *Wild* soon after receiv'd the forty Pounds due according to Law.

About the same Time *Richard Evans*, *William Elisha*, and *Richard Woodman*, were executed at *Kingston* upon *Thames*, *Push*, and *Field*, Two of *Wild's* Agents, being Evidences against them : Also at this same Assizes in *Sarry*, *Jonathan* caus'd a Prosecution to be commenced against one *Richard Gretoria*, a Victualler, at the Sign of the *Helmet* in *Red-Cross-Street* in *Southwark*, for Buying stoln Goods, especially a Gold Watch. 'Tis true, the Fellow was Rogue enough, as having been twice condemn'd for Robberies, and often Whipt at the Cart's Tail for *Petit Lerceny* ; and undoubtedly it had gone hard for his Life this Time, but *Jonathan Wild*, to agravate his Offences, giving him as odious a Character in Court as possibly could be, the Jury look'd upon *Wild* to be such a most vile unaccountable Rogue, that not believing one Word he said, tho' upon Oath, the Prisoner was acquitted.   But

But now *Jonathan Wild* having ran his most wicked Race, on *Monday* the 15th of *Feb.* 1724-5, he together with his Man *Quilt Arnold*, was apprehended at his House in the *Old-Baily*, by Mr. *Thomas Jones*, High-Constable of *Holbourn* Division, and carried before Sir *John Fryer*, Knt. and Bart. who sate up in his Bed, being Indispos'd, to examine the Prisoners, who being charg'd upon Oath with Aiding and Assisting one *Roger Johnson*, a notorious Highwayman, to make his Escape from a Constable at *Bow* near *Stratford*, in *Middlesex*, they were committed to *Newgate* for Felony : The Sessions beginning in a few Days after at *Justice-Hall* in the *Old-Baily*, *Wild* enter'd his Prayer according to custom, to be either Bail'd, Try'd, or Discharg'd ; and the last Day of Sessions, he moved by his Council to be admitted to Bail, as there had been no Proceedings against him : But an Affidavit of Mr. *Jones* aforesaid, being read in Court, importing that there were two Persons who had offer'd to charge *Wild* with Crimes of a Capital Nature, and a Warrant of Detainder sign'd by Twelve of his Majesty's Justices of the Peace for the County of *Middlesex*, and Liberty of *Westminster*, peremptorily charging him with being an Aider, Abettor, and Encourager of Felons, and other wicked Persons, being produced to the Court, he was order'd to remain in *Newgate* 'till the next Sessions.

About

About this Time, *Thomas Butler*, who had been formerly convicted for Robbing a Person at the *Feathers* Tavern in *Cheapside*, and who had been again lately taken up in *London*, and committed to *Newgate*, for privately Stealing about fifty Guineas from a Widow Goldsmith at *Winchester*, obtain'd his Majesty's most gracious Pardon for the last Offence, and gave Bail on *Saturdy* the 27th of *February* 1724-5, to plead to the same. This *Butler* made a long Information against *Wild*, charging him, among many other Crimes, with having seen in his Custody a Pocket-Book, which had been Stolen from a Corn-Chandler in *Gilt-Spur-Street*, and that *Wild* did commit the same to the Flames: So that these, and other Matters, being laid to his Charge when he came upon his Tryal, the Jury found him Guilty of the Indictment, and he was justly Condemn'd for the same.

Now *Jonathan Wild* being under Sentence of Death, his Condemnation put him upon the serious Thoughts of putting his House in Order, before his approaching Death, and to think often on this wholsome Saying of the Apostle, *Eat and Drink to Day, for to Morrow you shall Die.* Therefore knowing his Time was but short in this World, he improv'd it to the best Advantage, in Eating, Drinking, Swearing, Cursing, and Talking to his Visitants from Morning 'till Night ; whilst he was in the condemn'd Hold, he was (as well he might be) very Restless, and his Thoughts

fo very perplex'd, that he gave little or no
Attention to the condemn'd Sermon, that
the Pur-blind *Ordinary* preach'd before him,
to put him in Mind of his latter End : The
few Minutes he had to ftay upon Earth were
folely employ'd in contriving to get a Reprieve, but his very Name ftinking in the
Noftrils of all good Men, he could make no
Intereft at Court. So at laft the Day
coming that the under Sheriff and his Officers
went and demanded his Body in Order for
Execution, a Receipt being given for the
fame to the Keepers of *Newgate*, it was deliver'd up to them on *Monday* the 24th of
May, 1725.

Then *Jonathan* being decently feated in a
Cart, he was convey'd from *Newgate* to *Tybourn*, amidft innumerable Spectators, who
went to fee the Laft of him, who was abhor'd by the better Sort, loath'd by the middle People, and defpis'd by the Mob, who fo
much infulted him as he rid, that they pelted
him with Stones and Dirt all the Way, broke
his Head in feveral Places, and revil'd him
with the moft opprobious Language, for having Sold more human Blood at forty Pounds
per Head, than would fill the Canal in St.
James's Park. When he was arriv'd at the
Place of Execution, being dos'd beforehand
with Liquors, he made no Speech, nor did
he trouble himfelf to make any Confeffion of
his Sins to Mr. *Ordinary*, becaufe he could
not think of 'em all ; but requefted the
Hangman

Hangman to adorn his Neck with the Halter, place the Knot exactly under the left Ear, and to put him out of his Pain as soon as he could; then the Cart drawing away, he was, to the universal Joy of all that beheld his last Exit, turn'd off, and in the twinkling of an Eye, sent out of this World into another, where how he will Fare I will not pretend to judge; but shall present the Readers with the following Hymn to *Tybourn*, that was compos'd by some prime Wits, a little after the fatal *Catastrophe* which sent him out of the Land of the Living.

A I L! rev'rend Tripos, *tripple Tree*
            (of State,
Who arbitrates the grand Decrees of
            (Fate,
And is the chief Defender of the Laws;
Three Kingdoms joyfully give thee Applause;
And universal Praises to thee Sing,
Since Jonathan *upon thy Beams did Swing.*
Tybourn! *my Muse, thy most immortal Fame,*
In as immortal Verse shall soon Proclaim;
And that dear Halter *also Consecrate,*
Which did his Exit *in thy Presence date:*
For that, and you (I say) together hurl'd
The Rogue *of* Rogues, *into another World.*
Yet famous Arnold! *must not be forgot,*
In Newgate *Annals, who did tye the Knot,*
That precious Knot! which made the precious
            (Noose,
When Jonathan, *for haste, dy'd in his Shoes.*
                        Oh!

Oh! Tybourn, *Rogues, our Laws can never*
From all their Vices, quickly you reclaim; (claim
Men, who do once Acquaintance scrape with thee,
Will seldom (to displease you) vicious be;
Who'd then refuse to smell thy fragrant Wood,
When it will make a wicked Person good?
But yet too many Goodness do forsake,
Before they will this wholsome Tryal make.
Thy Limbs, which perpendicularly stand,
Are often the Supporters of the Land;
You safely prop the feeble State of Thieves;
A Bankrupt, who his Creditors deceives,
With Oath that's false; all Traytors you sustain;
And Murderers, to put 'em out of Pain:
Wives doubly Married for thy Succour fly;
All in thy Bosom quietly may lie:
And tho' a Coyner's Money shou'd be Brass,
Yet currently it doth at Tybourn pass.
    Great Tybourn *! thy most antient lofty Trine*
With Splendor o'er our Horizon does shine,
And from the British, *to the furthest Shore,*
Most celebrated Rogues thy Name adore:
The Church of Rome *her Orisons do pay*
To thee, and for thy future Greatness pray;
Since most of her prime Saints by you were bred,
To dye the Romish *Calendar with Red:*
For which Posterity unborn will see,
In Pilgrimage, thy sanctified Tree.
    Some Men pretend it is a foul Disgrace,
That Jonathan, *or any of his Race,*
Shou'd in thy pleasant sweet Embraces die,
Who was the very Source of Villany;

                              The

The very Name of most detested Wild,
Hath all thy Fame, and pristine Worth defil'd;
For Jonathan, *to meet his Shroud and Urn,*
Some Country Gallows might have serv'd his Turn;
Where little, petty, scoundrel Rogues depart
The World, upon a Ladder, or a Cart:
But these Reflections thy best Friends suppose,
Proceed from the Antipathy of Foes,
Who grudge to live in Unity and Love
With thee, who of a Rogue does well approve?
All Button's *Wits, and other Men of Sence,*
Unanimously join in thy Defence,
And say, which we acknowledge to be true,
Men must be Wild *before they come to you:*
Who do the Poor as well as Rich relieve;
And kindly all, alive, or dead receive:
Witness Old Nol, *and* Bradshaw *deifi'd,*
By each Blood-Thirsty, barb'rous Regicide.

Were all our Trees to bear such Fruit as you,
Or if thou only hadst but what's thy Due,
How blest wou'd most ingrateful England *be!*
That strives to cheat thee of thy lawful Fee.
The Cause of Justice bravely you'd maintain,
And shew she shou'd not hold her Sword in Vain;
For Men as strong as Sampson *you can tame,*
Or taller than Goliah, *bring to shame.*
But when such Courtiers *who their Taylors bite,*
Such knavish Lawyers *who their Clients slight;*
Stock-Jobbers, South-Sea *Bubles,* Tallymen,
Pawn-Brokers, Bailiffs, *who to Iron Den*
Their Fellow Creatures hurry, where they die
Between the frightful Scenes of Poverty,

And

And that Briſtolian *Knave, whoſe hanging Looks*
Men ſeeing, without turning o'er the Books
He ſells, from truſting him they do refrain,
For fear the cheating Pimp ſhou'd break again;
When theſe (I ſay once more) and you do meet,
Thy Glory's abſelutely then compleat.
But all in Time, long Look will come at laſt,
Before the Day of Judgment's here, and paſt.
Thy Fame is then at its Meridian Height,
On all Records 'till then you will be bright;
For 'twas by you that Wild *moſt juſtly fell,*
And fled into his native Orb of H-ll.

Never did any Malefactor die ſo much un-
pitied as this Fellow; his untimely End was
unlamented by all; every Body rejoyced to
ſee him dancing between Heaven and Earth,
as unworthy of either; and when his deteſtable
Carcaſs was cut down, ſo outragious were
the Rabble, that they had certainly *De-Witted*
it, or torn him to peices, but that it was by
a Stratagem of his Widow brought away by
two Surgeons, who pretended they had an
Order to fetch his Body to their Hall, to
Anatomize it; which upon this Account was
deliever'd to them, and they again deliever'd
it to them that were to Inter it; for truly
Jonathan's Carcaſs was not worth ſuch an
Operation, for he was ſo contaminated with
Venereal Performances with lewd Women,
that it was perfectly Rotten long before he
died; therefore to keep the much decay'd
Tenement in Repair, he was a conſtant
                                             Cuſtomer

Cuſtomer to an eminent Surgeon living not far from *Northumberland-Court* in the *Strand*. Where he was Buried we cannot learn, for the Funeral Obſequies were privately perform'd, leaſt the Mob knowing where he lies, they ſhould go and pull him Head and Shoulders out of his Grave. However, we have thought it fit to commemorate him with the following Elegy.

 H A T mournful Muſe *muſt aid me*
                            (in my Verſe,
          To pin on Jonathan's *dark ſable*
                            (Hearſe?
I know in Lethe *I muſt dip my Pen,*
To write againſt the very worſt of Men;
For none (I think) can write of him ſo well,
But what is brought from the Confines of Hell.
Each Jaylor, Strumpet, Pyrate, Bully, Thief,
Gameſter, old Bawd, *in Tears diſplay your Grief,*
But ye that can't cry, yet wou'd ſeem to weep,
Your Handkerchiefs in holy Water ſteep;
Then Snot and Snivel throw about his Grave,
And wiſh Old-Nick *may Soul and Body have.*
How happy is his unlamenting Wife!
Nothing but lucky Stars ſmile on her Life;
Some Planet has contrived, in a Trice,
To make poor Moll *a hempen Widow twice:*
For this good Fortune Women Molly *hate,*
And think their Husbands deal with Death and
But daily live in joyful Hopes, to be (Fate;
Widow'd like her at the ſame Triple-Tree.
                                      Ob!

Oh ! Jonathan, *of thee I'll write no more,*
No more Parnaſſus *will exhauſt its Store ;*
But Jonathan, *art thou ſincerely Dead ?*
Yes, yes, I ſee ; and to the D---l *Fled.*

I ſhall here take Notice, that every Execution-Day, *Jonathan* being mounted on Horſe-
Back, he would in great Triumph ride a little
before the Criminals that were going to die,
and at ſome Taverns in the Way call for
half a Pint of Wine, telling the People about
him, with the greateſt Exultation, and Joy
imaginable, that ſome of his Children were
coming, they were juſt behind : So when he
went deſervedly to be hang'd, ſeveral Thieves
went a little before the Cart, telling People,
their Father was coming, he's juſt behind.
'Tis ſaid he made a Will before he departed
this mortal Life, wherein he left nothing to
an own Brother of his, who at preſent lives
pretty Handſom and Comfortably, upon the
Reverſion of ſome Whores living in the de-
ſolate *Mint* in *Southwark* ; but to his Son, who
is at Man's Eſtate, and whom he had by
his firſt Venture, he bequeath'd one hundred
Pounds, at which the Orphan is ſo overjoy'd,
that he wiſh'd his Father had been hang'd
Seven and Seven Years ago ; and to his
Widow he left all the Reſt of his Subſtance ;
at whoſe Requeſt ſhe deſir'd the following
Epitaph to be wrote, which ſhe will cut on
a Stone, and have laid over the Deceaſed's
Grave, when ſhe thinks the Mob will be ſo far
pacified as to let him lie at Reſt.   *Here*

ERE Jonathan, *for want of Breath,*
Lies in the Folds of Icy Death;
The Catcher's Catch'd, *we plainly see,*
In that same Trap *he kept, to be*
His Bank, *which him and* Moll *supply'd*
With Gold *enough, before he dy'd.*
But if it's ask'd, why he's confin'd
So close, who has to Death *been kind ?*
We only can reply but this,
B'ing Wild, *if* Loose, *he'd do amiss.*

* * *

ARNOLD POWELL, *a Housebreaker.*

THIS Criminal, and the Four which suc-
cessively follow, we have thought fit to
link together, because they being very inti-
mate with *Jonathan Wild,* many Passages
will occur relating to the said *Thief-Takers's*
Life and Conversation : Therefore you must
understand, that *Arnold Powell* was born of
very poor and mean Parents, in *Rosemary-*
Lane, famous for the celebrated *Rag-Fair,*
that is continually kept there, excepting upon *Sundays,* and some particular *Holy-Days.*
Under such stress of Poverty was his Father,
that being not able to give this their Son any
Learning, nor a Trade, his want of both
these Advantages which might have brought him
C   to

to have got his Bread honeſtly, ſoon corrupted his Manners, for he very early took to Pilfering, and in his very juvenile Years could not leave it off, tho' he had undergone the Diſcipline that is uſed in *Bridewell*, with Perſons of his Rank and Quality ; and twice underwent the Correction of being well flaug'd at the Cart's Tail.

He was now rather harden'd in, than terrified from Villany, therefore it ſignified no more to give him good Council, than to ſing Pſalms to a dead Horſe : Ill Courſes he ſtill purſu'd, 'till he was once burnt in the Hand, which looking upon to be rather an Honour, than a Diſgrace, he was obſtinately bent to tempt his Fate to the Uttermoſt, and ſo became a moſt notorious Houſebreaker, committing great Depredations in and about *London*, *Weſtminſter*, and *Southwark*.

At laſt this Villain being ſeiz'd near *Golden-Square* in attempting to break a Houſe in the Night Time, after wounding two Watch-Men with a Pen-Knife, was committed to *Newgate*. Now *Jonathan Wild* hearing this Robber was poſſeſs'd of a round Sum of ready *Rhino*, gave him to underſtand he expected a Pair of Gloves, by way of *Huſh*, or if it pleas'd *God to take him to himſelf*, to be remember'd in his laſt Will and Teſtament; but *Powell*, deaf to theſe Hints, defy'd the *Thief-Taker*, and all his Works, as believing it was not in his Power to do him either Harm, or Good.

Hereupon

Hereupon *Wild* grew very affiduous to find out the Perfons whom he had robbed, and foon found out a Fact that would foon make him exchange this Life for a Better, or a Worfe. Mr. *Eaftlick,* a Glafs-Maker at *Fleet-Ditch,* was the Perfon whofe Houfe he had broke open, and robb'd, and at the next Seffions an Indictment was found for this Burglary and Felony: Mr *Eaftlick* altogether unacquainted with Affairs of this Nature, leaves the Profecution to be manag'd by *Jonathan:* Now *Powell's* obdurate Heart, by this Time, began to relent, and he foon ftruck up a Peace with *Jonathan,* who had his own Terms: Alfo *Jonathan* finding he had already made a fad Havock and Wafte among the *Brethren,* and that *Powell* being a very ufeful Hand, it would be carrying the Jeft too far to cut him off; he therefore retracted his Zeal, and thought of an Expedient to work his Deliverance. The Seffions came on at the *Old-Baily,* and Mr. *Eaftlick* came with his Witneffes to proceed againft the Prifoner; *Wild* told them the Court would be taken up all the firft and fecond Days with other Tryals, and orders them to wait at an Alehoufe in the *Old-Baily,* keeping one of his Agents to ply them well with Liquor.

In the mean Time *Wild* manages *Powell* to be fet to the Bar and Arraign'd, the Witneffes were call'd Time after Time; *Wild* being in Court, declar'd he knew not what was become of them; and after the Prifoner's being

fet

set several Times to the Bar in that Manner, and the Witnesses call'd, and none appearing, the Lord Chief Baron *Bury* declar'd him acquitted, and order'd the Prosecutor's Recognizances to be estreated ; and the next Day there was to have been an Order of Court for the Prisoner's Enlargement : But in the mean Time, this dark Transaction coming to the Prosecutor's Knowledge, he the next Morning apply'd himself to Sir *William Thompson*, the Recorder of *London*, who call'd upon *Wild* in Court, and after a severe Reprimand for stifling the Prosecution against so notorious an Offender, order'd him to stand committed to *Newgate* ; but Mr. *Eastlick*, not willing to proceed against him, the Matter dropt : However, *Arnold Powell* was continu'd 'till the next Sessions, when he endeavour'd to elude his Tryal by putting himself into a Salivation ; but that not availing him, he was Try'd, Convicted, and Executed at *Tybourn* for Mr. *Eastlick's* Robbery.

JAMES PARQUOT, *a Highwayman.*

J Ames Parquot, was born of good and honest Parents, near the *Pont Neuf*, or new *Bridge* in *Paris*, but they being *Hugonots*, were forced to leave that Kingdom, for fear of the great Persecution that was rais'd against them

them by the late King of *France*, *Lewis* the Fourteenth, and came for *England:* His Father was a Jeweller by Trade, and brought up him to the same Occupation ; but being of a light, wavering, inconstant Disposition, he could not heartily be settled to any Business, which brought him to an unaccountable habit of Idleness ; to support which, he took to ill Courses, and bad Company, who soon enveigled him to those Vices, which at last brought him to his Ruin.

His first Step to Destruction was picking Pockets, and to become an expert Diver, he got into the Acquaintance of *Roger Johnson*, who was the Downfal of *Jonathan Wild*, as *Jonathan Wild* had been the Downfal of others. This *Roger Johnson*, who is now in *Holland*, to avoid the Justice of his Country, is the Son of a Broker, formerly living in *Peter-Street* by *Clare-Market*, but when he swore his Mother to be a Coiner, for which she was committed to *Newgate*, and there died before she came to a Tryal, the Father left off his Business, and went no Body knows where, for fear his Son should also have sent him thither to bear her Company. After this he Married (or else they took one another's Words, as most of this Sort of Cattle do) the Carrot-Pated Daughter of old Mrs. *Whittle*, living in one of *Dunbar*'s Houses, in *White-Horse*-Yard, in *Drury-Lane*; which Mrs. *Whittle* was the greatest *Fence*, or *Lock* of her Time, for she has bought as much

stoln

ftoln Goods as will fill a firft Rate Man of
War, or Two, to the great and unexpreffible
Damage of thofe honeft People who unhap-
pily loft them.

Now *Roger Johnfon* (to whom the abovefaid
Parquot became a Pupil in Iniquity) being the
beft Pick-Pocket *England* ever could brag of,
he went at fuch a flaunting Rate in fine and
rich Apparel, that fcarce any Perfon of Quality exceeded him; and going thus richly
dreft, he committed many Villanies with the
lefs Sufpicion. In this fine Equipage he made
fad Havock among the Gold Watches, and
Snuff-Boxes of the Nobility, when any Knights
of the Garter were Enftall'd at *Winafor* : At
the laft Enftalment there, a Perfon (the
Highnefs of whofe Character it is not here
proper to mention) going into St. *George's*
Chapel, upon the Steps, *Roger Johnfon* putting
his Leg a-crofs his Legs, tho' in the midft of
his Attendance, which made him give a great
Stumble, but the faid *Roger* being a very com-
plaifant Gentleman, with one Hand fav'd him
from falling, and with t'other Hand very
mannerly pick'd a Gold Watch out of his
Fob, worth above a hundred Guineas, for which
extraordinary Piece of Civility the lofing
Perfon mov'd his Hat to him, and return'd
him Thanks: However, the Watch (as I am
inform'd) was return'd again but for half its
Value.

Alfo in this fine Equipage Mr. *Parquot's*
Mafter, *Roger Johnfon*, had oftentimes committed

mitted several Court-Robberies unsuspected ;
but One in particular was thus : There being
to be an extraordinary Ball at St. *James's*
Palace , the Day being come, *Roger* was drest
as fine as Hands, and good Cloaths could
make him, then taking Chair he went to the
Duke of *Gloucester's* Tavern in the *Pall-Mall*,
and sending for One of the Knight-Marshal's
Men to him, to whom (after drinking a Bottle of Wine) imparting his Business, he presented him five Guineas for Hush-Money.
The Provest knew his Meaning by his Gaping,
and assur'd him he would be very serviceable,
so steping again into his Chair, the Marshal's
Man went before it into St. *James's-Court*,
and alighting at the Foot of the Stair-Case
which leads into the Royal Lodgings, he conducted him through the Guard-Chamber, and
out of one Room into another, 'till he put
him into the Chamber where the Ball was to
be perform'd, and there left him. His Con-
ductor returning back, the Yeoman of the
Guard ask'd him what Person of Quality that
was he conducted along, for they did not
know him? Quoth the Marshal's Man, D—n
him, nor I neither, but he's some Foreign
Ambassador. Presently after the Ball-Room
was full of Persons of Quality, of both Sexes,
among whom, *Roger* without Respect to any
Person, made such a promiscuous Slaughter,
that next Day there was a general Outcry of
stoln Watches, Snuff-Boxes, and Jewels, in
the Advertisements of the *Daily-Courant*, *Dai-*

ly *Poſt*, *Daily-Journal*, and other News-Papers, which *Jonathan Wild* advis'd him to bring to his Houſe, becauſe, quoth he, Methinks I would have them ſafe. And quoth *Roge-* to himſelf, So would I too, therefore I ſhan't truſt you with 'em : For he brought them but by Piece-meals, leaſt *Jonathan* ſhould have made but one Premium ſerve for ſeveral Rewards.

By this famous Pick-Pocket, *Parquot* had gain'd great Experience that Way, and got a great deal of Money, which he moſt riotouſly ſpent in Gluttony, Drunkenneſs, and Whoredom, for he was of a moſt lacivious Inclination, caring not what Villiany he committed, ſo he could but have his End of a Woman : He would Cloath her, Feed her, give her Money, or Marry her, if ſhe would not comply with him upon any other Terms, tho' he left her the next Day ; but Adultery, and Fornication, were moſt agreeable to his Palate ; which puts me in Mind, he was like *Antonio* in the *Succeſsful Stranger*, when to ſave the Prieſt the Labour of making them *One Fleſh*, but more likely Charges, he ſaid ;

That I might the Prieſt a Labour by it ſave;
Fornication would ſerve my Turn as well,
If ſhe'll be kind, and ſave the Form of Wedding,
She'll have the Advantage of a Wife in Bedding.

But

But *Porquot* looking upon Pocket-Picking to be but a diminutive low Sort of Thieving, he was resolved to follow Enterprizes more Honourable, as he thought 'em, and Daring; therefore becoming aquainted with *Prior*, and *Vickars*, two as great Rogues as himself, they committed several Robberies upon the Highway; but one Time above the Rest, Mr. *Squire*, One of his Majesty's Messengers, riding upon extraordinary Business into the Country, these three Villains and another, set upon him, and robb'd him of a Silver-Watch, Silver-Hilted Sword, and some other Things of Value: Some short Time after they were apprehended, and committed to *Newgate*, whereupon *Parquot* to save his own Neck, would have made himself an Evidence against his Comrades: In order hereto *Parquot's* Father apply'd himself to Justice *Margate*, a *French* Apothecary near *Covent-Garden*, lately deceas'd, and for the Sake of his Countryman, he used his best Offices with Mr. *Squire*, to permit *Parquot* to be an Evidence against his wicked Associates; but Mr. *Squire*, having more Honour and Justice in him, rejected the Proposal, because as *Parquot*, *Prior*, and *Vickars*, would have Murder'd him, if they had not been prevented by the other Rogue, therefore he made him the Evidence, who convicted the other Three, and they were accordingly Hang'd at *Tyborn*, on the 13th Day of *February*, 1718-19: The Evidence was shortly after Transported.

C 5 *James*

JAMES WRIGHT, *a Highwayman.*

THIS unhappy Person was descended of
Parents more Honest, than Wealthy,
however they put their Son to School, where
he had acquired Reading, Writing, and a
little Skill in casting Accompts : Afterwards
he was put Apprentice to a Perruke-Mak
for seven Years, which Term he served o..
as a faithful Servant should do, and then let
up for himself upon *Ludgate-Hill.* But Things
not happening right to his Expectation, he
very much neglected his Business, which
brought him to labour under great Difficulties,
all which to avoid, he was resolved to run a
worse Risque, by taking ill Courses ; accordingly he became acquainted with one *Blueskin,*
a notorious Highwayman, and in his Company had taken many a Purse on the Road, by
frighting People with these scaring Words,
Stand and Deliver.

Tho' this *Blueskin* was the greatest Rogue
of the Two, yet he surviv'd the other some
few Years, when being apprehended, and
committed to *Newgate,* he came to take his
Tryal at the *Old-Baily,* where *Jonathan Wild*
stuck so close to his Skirts, that he was convicted of a capital Crime, *Blueskin* took it
all

all in good Part, but as going up to *Newgate*
to be put into the Condemned Hold, efpying
Jonathan Wild among the Mob, he beckon'd
to him : The *Thief Taker* thinking he had
fomething to fay which might be of Service
in the further Difcovery of other Rogues,
went up to *Blueskin*, who with one Arm
taking *Jonathan* about the Neck as if he
would whifper in his Ear, with a Penknife
in t'other Hand, he gave his Throat fuch a
Wipe, that every One thought it really cut
to the Purpofe. *Jonathan* dropt down, loft
a great deal of Blood, was carried Home,
and lay under the Surgeon's Hands for above
a Month. The Fact was highly extoll'd by
all that faw it ; and if *Blueskin* did ever deferve Hanging for any Thing, it was purely
for not cutting *Jonathan*'s Throat effectually.

But to return again to *Wright*, he having
been pretty Succefsful in feveral Robberies,
at laft he robb'd the Earl of *Burlington*, and
the Lord *Bruce*, in *Richmond-Lane*, of a Gold
Watch, and a Blue Saphyre Ring of great
Value, befides Money. Now *Wild* knowing
the Rogues, and being inform'd of the Haunts
of *James Wright*, formerly a Perruke-Maker
on *Ludgate-Hill*, apprehended him at the
Queen's-Head Tavern on *Tower-Hill*, in
the Kitchen, before a great Number of Men,
after the greateft Refiftance that could be
made by the Robber, who drew his Piftols ;
but *Wild* being clofely engag'd with him, he
had not an Opportunity to Cock them, and
the

the *Thief-Taker* held him faſt by his Chin,
with his Teeth, 'till he dropt his Fire-Arms,
Surrender'd, . and was brought to *Newgate* ;
and being convicted of other Robberies in
Middleſex, he was Executed at *Tybourn*, being the firſt Malefactor that ever went thither
in his burial Shroud, but ſince he brought up
that Faſhion, ſeveral Rogues has ſince follow'd
it.

The aboveſaid *Wright*, being once to viſit
St. *James*'s-Palace, when indeed he was very
well dreſt, more like a Perſon of Qualty than
a Tradeſman, with a Footman after him in a
very good Livery, tho' they were Hail Fellow
well Met, when together, gazing and ſtaring
about, he at laſt came to the King's Kitchen,
into which earneſtly Peeping, and ſtill ſtanding at the Door, One of the Cooks thinking
him to be a ſtrange Gentleman, told him he
might ſtep in if he pleas'd ; accordingly *Wright*
goes in, and his ſuppos'd Footman with him,
and it being early in the Morning, when little
or nothing was then to do, there was no Body
yet in the Kitchen but this Cook, and a Turn-
Broach, the Former of which, *Wright* inviting
to take a Glaſs of Tent and a Toaſt for a Breakfaſt, the Cook accepted of the Motion, and
to the neareſt Tavern they went in St. *James*'s
Street ; in the mean Time the ſuppos'd Footman goes back to the Kitchen again, with a
Piece of Paper in his Hand, Seal'd up like a
Letter, and Superſcription upon it, directed
to *Jack-a-Nokts*, or *John-a-Styles*, living with
              ſome .

some Person of Quality in the Palace, and
tells his Turn-Broach It was his Master's Orders, as he knew all the Families lodging
there, to deliver that Letter, and bring him
an Answer immediately.

The Turn-Broach thinking no Harm in the
Matter, carries the Letter to where it was
directed, in the mean Time *Wright's* sham
Footman fills a Hand-Basket he found in the
Kitchen full of Plate, to the Value of Two
Hundred and Fifty Pounds. Presently comes
the Cook, and just at his Back was the Turn-
Broach, whom asking where he had been,
he told him to carry a Letter to the Lord
such a one's Lodgings, as he had order'd him,
but there was no such Person liv'd there as
the Superscription mention'd; the Cook said
he knew nothing of any Letter, so breaking
it open, and finding it all a Blank, he then
began to smell a Rat, and hunt about the
Kitchen, when to his Sorrow he soon found out
that the Gentleman's Man had been too busy
with his Majesty's Plate; but not knowing
which way to go after Master, nor Servant,
he apply'd himself to the Care and Direction
of the late *Jonathan Wild*, who was civil
to him, because he belong'd to the King, to
abate him the Fashion, and let him only pay
the bare Weight of the Plate, which came
to One Hundred and Ninety Pounds.

JOHN

✿✿✿✿✿✿✿✿✿✿✿✿✿✿

JONH JAMES, *a Highwayman.*

THIS *John James* was defcended of as good Friends as any could be expected, who live in *Parker's-Lane*, in the antient Hundreds of *Drury*, his Father being a Drummer in the *Coldſtream*, or Second Regiment of *Foot-Guards*, and his Mother a Bunter, or Flatcap, ſo that got he was among 'em, but how to bring him up his Parents never troubl'd their Heads about it. However, the Boy being naturally Sharp, without pow'ring any Vinegar into his Ear, as ſoon as he knew what was what, which was by that Time he was in the Teens, for he was then ſharp enough for to be a Tapſter of an Inn, a Stock-Jobber, or Jockey, he would never let any Thing be loſt that lay not out of his Reach, ſo that with taking Pains early and late, he made ſhift to maintain himſelf without being beholden either to Father, or Mother, who (he vould often ſay to their Faces) were more lke Rogue and Whore, than Man and Wife. He by that Time he was arriv'd to Man's Eſtate, had ran through all the Degrees of *Newgate*, but Hanging, for he had *Shov'd the Tumbler*, that is to ſay, had been Whipt at the Cart's Arſe ; he had been *Glimn'd in the Muns*,

Muns, that is to fay, had been Burnt in the Face, he had been *Glimn'd in the Paw*, that is, Burnt in the Hand; and he had been *Tranfported*, but found the Way home again from *Virginia*, three Years before the Time of his *Tranfportation* was expired.

Now *Jonathan Wild*, and *James*, could never Saddle their Horfes together, therefore when at his Majefty's Acceffion to the Throne, the Tranfportation Act paffed, wherein amongft other wholefome Things, was the Claufe following, *viz. And whereas there are several Perfons who have fecret Aquaintance with Felons, and who make it their Bufinefs to help Perfons to their Stoln Goods, and by that Means, gain Money from them, which is divided between them and the Felons, whereby they greatly encourage fuch Offenders, be it enacted by the Authority aforefaid, that wherever any Perfon taketh Money, or Reward, directly, or indirectly, under Pretence, or upon Account of helping any Perfon; or Perfons, to any fuch Stoln Goods, or Chattels, every fuch Perfon, fo taking Money, or Reward, as aforefaid (unlefs fuch Perfon doth Apprehend, or caufe to be Apprehended, fuch Felon who Stole the fame, and caufe fuch Felon to be brought to his Tryal for the fame, and give Evidence againft him) fhall be guilty of Felony, and fuffer the Pains, and Penalties of Felony according to the Nature of the Felony committed in Stealing fuch Goods, and in fuch and the fame Manner as if fuch Offender had himfelf Stole fuch Goods and Chattels,*

Chettels, in the Manner, and with such Cir-
cumstances, as the same were Stoln. Why
then (as before said) *James* concluded that
Jonathan Wild's Way of Business was now at
an End ; but seeing he was not to be so easily
joaked out of his Livelihood, he still waited
a farther Opportunity to stick in *Jonathan*'s
Skirts.

Afterwards a Clause was inserted in another
Act of Parliament, for paying a Reward of
Forty Pounds to any Person, or Persons, who
should Convict any One of taking Money,
or Reward of Persons, under Pretence of
helping them to Stoln Good. *Wild* went still
on in Defiance of both these Laws, and fatal
was it to *Jack James,* for threat'ning to put
One of the Acts in Execution against him.
James was a private Dealer on the Highway,
always doing Business by himself, and sup-
ported a Wife, three Children, and two
Harlots, very comfortably. *Wild* would suffer him no longer, vows Revenge, and that
he should *Rest from his Labours* ; and on the
9th of *September* 1721, he surpriz'd him, at
Noon, in a Court in *Monmuth Street*, in Bed
with One of his Mistresses; and tho' he was
a bold desperate Rogue, and capable of any
Villany, he was so intimidated at the Sight
of *Wild*, that he patiently surrender'd, was
carried before Justice *Ward*, and committed
to *Newgate*. *Wild* not being ready with Pro-
secutions, he was carried before a Judge by
his *Habeus Corpus*, and had like to have es-
caped

caped by Bail, but the Persons, whose Names he had given in to be his Sureties, not appearing, he was remanded back to *Newgate*, and at the Sessions ensuing, there were several Indictments against him for the Highway, and being fully Convicted, he suffer'd at *Tyburn* the Twenty First of *November* 1721.

A little before he was this last Time in *Newgate*, being one Day habited like an Attorney, in a tufted Gown, and a black Suit of Cloaths, with a Bag under his Arms, seemingly full of Writings of Concern, he steer'd his Course to St. *James's* Palace, and going into the Guard-Chamber, he requested One of the Beef-Eaters, or Yeoman of the Guard, to shew him what he could of the Royal Lodgings ; it was pretty Early in the Morning, and the King not stirring, however, he gave him a sight of the Council-Chamber, the Oratory where the Royal Family sate to hear Divine Service, the Gallery, the Presence-Chamber, an Anti-Chamber to it, the Billiard Room, the Ball-Room, and several other Apartments, for which Civility he gave the Yeoman half a Crown, and went about his Business.

In less than a Quarter of an Hour, *James* returns again, telling the Yeoman he had left his Silver Snuff-Box, he believ'd, in the Window of such a Room, therefore desir'd the Favour of him to go and fetch it him : The Yeoman being set upon Duty, could not stir from his Post, but told him, if he pleas'd,
he

he might ftep in himfelf for it. Accordingly
James went in, and quickly with a Pen-Knife
cut down about Twenty Yards of Cloth of
Tiffue Hangings, valu'd at about One Hundred Pounds, which he cramn'd into his Bag,
after emptying it of his feeming Writings,
which were only brown Paper, and return'd
into the Guard-Chamber again, with the
Snuff-Box in his Hand ; where he return'd
the Yeoman Thanks, gave him another Half
Crown, under a Pretence of great Joy for
finding his Box, and then went off with his
Booty, which he Sold to one Old *Glanifter*,
an old *Fence*, or *Lock* in *Holbourn*, for Twenty
Five Pounds : But the Yeoman loft his Place
for *James*'s Crown, and was forc'd to live
folely upon the Retailing of Beer and Ale, he
keeping an Ale-Houfe not far from *Dever-
eaux-Court* in the *Strand*, when this Misfortune happen'd.

JOHN ALLEN, *a Highwayman.*

THE Subject of our following Difcourfe
is upon an unfortunate Perfon named
John Allen, the Son of a wealthy Citizen in
the City of *Gloucefter*, who left him at his
Death betwixt four and five Thoufand Pounds,
which inftead of rafing his Fortune in the
World, prov'd his Misfortune. For tho' he
was

was set up before his Father's Decease in a
very good House in *London,* being a Haber-
dasher of Hats, and had full Business, yet instead of improving his Stock, he Daily de-
minish'd his Substance, by leaving off his
Trade to turn Gentleman.

Now the Play-House is constantly made
his Nursery of Vice, the Tavern his Recrea-
tion, and a Bawdy-House his chief Place of
Pleasure ; for Whoredom, Gaming, and
Drunkenness, were the darling Sins, in which
he was resolv'd to live and die, in spite of all
the wholesome Council, and serious Admoni-
tions, that were given him to the contrary.

Allen being once committed to the *Mar-
shalsea-*Prison in *Southwark,* for desperately
wounding One of his Cronies in a Tavern-
Fray, one *Frances Thompson,* a beautiful Woman, but One of the most Cunning, Tricking,
Intrieguing Jilts of the present Times, desirous to make a Prey of him, procur'd herself to be arrested in a sham Action, of Fifteen
Hundred Pounds, and to be sent Prisoner to
the same Jayl, where she liv'd at a splendid
Rate, both in Respect of good Eating, Drink,
and Lodging. *Allen* insinuates himself into
her Acquaintance, being so much Enamour'd
with her Person, and Conversation, that he
promis'd to pay her Debt, that she might
have her Liberty. At this Promise she shak'd
her Head, and sighing said, Dear Sir, my
Action, which is Fifteen Hundred Pounds,
therefore too great a Sum for so generous a
Gentleman

Gentleman to disburse for a meer Stranger;
neither should he if he would, because it
was no real Action against her, for she ow'd
not a Farthing in the World ; but because she
would not resign up her Writings of her
Estate, which was Three Hundred and Fifty
Pounds *per Annum*, to a covetous, barbarous
Uncle, he had laid a sob Action on her, in
hopes Confinement may bring her to a Compliance with his exorbitant Humour.

So bewitch'd was *Allen*, with the Passion
of Loving this Crocodile, that he have believ'd
more unlikely Things than these ; and the
Effect of this doleful Narration was, that he
assur'd her of all the Favour, and Affection,
she could expect from him, even his Personal
Estate (which as yet he had reduced but to
four Thousand Pounds) Life, Heart, and
Soul ; intreating her to forget all her Misfortunes, for he would (if she pleas'd) make her
absolute Mistress of all he was possest of.
Mrs. *Frances* returns him many Thanks for
his generous Offers, concluding her Compliments with a Shower of Tears ; which she
had at Command whenever she pleas'd, or
stood in need of 'em. With these Artifices
she became Mistress of *Allen*'s Heart, so that
she might dispose of him as she pleas'd ; her
Beauty had wounded him, and he was mighty
desirous to try whether she would Cure him :
But he could not contrive how to acquaint
her with his Malady ; for she pretended so
much Reservedness and Vertue, that he was
                                    afraid

afraid to break his Mind to her, by asking
her the laft Favour in an unlawful Way;
befides, as fhe had Beauty, Wit, and an Eftate,
as he thought, he lays afide the Thoughts of
prevailing upon her Submiffions, and Prefents,
and would ufe the laft Remedy, which was
to Marry her; for this is a Bait that many
Times Catches the moft Subtle of the Female
Sex, but he that ufes it, his Caufe moft commonly to repent. At the fame Time the
cunning Baggage had no other Defign than to
examine his Bags; and would be no way
engaged, 'till fhe was fecure of the Prize.
Allen being now up to the Ears in Love, he
daily treated her in a very extraordinary
Manner; fhe could play well on the Spinnet,
and Sing as fine; fhe had fuch an Inftrument
brought to her Chamber, on which one Day
playing, and to it joyning her Voice, fhe Sung fo
fweetly, that *Allen* being ravifh'd at the Mu-
fick, he made her this high Compliment,
That he could not imagine it to be the Voice
of any mortal Creature, but rather that of
an Angel defcended from above; and coming
towards her Tranfported with Joy, How
(fays he) hath my Confinement made me fo
happy, as to be bleft with the Converfation of
fo adorable a Creature! What Happinefs hath
your Arrival crown'd me with, who never
knew any before? What Felicity have I received in beholding your tranfcendent Beauty,
and to obferve in you a Thoufand unknown
Excellencies, which I never beheld in any
Woman

Woman before? Mrs. Quality in Difguife
reply'd, You prefs (Dear Sir) too hard upon
me, and put me to the Blufh with your ex-
ceffive Praifes: I am not fuch a Stranger to
my felf, but that I muft account it Flattery,
to beftow fuch extraordinary Commendations
on a Perfon that deferves fo little ; unlefs
generous Natures have an Inclinalion to favour
Perfons of mean Performances, and perfuade
them their Accomplifhments exceed what indeed they are : No more Compliments, I
befeech you, Dear Madam, fays *Allen*, now
raifed up to the higheft Pitch of befotted
Love ; My Expreffions proceed from my
Heart, and I can affure you, Madam, that
tho' I have heard celebrated Voices at St. *Paul's*
Weftminfter - Abby, the *Play - Houfes*, and
the *Opera-Houfe* in the *Hay-Market*, yet
yours is beyond any of them.

In a fhort Time the Man whom *Allen* had
wounded being well again, he was difcharged
and was at Liberty. The next Day he Bail'd,
out his adorable Creature, and was Married
to her: Within a Fortnight after the Nuptials
fhe pretended to be very Ill, but at the fame
Time fent her Husband into *Norfolk* to receive about Two Hundred Pounds due to her
for Rent. He rid to the Place directed, but
none of the People acknowledged him for
their Landlord, nor his Wife for their Landlady. Now fmelling a Rat, he made the
beft of his Way Home again, but before
his Arrival, fhe had packt up Bag and Baggage,

gage, taking all his Money, 'Plate, Cloaths, and Linnen, and went with her Bully to *Holland.*

Allen at his Return finding what had happen'd, was in the greateſt Surprize, and Confuſſion, as ever Man could be, at his being utterly Ruin'd and Undone, before Honey-Moon Month was over; and by Way of Reprizal he was reſolv'd the Country ſhould pay for it, by making Depredations on the Highway. This Courſe he follow'd ſome Time with pretty good Succeſs; but in 1723, towards the latter End of *December*, he, with *Edward Frazier*, and *Peter Levee*, Robbing one Mr. *Waſey*, a Surgeon, as he was paſſing through *Lincoln's-Inn-Fields* at Midnight, of a Gold-Watch, a Twezer-Caſe, a Sword, and Money, the next Day the Loſer waited on *Jonathan Wild*, and acquainted him with his Misfortune, who, after asking him ſeveral Queſtions, told him, he ſhould be glad to ſee him in Two or Three Days, by which Time he hoped to be able to give him ſome Account of the Robbers: *Peter Levee*, was immediately ſent for, *Wild* giving him a ſafe Paſs-Port, upon the Faith of his Word and Honour, that not a Hair of his Head ſhould be hurt; *Levee* comes, and agrees to betray his Comrade *Allen*, and ſets him accordingly at an Ale-Houſe in a little Court near *Newgate.* Mr. *Waſey* had his Watch brought him again by a Porter, he paying Five Guineas, as a Reward for the

Care

Care that had been taken of it : *Allen* was for this Robbery Convicted, and Executed at *Tybourn*, on the Third of *February*, 1724, and *Wild* soon after receiv'd the Forty Pounds due according to Law. But the Death of these Five foregoing Malefactors, was not all the Blood he had dabbled in, by a great many, but as what he did therein was meerly out of Self-Interest, not Honesty, he hath deservedly met with the like Fate, at the same Tree.

The

The Life of *JOHN HAWKINS*, that was Hang'd in Chains for Robbing the Bristol-Mail. With a Detection of *WILSON's* Account of Robberies.

Written by *WILLIAM HAWKINS*.

THO' many Books have been Publish'd in most Languages, to set forth Biography, or Writing the Lives of unhappy Persons, for the blazoning Vice in the foulest and blackest Colours as may be, as well as writing the Lives of good Men, to paint Vertue with the greatest Beauty and Glory it can be describ'd in ; yet when Men undertake such Matters, they ought to write with the greatest Candour, and Sincerity imaginable, because upon their Writings depends eternal Infamy, or Honour, which stand Recorded to future Ages : In the first Place he begins with a Lye, in saying my Brother, (whom he counts as Famous as *Cartouche*, the *French* Robber)

D   was

was thirty Years of Age when he dy'd, when
he was but Twenty-Eight ; but if that
was all his Lying, the Miſtake of Age was
ſo inſignificant, that had he kept up to the
Truth of my Brother's Character, it was
impoſſible for him to tarniſh his Reputation in
the moſt minute Circumſtances whatever.

As for my Brother's Parentage, it was good
and creditable ; ſo paſſing by that, and the
Place where he was Born, and ſpoiling his
Reputation in Sir *Dennis Dutry*'s Service,
(which laſt Article is plainly contradicted in
the *Preface* of my Printed Book) I ſhall proceed to acquaint you of his other lying Para-
graphs, eſpecially to tell you Firſt, that my
Brother was in ſuch good Circumſtances, when
he left Sir *Dennis Dutry*, upon his own volun-
tary Account, that he was not neceſſitated
to be put to a *Nonplus* for Horſe and Piſtols
to get his Living by irregular Actions.

As for my Brother's firſt Beginning to rob,
his firſt Exploit was upon the *Richmond* Coach
in the County of *Surry*, and not upon *Hounſlow-Heath*, in the County of *Middleſex*,
which ſhews that though he was right in my
Brother's taking the Eleven Pounds, yet was
he miſtaken in the Place of obtaining it, as
well as loſing it at Play at the *Phœnix* Ale-
Houſe in the *Hay-Market*, which is ſome
little Diſtance from the King's-Head at *Temple-Bar*.

If a Man, as he ſays, *Page* 3. did loſe by
Play, what he got upon the Highway, which
may

may not be improbable, yet it is more than the ingenious *Ralph Wilson* knows; for he had not then the Honour to be acquainted with my Brother, who never did a barbarous Action, I mean in Relation to Bloodshed, which he always scorn'd, tho' oppos'd to the very highest Degree, that might cause a Provocation to Murder.

As for that *Irish* Captain Mr. *Wilson* talks of, is Captain *Lennard*, who, tho' he was under Displeasure of the Government, was no Highwayman, nor did he ever go Abroad with my Brother upon any such Account; besides, my Brother, when he did undertake such dangerous Enterprizes, for which the Laws of his Country cut him out of the Land of the Living, in the Prime of his Youth, he always was so far above wanting, that he had no Occasion to become a *Cannibal*, or *Man-Eater*.

I am proud that Mr. *Wilson* says my Brother was a Prisoner of State, upon the Account of rescuing Captain *Lennard*; but the Matter could not be prov'd against him, because, although he offended against his Majesty's Laws, in plundering his Subjects, yet was he always affectionate to the Government: And as for *Reeves*, *Cummerford*, and *Riley*, what ever their Misfortunes were, had but Mr. *Wilson* have come under the like Dilemma, the Fellow had but had his Deserts, for brave Men that were less culpable than him upon any Account whatever.

D 2   The

The Fellow (*Wilson*) being now in Custody, his simple Judgment incites him to believe his Confinement is Protection to screen him from Justice, in casting his scurrilous and unjust Reflections upon the Magistrates of *Westminster* ; but having taken Notice of that Piece of unparrallel'd Impudence in my *Preface*, I shall only say, that Mr. *Wilson* was so much from being spoil'd before his coming acquainted with my Brother at the Gaming-Tables, that he was spoil'd to his Hands, and by his Behaviour, and Actions, shew'd as if he had been bred a Villain in his Mother's Womb, and so came an acute R------- into the World.

In *Page* 5. *Wilson* says he was Born in *Yorkshire*, and is now but Two and Twenty Years of Age; which plainly proves he was Born far *North*, or otherwise he could not be so ripe in Villainy, at those early Years; but yet in such Sort of petty Villainies, which will give him only the Characteristick of a petty Thief, or at most to the Stealing of a Horse, which is very Natural to all Men in his *Northern* Climate.

When my Brother was Try'd for Robbing a Coach in *Monmouth-Street*, *Wilson* was not then acquainted with him ; so as to his extravagant Living, when a Clerk, it was the Infection of his early Vices, which broke out afresh upon him ; for he was never Heal'd of his most exorbitant Wickedness, so had no Abborrence of Villainy, which was rivetted

to

to his vile Nature from the very Font, to his Confinement now in the *Poultry-Compter*.

If *Pocock*, as *Wilson* owns, *Page 6.* became an Evidence against his Companions, he cannot justly Reflect on others making themselves so, to avoid a Fate of the greatest Consequence ; that is to say, the Loss of Life, Goods, and Chattels : As to *Ralphson's* running away with a Gold Watch of mine, to *Holland*, Mr. *Wilson*, is false again, for he ran away to *Ireland*, where he Marry'd well, and shortly after dy'd of a Pleurisy, in that Kingdom ; and his former Wife now lives in *Grub-Street*, in *London*. Again, at this Time, *Pocock* made a false Information against me, for which I was committed a Prisoner to the *Poultry-Compter* in *London*, in 1720, from thence remov'd to *Newgate*, and at *Justice-Hall* in the *Old-Baily*, taking my Tryal, I was honourably Acquitted ; as well I might be, as 'till then having a most unquestionable, and unspotted Reputation, which being (tho' Innocent) somewhat then sully'd, despair of ever retrieving it, did tempt me to irregular Practices : of which more hereafter.

As for my deceas'd Brother's being in the Robbery attempted upon Col. *Floyer*, when he shot *Wooldridge* the Broker of *Hanp-Alley*, he was not in his Company at that Time ; nor (as my Brother has often told me) was he ever Guilty of Killing any Man, much less General *Evans's* Footman ; which was the greater Satisfaction to him, when he was going to

launch

launch out into Eternity, that he dy'd with a clear Conscience from Blood Guiltiness: But as for the Matter about the Robberies committed by *Wright*, and my Brother *John*, after their Re-union, they were First attacking a Coach, and Two Horses, but the Right Honourable, the Earl of *Burlington*, and the Lord *Bruce*, coming by at the same Time in *Richmond Lane*, with several Gentlemen on Horse-Back, taking them to be a greater Prize, they attack'd them, and took Three Watches, a plain Gold One, which the Lord *Bruce* had again, and a Gold One of the Earl's, the Case all Enchas'd outwards, and finely Enamel'd within, and another Gold Repeating-Watch, taken out of the same Coach ; but the Earl's was Sold at *Amsterdam*, and the Repeating Gold Watch is pawn'd at the *Stadthouse* in the same City, for an Hundred Livers, and the Earl's Saphyre Ring, for Thirty Pounds, to a Jeweller at *Amsterdam*, (not Forty Pounds, as he asserts) as was also a Gold Watch, that was taken out of a Coach, wherein Mr. *Blackstone* was Robb'd in *Fig-Lane*, to a *French* Watch-Maker at *Amsterdam* ; but since the Disposal of those Moveables there, they did not afterwards go to *Holland*.

As for *Wright*, the Barber's Fidelity, which *Wilson* so much Extols, it evidently appears, by what I am now going to recite : It was a Day or Two after *Wilson* had shot his own Hand, as not being expert in the Use of Pistols, any

any more than he is at Sword ; that *Wright*
being in the *Marſhalſea*, he wrote to me, my
Brother, and *Wilſon* for Money, telling us
in plain Terms, that he would not live any
longer without ſome, and that he had very
great Offers made him by *Jonathan Wild* ;
but at the ſame Time ſwearing *D----n him,
he would not accept of them.* This Letter put
us into a pannick Fear, and made us bid Adieu
to *London*, my deceas'd Brother flying to
Shaftsbury in *Dorſetſhire* ; I went to *Sraines*,
near *Windſor*, and the ſham-brave *Wilſon*,
took his Horſe for *Whitby* in *Yorkſhire*, to de-
ſert his Villainy, as he pretends, 'though he
had then, and ever will have, as great Affection for any Thing that is R——ſh, as a
Welſhman has for Toaſted Cheeſe, a *Scotchman*
for Oaten Bannock, an *Ireſhman* for Bonny-Clab-
ber, a *Spaniard* for a patch'd Cloak, an *Italian*
for Buggery, a *Dutchman* for Butter, or a
Frenchman the Pox. Now this is the *Wright*
that *Wilſon* ſo much Extols for a faithful
Companion ; and in his erroneous Book ſets
out, that *Wright* follow'd an honeſt Employment, 'till I impeach'd him ; but this inſignificant Author would do well to ſatisfy the
World, what was the deceas'd *Wright's* honeſt
Occupation : If he did any Thing under a
Screen of Honeſty, it was only to palliate
thoſe irregular Courſes he purſued, which
brought him to his untimely *Exit*. And
when *Wilſon* went into *Yorkſhire*, I took Leave
of him on the 1ſt of *February*, and did not

ſee

ſee him 'till the 4th of *November* following, which was the unhappy Night I was taken into Cuſtody, and am ſtill under Confinement, to the great Detriment of my wanting Wfe and Children.

Wilſon, in *Page* 8. ſays, He uſed to preform his Part ſo well, that *John Hawkins* never car'd to part with him afterwards. As to this Article, I muſt ſay, this Hero was firſt Porter to the Gang, and being very tractable, through his wanting Bread, he was made *Aid-de Camp* to them; but truly when he came to be brought into Action, if the Engagement prov'd too ſharp, let who would loſe the Day, he won the Race, for he always run away Firſt; ſo as for what he ſays about taking Three Pounds in Money, a Snuff-Box, and Pocket-Book from Sir *David*, for which Sixty Pounds was offer'd to *Jonathan Wild*; but my deceas'd Brother being always too generous, to deſtroy Papers, or Notes, he ſent them back *Gratis* to the Owners, without any Reward, which is a Principle above *Wilſon*'s Bravery, which never exceeded (though he was in this Action, and the Snuff-Box was found upon *Wright*) that of *Domitian*, Emperour of *Rome*, catching Flies all the Day long, and thruſting out their Eyes with Bodkins.

He ſays, *Page* 8. That after the Commiſſion of this Robbery on Sir *David*, he led a Dog's Life; and ſo he ought, for the Dog that Barks, and will not Bite, ought to be kick'd; and

my deceas'd Brother was too brave a Man to
give *Wilson* any other than decent Correction
for his Cowardice, and not have made a Property of him for a Tool, in Hanging his Comrade, to save himself, for he had that Opportunity several Times, but scorn'd to take
away the Life of any Companion, nor to
reflect on any Person, to the last Moment of
Living on this side the Grave.

I will farthermore do Mr. *Wilson* the Justice
to say, He was concern'd in the Robbery of
Mr. *Hide* of *Hackney*, of Ten Pounds, and
a Watch; but as for Robbing a Coach against
the *Dead-Wall* in *Chancery-Lane*, at Night,
in *August* 1720, and the same Night another
in *Lincoln's-Inn-Fields*, it is notoriously False;
and as the Month, and Date of the Year
are mention'd, I defy any Person Living to
prove such a remarkable Transaction committed then: But as for the Earl of *West-
moreland's* Coach being Robb'd, out of which
they took a Purse, with Sixty Shillings in it;
that was done in *Broad St. Giles's*; so they
could not stumble upon the Booty in *Lincoln's-
Inn-Fields*, however, *Wilson* was in this Exploit, and Two, or Three more above-mentioned, never in any more with *John Hawkins,*
and *Wright,* who brought him off from the
Watch, for a Staff is as dreadful a Thing as a
Pistol, to the Eyes of *Wilson,* who never
cares to be in any desperate Rencounter where
Death appears before his graceless Eyes.

This fham Penitent pretends he had a mighty Itch to Gaming, tho' the Chub knew nothing of the *Levant* at Dice, the Difference betwixt Loaded, and Mathematical ones; the Slip at Cards, the Palm, and other Bites. But paffing by his little Skill at thofe Paftimes, dreading that when I, and *Wright*, were in Prifon together, he fled with my Brother to *Oxford*, who went along with him to give him the leaft Sufpicion of being inform'd againft by *Wright*. When arriv'd at this moft famous Univerfity, they came into the *Bodleian* Library, where being feveral curious Pieces of Painting, it was the honeft Mr. *Wilfon* defac'd a great many; and coming to One of our bleffed Saviour's Crucifixion, with his bleffed Mother beholding her Son's Death, thruft his Cane thro' it; and being Reprimanded by my deceas'd Brother, for committing fo impious an Action, quoth the blafphemous Fellow *Wilfon*, D----m---ye, *Was my Redeemer here now upon Earth, I would* ------- *him*; and as for his Saviour's Mother, the Virgin *Mary*, he would ------ her. Oh Impiety unparallel'd! and for his vile Expreffions ought to be fton'd to Death.

In relation to *Butler Fox*, who was Hang'd at *Croyden*, *Lent* Affizes laft, *Wilfon* never knew him; fo what he fays in Print betwixt that Perfon, and me, is utterly Falfe, about making him a Tool, when necessity oblig'd me. But fee how this bold harden'd Fellow *Wilfon*, reflects upon Sir *Edward Lawrence's*
trying

trying the aforesaid *Butler Fox,* at the *Old-Baily,*
for a Fact of which he was really Guilty ;
but bringing many Persons of Reputation, to
give him a fair Character, he was acquitted.
But yet the Honourable Sir *Edward Lawrence,*
nor his Servants (tho' just in his Profecution
against him) never trumpt'd up Colonel
Archibald Hamilton's being Robb'd by *Butler
Fox,* for neither Sir *Edward,* nor any of his
Servants, knew of it 'till after he was taken
up, purely upon my Information, as being
the best Informer, when none but *Butler Fox,*
and I, committed the Fact, and not my deceas'd Brother, and *George Sympfon* ; but as
Wilfon's Reflections are False upon the Honourable Sir *Edward Lawrence,* fo 'tis well
known (I believe) to that worthy Gentleman,
and other good Gentlemen, that I never
threw away the rifled Barrel Gun, we took
away from Colonel *Archibald Hamilton,* as
Wilfon pretends to have had in his Hand,
when it was prov'd in the Court to the Contrary. As for the Silk, I fuppofe he might
have Handled, as having given it to my deceas'd Brother to pawn, and accordingly it
was pawn'd at a Broker's in *Alderfgate-Street* ;
but when the Owner went thither for it, it
was not to be found, by Reafon the Pawn-
Broker hearing of my Misfortune, he had
convey'd it away before his Houfe was fearch'd.
Befides, Colonel *Hamilton* came to me to the
Gate-Houfe at *Weftminfter,* where his Honour's
Eyes were fo good, that he was pofitive I
was

was One of the Men that Robb'd him; and
therefore I admire that his Coachman could
not have as good Eyes to know *Butler Fox*,
when he was so positive to his being in that
Robbery of his Master, in Company with
me; and I had no Manner of Conversation
with him, about the Certainty of knowing
him, 'till he came upon his Tryal at *Croyden*,
and there prov'd the Colour of the Horses,
on which we committed that unhandsome
Action, by the Honourable Colonel; by the
same Token that *Butler Fox* return'd the Man
his Horses, without paying the Hire of them:
The Owner of the Grey-Horse keeping a
Cook's-Shop, and Ale-House, at the Sign of the
Plough in *Forestreet*, by *Moorfields*; and the Bay
Horse in *White-Horse-Yard*, in *Finsbury*: Besides,
to prove this, the Honourable Sir *Edward's*
Servants were with Mr. *King*, and the other
Man, who did Lett them to *Butler Fox*, and
who testified that they had such Horses of
them, as I had declar'd in my Information.

As for a Villain calling me heedless Villain,
Page 12. His lying Tongue is no more Scandal, than that of my cheating *Wright* of 50
Pounds, when he was starving in Prison. As
for his Estate left him, which was Sold for
350 Pounds; his being a Cull at a Gaming-
Table, as above-mention'd, he consum'd it
there, and not in Buying Horses for me, and
my deceas'd Brother; to which deceas'd One,
he ow'd then Nine Pounds. Perhaps now
and then he might be a Groat, or Six-Pence
                                        out

out of Pocket for B - gg--ring a poor Hoftler,
or Boy, belonging to the Stables where we us'd
to hire Horfes: But yet fuch was Mr. *Wilfon's*
Prudence in faving his Money, that he would
rather make Ufe of a Mare, in his Sodomitifh
Way, which he faid was more pleafant Le-
chery, than lying with the fineft Woman in
Chriftendom. As for his lying Bravados that
I never was a Man of any Courage, the
World knows fo much to the Contrary, that
I fhall not here prefume to blow a Trumpet
in found of my own Praife: But as he owns
himfelf, *Page* 13. That in a Robbery attempted to be committed in *Fig Lane*, he,
and his Affociates, tho' all brave Men, excepting him, did not go out with a Defign to
Kill, any more than the Gentlemen attack'd
defign'd to have been Robb'd, by putting
their Heads out of the Coach, which fhew'd
Wilfon to be born in a Wood, to be fcar'd
by an Owl; I fay, upon this cowardly Action
of his, he did not care to venture his Life
upon fuch Chances; and therefore went and
took my Mare, from my Lord *Frame's* Stables
in *Swan-Alley*, in St. *John's-Street*, which I
never faw to this Day, altho' I give him a
Note of Ten Pounds, payable as Money was
got; and fo I never afterwards went abroad
with him, to rob any more in fuch a Scoundrel's Company.

As for that faying of *Wilfon*, That our
Horfes Heads were fwell'd fo much, we cou'd
not get 'em out of our Stables, that's an old
Story

Story borrow'd from mad *Ogle,* the Life-
Guard-Man, when he had brought his Horfe
to live upon a Bean a-Day, and juft then it
died ; and a dead Horfe, is as good to *Wilfon,*
as a live One ; rather than be taken Prifoner,
he will make ufe of his own Heels, as well
as any Creature with Four Feet ; fo his
Cowardice never fpoils his running away,
whether on Horfe-Back, or Foot. As we
always had brave Men in our Company, there
was no Occafion for my deceas'd Brother, and
Sympfon, to ride into *Yorkfhire,* to fetch up a
Coward for their Companion.

As for the Houfe kept by one Mr. *C------,*
by *London-Wall,* I fuppofe he means one *Car-*
ter, whom (I'm affur'd) he cannot afperfe
for any bafe Action, as having little, or no Acquaintance with the Man ; as little Acquaintance as he had Knowledge in Robbing the
Cirencefter, Gloucefter, Oxford, Briftol, Ip-
fwich, Colchefter, Portfmouth, and *Berry* Coaches,
in attempting which to rob fo often, as he
fays, he was no more prefent at, than old
King *John,* who has been dead, and gone, as
our Chronicles fay, above 500 Years ago.

Thefe, he fays, were Morning Exercifes,
the Evening Ones were generally between
Hampftead, Hackney, Bow, Richmond, and
London, and behind *Buckingham* Wall, and
other Places adjacent to our moft famous
Metropolis ; but yet they knew fuch Exercifes that *Wilfon* never dare to commit, without the Affiftance of fuch brave Fellows as
he

he calls *Sympſon*, and my Brother, who would
never venture ſuch a Pea-Hearted Raſcal as
him in any Thing great, and daring.

Wilſon is Falſe in his Account about the Robbery committed on *Richard Weſt* Eſq; behind
Buckingham-Houſe, in which my deceas'd
Brother, and *Sympſon*, had no Hand. And
as to his ſaying he had his Horſe kill'd under
him from a Coach, one Morning in *Portſmouth*-Road, I can only ſay to that Misfortune
of *Wilſon*, our *Engliſh Don Quixot*, or Knight
Errant, that had he been kill'd inſtead of
the Horſe, the moſt rational Creature of the
Two had been ſtill ſurviving.

As for Mr. *Green*, the Brewer's being
Robb'd, with his Lady, as riding in their
Coach behind *Buckingham*-Houſe, I know
nothing of it, nor will I believe that *Wilſon*
does, tho' he was upon Oath ; and it is a
Paradox to me, that my Brother, and *Sympſon*, ſhould take ſuch a mean-ſpirited Fellow
as he, to go upon a deſperate Attempt, as
Robbing the *Harwich*, and *Briſtol* Mails ; and
then pretends he had not turn'd Evidence
againſt my deceas'd Brother, but that he was
inform'd I had acquainted the Poſt-Maſter-
General, that I had impeach'd him, and
would certainly convict him ; all which is
utterly Falſe : And again, to diſſolve the
ſolemn Vows, and Proteſtations, he had made
to his betray'd Comrades, he trump'd up a
Letter, as if written from *Sympſon* to the
Poſt-Officers, for diſcovering the Perſons concern'd

cern'd with him in the laſt Robbing the *Briſtol* Mail, for which my Brother, and *Sympſon* dy'd, on *Monday* the 21ſt of *May*, 1722: And I hope their poor Souls are at Reſt in Heaven; which *Wilſon* will never arrive at, but from a Gibbet, inſtead of a Church Yard.

But to make the Title of my Book, in point of diſcovering ſuch bold Robberies, which never were yet ſo publickly tranſacted in Places of the greateſt Dangers, to be the ſooneſt apprehended, it will be proper for me here to ſay ſomewhat of my Birth, and Parentage, before I come to my Life, and Converſation.

The Life of WILLIAM HAWKINS, a Highwayman.

With an *Account* of *Robberies committed in City, Town, and Country, in Company* of his *Brother* John, *Butler* Fox, Wilfon, George Sympfon, Tom Davy, *and others. Wherein he difcovers the moft Surprizing Robberies ever done on the Highway.*

Written by himfelf.

THEREFORE this is to inform my Readers, that I was Born at *Staines* in the County of *Middlefex*, of Parents Honeft, Reputable, and of fo good Circumftances, as to have given a handfome, and genteel Education, had my Inclination led me to Learning ; but attaining no higher a Pitch than Reading, Writing, and cafting Accompts, I was, at about Thirteen Years of Age, put Apprentice to one Mr. *Richard Bruges,* of the City

City of *London*, Plaifterer, to whom I had
faithfully ferv'd my limited Time of Seven
Years more, and then follow'd the fame Occupation my felf for about Eight Years, when
unhappily becoming acquainted with lewd,
and loofe Perfons, they unfortunately brought
me too foon to be as Bad as themfelves.

When I became a Man for my felf, I kept
a very creditable Houfe, in the Neighbourhood where I liv'd, which was in *Crown-Court*
in *Grub-Street*, near *Morefields*, where then
unhappily becoming acquainted with bad
Company, not fo much as *John Hawkins*, my
deceas'd Brother, as *James Wright*, whofe
Friends liv'd at *Enfield* Town, and then, by
their Perfuafions, being fworn to take ill
Courfes, they over-perfuaded me to hire
Horfes for them, with a Pretence of going
to fee their Friends, which they feemingly
frequently did; and the Perfons who lent
them out, came always to me for the Money,
which I duly paid them ; but I folemnly
Proteft, I did not know, upon what Account
they were really upon, 'till one Day a Man
came to tell me, he had loft his Horfes;
and as I had hir'd them, I was oblig'd in
Point of Honefty, to go, and fee after the
Perfons I deliver'd them to ; when going
immediately to *James Wright*'s Houfe, who kept
then a Perruke-Makers Shop, in the *Old-Baily*,
I found him, and my now deceas'd Brother,
in Bed together ; and on a Table, in the
fame Room, I faw Two Great Coats, and
Piftols,

Piſtols, which gave me ſtrong Suſpicions, that they were going upon ſuch Expiditions, of which they had given ſome Inkling, as above-mention'd ; that is as much as to ſay, an Invitation upon the Highway. However, I aſk'd them where the Horſes ſtood, which they refuſing to tell me, I told them I believ'd they got their Living upon the Road ; but in ſhort they would not deliver me the Horſes, upon the Account of proving the Goodneſs of 'em farther, in order to pay the Hire of them : I muſt confeſs, that my Brother would *Nolens volens* have them ; to which Reſolution, *James Wright* anſwer'd ; *That it being Chriſtmas-Eve, he could not then leave the Buſineſs of his Shop,* and therefore begging his Excuſe for not going Abroad that Day, my Brother then ſaid, he would have his Horſe, and give it, (according to Captain *Bew*'s Expreſſion, who was barbarouſly Murder'd at the *White Swan,* at *Knight's-Bridge* ; *That he would give his Horſe an Airing* ;) that is to ſay, by taking a Purſe, or robbing the Stage-Coaches upon *Hounſlow-Heath.* At that Time, my Circumſtances being very low, as not daring to ſhew my Head, (but not through irregular Living then, but by having been involv'd in Debt, through ſeveral Croſſes, and Loſſes in the World ;) beſides being brought into *Premunires* for my Friends, by being engag'd for them : I told him I would go along with him upon the Lay ; whereupon he had ſuch a Check upon him, as being ſo

nearly-

nearly related to him as I was, and having
also a due Sense of Honour in him upon the
same Account, he generously told me, that
One unfortunate Person in a Family, was too
much to suffer an untimely *Exit*; and therefore, he would not permit me to bear a
wretched Fate with him; but upon pressing
my Circumstances were very hard, (and then
with a great deal of Regret, and Concern)
he gave his Consent, upon Promise, that none
but I, and he would Rob together; and being
provided of a Pair of Pistols by *Wright*, we
set out upon our First Expedition, to *Hounflow-Heath*, where it so happen'd, that on
the 24th of *December*, 1719, going over the
said *Heath*, we there stopp'd in a *Lane*, on
this Side *Longford*, in the County of *Middlesex*, Three Stage-Coaches, all together, in
which were Eighteen Persons, besides those
without, being Six more, the Coachmen
excepted, from whom we took Twelve
Pounds in Money; then riding to *Twittenham*,
and ferrying over to *Richmond*, being a little too
soon, (altho' we baited our Horses there) we
miss'd of our Design of Robbing the *Richmond* Coach, and so we made the Best of our
Way to *London*; where paying the Hire of
our Horses, it made me easy for some Time,
as keeping then a good *Christmas*.

In *January* following, (to begin the Year
well) my Brother, and *James Wright*, came
to me to procure them the same Horses,
which I procur'd, tho' I told them, I would
not

not run any such Risque again ; but upon
their earnest Entreaties, they prevail'd with
me, and accordingly on the 8th of *January*
(being *Sunday*) I mounted with them, when
at *Mile-End*, stoping Two Gentlemens
Coaches, we took from them Three Silver
Watches, Two Swords, a plain Gold Ring,
a Cypher Ring, and about 15, or 16 *l.* in
Money ; but One of the Watches, I return'd
to the Owner since my Confinement, and
the other Two were dispos'd of in *France*,
where we us'd to carry such Moveables for
Safety.

On the 22d of *January* following, we went
Abroad again, with Intent to rob the Coaches
in the Streets of *London* ; and accordingly
in *Marlborough-Street* we met with a Coach,
in which was one Mr. *Samuel Towers*, and
Two Ladies, whom we stopp'd, and took
from them Two Snuff-Boxes, and a Silver
Watch, and about 1 *l.* in Money. Since my
Confinement in the *Gate-House*, at *Westminster*, the abovesaid Mr. *Towers* told me, he
had at the Time he was robb'd, 60 Guineas,
and a Diamond Ring, which he sav'd, by the
Opportunity of the Watch coming at that
Time to his Assistance ; but obliging the
Watchmen to lay down their Lanthorns, and
Staffs, and stand by to see the Persons robb'd,
and then going off, we put up our Horses ;
however, I return'd the Watch since to him,
and for this Robbery *James Wright* was
Executed.

The

The Night following, we Three ſtopp'd a Coach with one Gentleman in it, near St. *James's-Street*, and took from him Five Guineas, and a Pocket-Book ; but riding off, One of my Companion's Horſe ſtumbling, the Pocket-Book was dropt ; at the ſame Time Centries ſtanding at the End of every Street, upon the Account of ſuch unaccountable Robberies, as were then committed, beſides the Patrole going about the Town, at the End of *Bond-Street*, we were prevented our alighting, and taking it up ; tho' I am inform'd ſince, that thoſe who came to the attack'd Gentleman's Aſſiſtance, took up the ſaid Book, wherein were ſeveral Bank Notes of conſiderable Sums.

The ſame Month, and in like Manner, going out, we gave the Word *Stand*, to a Gentleman's Coachman in *Tybourn-Road*; but he being a reſolute Fellow, and imperiouſly diſobeying the *Word of Command*, he turn'd ſhort up a Street, and got off, with no greater Damage than our ſhooting One of his Horſes, which dropt down dead (as I was ſince inform'd) before he got Home : However, by this Coachman's Reſolution, we loſt our Booty ; and the ſame Misfortune we met with about a Night, or Two after in *Red-Lyon-Square*, by killing another Horſe belonging to 'Squire *Thorold*, Brother to Sir *George Thorold*, Kt. and lately Lord - Mayor of *London.*

However,

However, the Dice turn'd shortly, and
Fortune smil'd favourably upon me, and *James
Wright*, when only we Two stopping a Coach
in *Monmouth-Street*, with Two Gentlemen in
it, about Eleven of the Clock at Night, we
took from them about Eight Pounds in Money, a Ducat, a Case of Instruments, Two
Mourning Rings, Two Tye-Wiggs, and a
Pair of new Stockings. In this audacious
Action, whilst *Wright* was rifling the Coach,
I stopp'd the People on Foot; for though it
was so late, the Street was very populous; and
yet, considering how many Spectators look'd
on, it was the quietest Action I ever was in,
for there was not one Word spoken, so that
we rid off without the least Danger imaginable; which gave us such Encouragement,
that the very same Night, riding through
Hog-Lane, towards St. *Giles's Pound*, we
turn'd up *Great Ruffel-Street*, *Bloomsbury*, and
stopt a Hackney-Coach, in which was one
Gentleman, from whom we took Six Guineas,
his Watch, and a Silver-Hilted Sword; but we
were not so quiet in the Action just before,
but we were as badly Mob'd in this, for just
by *Mountague-House*, my Comrade *Wright* had
like to have been knock'd off his Horse, by
a Chairman's making a Blow at him with his
long Pole, and crying out *Stop Highwaymen, Stop
Highwaymen*; however, it was our good Luck
nevertheless to come off with flying Colours.

Now

Now you muft underftand, that *James Wright*, and my deceas'd Brother, having had fome Difference, *Wright* would not go with us for fome Time, but went to feek his Fortune in the Company of one *John Scultrop*; but they Two had not got their Living long upon the Highway, before they alfo differ'd, when *Scultrop* going upon fuch dangerous Exploits by himfelf, within a Week after his bold Enterprizes, he was taken at *Newington* Turnpike, and, to fave his own Bacon, impeach'd *Wright*, and *John Wilfon*, and one *Buckmafter* ; tho' ('tis my Belief) that not either of the two Latter had follow'd that Courfe of Life : But upon this Information, *Wright* keeping out of the Way, was not apprehended, tho' *John Wilfon*, and *Buckmafter*, were in Cuftody ; but at the Affizes held at *Croyden*, they being acquitted, *Scultrop* was then Executed, tho' to fave his Life, he had fent feveral Letters to *Jonathan Wild*, to come and be an Evidence againft me, tho' I never knew, or faw him to my Knowledge in all my Life : This occafion'd me to fend a Man the Day he was Executed, to *Croyden*, who faw the Criminal juft as he receiv'd the Sacrament, when he declar'd to my Friend, that *Wright*, and I, were the firft Perfons that had feduc'd him to thofe Irregularities, for which he had then, by the Laws of the Land, forfeited his Life : This I infert here, tho' a Degreffion, to let the World fee, how a Man would die with a Lye in his Mouth;

for

for I folemnly declare, before God, and all Mankind, that I never was in *Scultrop*'s Company ; tho' he was the Occafion of my Confinement in *Newgate* for 13 Weeks, on Sufpicion of Robbing Mr. *Blackfton,* an Apothecary in *Newgate-Market,* when he was Robb'd by my Brother, and *Wright,* upon the 5th of *June* 1720 ; of which the Reader will have an Account in the Particulars which follow.

But during *Wright*'s Abfence (as above-mention'd) I got a new Companion, namely, *Thomas Davy* ; and the firft Enterprize he, I, and my deceas'd Brother went upon, was in *February,* 1720 ; when in *Denmark-Street,* near St. *Giles's-Church,* we ftop'd a Coach, in which was a Gentleman, and three Ladies, from whom we took about 25 *l.* in Money, a Gold Repeating-Watch, feveral Cornelian Seals fet in Gold, a fmall Landskipt in Gold, a Silver-Hilted Sword, a Chriftian's Tooth, and a little Agget-Shoe fet in Gold. As for the Two latter Things, I very well remember ; for when we were in Company by our felves, we ufed to toaft the Tooth, and Shoe, as a Health, as we always did all our other Benefactors. However, it was Advertiz'd in the News-Papers, that 2 Watches were loft in this Robbery ; but I fincerely declare (as no Danger can befal me now for my Life) that I never faw but One. The Cornelian Seals, and all the other Things, after we had unfet 'em, were fent to the Gold-Ring, oppofite to St. *Dunftan's-Church*

E   in

in *Fleet-Street*, according as the Advertisement
directed ; which was a piece of Civility un-
merited, considering how troublesome the
Footman was, when he came from behind
the Coach, to oppose our rummaging his
Master, and the Ladies, making Offers several
Times to strike us with his Stick ; and by
that Time I had oblig'd him to quit his Wood-
en Weapon, the whole *Posse* of the Watchmen came to their Assistance, so that I had
my Handful then to keep off those Tatterde-
malions ; but firing a Couple of Pistols over
their Heads, they all tumbled Head over Heels
in their Retreat, which gave us the favourable
Opportunity of riding off clear : When making the Best of our Way towards *Hampstead*,
we turn'd down *Fig-Lane*, and came again
into Town, where two Watchmen standing
at the End of *Gray's-Inn-Lane*, saluting us
with the usual Question, *Who comes there?*
We answer'd, *Friends :* However, they were
so unfriendly, as to take hold of the Horse-
Bridle of One of my Companions, saying,
They would know who we were : One of us
cocking a Pistol to One of their Breasts, saying,
*We would Shoot him, in case he did not let go
his Hold* ; but he still held the Reins fast, 'till
a Pistol was snapt at his Breast, but as good
Luck was, it did not go off, the Fright made
him loose the Bridle, and we got them clear
without any Harm.

The second Enterprize we did with *Day*,
was in *Battersea-Fields*, on the 19th of *Feb.*
1720,

1720, when ftopping a Coach, in which were two Gentlemen, two Gentlewomen, and a Child, we took from 'em a Gold ftriking Watch, a Silver Watch, and Chain, a Gold Seal Ring, a Diamond Ring in a Shagreen Cafe, two Mourning Rings, a Silver Tooth-pick-cafe, a Pocket-Book, with feveral Notes of Value, and about 23 Pounds in Money. Moreover, the Lady had her Brother's Picture hung to the Watch, which valuing very much, was put in an Advertifement, and according to the Directions thereof, we fent it Home, with the Pocket-Book, and feveral other Things, which were of no Value to us: In this Exploit *Davy* had One of our Horfes to hold, whilft I, and my Brother plunder'd the Coach, and the faid *Davy,* by fome Accident, firing a Piftol, the led Horfe broke out of his Hand, befides the Bullet flying through the Coach Door, and fhooting my Brother thro' the Coat, which had like to have prov'd the Deftruction of us all; for we were oblig'd to keep the Gentlemen, and Ladies, half an Hour, whilft I was endeavouring to catch the Horfe, which taking the Road, went to *Vaux-Hall* Turnpike; upon which we then let the Gentlefolks go, and at the aforefaid Place, two Men affifting us on Foot to catch him, we gave 'em a Shilling to drink, and being again mounted, we return'd fafe to *London.*

The latter End of *February* following, *Thomas Davy,* with me, and my Brother, having

E 2   many

many Things of Value, went on Board the
Mary Yacht, and setting Sail for *France,* a
favourable Gale carry'd us safe to *Calais,*
where going up the Country to dispose of our
Goods to the best Advantage, we steer'd our
Course to *Dunkirk,* at which Place we sold
the Silver Watch, taken in our Exploit in
Battersea-Fields, as in the Relation last mention'd ; but the Gold striking Watch, which
we had out of the same Coach, and the Gold
repeating Watch, taken out of the Coach in
Denmark-Street, we pawn'd at *Calais* for 62 *l.*
and three Hogsheads of *French* Claret, at 4 *l.*
10 *s. per* Hshd. for at that Time the Merchants,
as well as others, car'd not to go the Price
of Guineas, which then went at 43 Livres
a-piece. Having thus dispos'd of all our Goods,
we then fell to Merchandizing ourselves, buying Wines, Brandy, Silks, Cambricks, *&c.*
and then return'd to *London,* where about
the latter End of *March* following, we dispos'd of all our exotick, or outlandish Commodities, and then fell to trading in our
English Ones; 'till having gain'd a sufficient
Cargo, we then Shipp'd off, in *July,* or *August,* for *Holland.*

Not long after returning to *London,* honest
Davy, not wanting Money as usual, deny'd
going along with my Brother, and me, 'till
bad Circumstances, as not being able to hire
a Horse at his own Charge, oblig'd him constantly to hunt all the Town over after us, to
be reliev'd ; in order thereto, he propos'd to

us,

us, the dangerous Attempts of robbing in the
Streets of *London* again, if we would take
him into our Service; which we denying, he
laid the mean rascally Schemes of robbing
Foot-Passengers about *Islington,* and *Hoxton,*
telling us, that from the great Number of
People that went that Way by Night, we
might get abundance of Money, saying at the
same Time, he would find *Gag,* and *Cord*:
Farthermore, to shew the Rascality of this
Fellow, who was never yet taken up, he propos'd to us to rob Mr. *Leach,* the best Friend
he had, and I doubt not but some Murder
was design'd by *Davy,* in saying, that whenever Mr. *Leach* was dead, his Child, own as being
somewhat related to him, would be the Better. He likewise told us, Mr. *Leach,* went
frequently to the *Royal Exchange,* and had a
Pocket in the Bosom of his Coat, in which
he kept his Pocket-Book, with several Bank-
Bills. At this Prize, as *Davy* thought it, he
often shew'd me the said Mr. *Leach,* at the
Paul's-Head, in *Lawrence-Lane,* at the *Exchange,* and at his own House in *Grub-Street*:
These, so very base Things, we could not
agree to; and telling him, we were too brave
to attempt any Thing on Foot, and he not
daring to perform any Thing brave on Horse-
Back, we quite discarded him: But still
about the Middle of last Summer, he came
and told me, Mr. *Leach,* was going into the
Country, in the *Huntingdon* Stage-Coach,
which Inns at the *Red-Lyon* in *Aldersgate-*

Street;

Street; to confirm the Truth of which, he tells me, (like a Villain as he was) that the said Mr. *Leach*, had given him the Money for the Coach-Hire; and the Morning he went, flung a Stone out of his Yard, through my Window, where I lay; and asking what he wanted, he defir'd to fpeak with me prefently, when coming to him, he told me, as above, he would have me go along with him to rob old Mr. *Leach*; but I fo much abhor'd his Barbarity, of robbing his own Friend, that I, and my Brother, difcarded him our Service ever after.

About the latter End of *April*, or Beginning of *May* laft, I, and my Brother, went on pretty fuccefsfully by our felves, committing 'till near *Whitfontide*, feveral Robberies betwixt *Hampftead*, *Bow*, and *Hackney*, and particularly we robb'd a Gentleman's Coach between the two Watch-Houfes, upon *Cambridge-Heath*, the Perfon in it, if I miftake not, was Mr. Juftice *Ward*, from whom we took the Trifle of about 20 *s*. in Money, his Tye Wig, and fcarlet Rocquelaure, which we compaffionately gave to that ingenious Gentleman, Mr. ――――, the bright *Poultry-Compter* Author, fent now to the Seminary of *Newgate*, for his better Education in Villainy; he being bare in Cloaths, and a Hanger on us to learn our Art, and Myftery, (for at that Time he never, to my Knowledge, had been Abroad) to make him a Waftcoat, and Breeches : But by the Way, when my Brother,

ther, and I attack'd the abovefaid Worfhipful
Gentleman, if it was he, my Brother, thinking we had not Booty enough, breaks the
Coach-Glafs, and opening the Door, demands
his Worfhip's Pocket-Book, and Watch,
which putting the Gentleman into a Fright,
he flings the Coach-Door againft the Nofe of
my Brother's Horfe, leaps out, and crying
out, *In the Name of God, do you defign to
Murder a Man; you fhan't have my Pocket-
Book, I will fooner lofe my Life;* fo running
along the Road, crying, *Murder, Murder,*
he fell flat on his Face; upon which my
Brother cry'd out, *Shoot the Rogue;* at which
Words, he nimbly got up, and tumbled over
a Bank quite out of the Road, where we
could not follow him, his Footman, and
Coachman, crying out alfo, *Highwaymen,
Highwaymen,* which Alarm, made us return
back, and Shooting One of his Coach-Horfes,
we rode off.

About this Time, being *Whitfun-Eve,* going
up *Fleet-Street, Wright* meeting me, and my
Brother, told us, he had robb'd a *Quaker* of
about 20 Pounds, and a Pair of Silver Spurs,
in Company of *Scultrop,* whom we never
knew, as I have faid before, and whatever
the Difference was I cannot tell, but *Scultrop*
would go with *Wright* no more; however,
my Brother, and I, went to the *Grey-Hound*
Tavern in *Fleet-Street,* where we appointed
to meet the *Monday* following, at the *Caftle-
Tavern,* in the fame Street, and being all as

good as our Promife, when together, my
Brother told him (it being Holy-Day-Time)
he would take a Ride out with him, which
Propofition he accepting, faid he would go
out with him if he had a Horfe, whereupon
I fent him mine, upon paying me for the Lofs
of my Time, as being engag'd upon honeft
Affairs, with other Company that Day ; fo
they went out together, had good Bufinefs,
and I met them at the laft mention'd Tavern,
where they fhew'd me what they got from
Mr. *Blackfton*, namely, a Gold Watch, a
Silver Watch, a Silver Snuff-Box, a Silver-
Hilted Sword, a Cafe of Inftruments, a Diamond Ring, with Ten fmall Stones, and a
large One in the Middle, and about 40 Shillings in Money : Upon which Booty, I got
a Crown of *Wright* for the Hire of my Horfe,
and a good Supper, and truly that is all I did
get, for 13 Weeks Imprifonment, for a Crime
I never was Guilty of ; but however, it was
fome Satisfaction, becaufe *Scultrop* was then
Hang'd for his falfe Induftry, as abovefaid, which
made me digeft my Supper the better, upon
the Account of his receiving our bleffed Lord's
Supper, upon the telling a notorious Lye, at
going out of the World.

On the 9th of *June* 1620, the faid *Wright*,
with me, and my Brother, took a Ride to
Epping-Forreft, and on the Back-Side of *Woodford* Town, we met One of his Majefty's
Coaches, and Six, we ftopt them, and took
from the two Gentlemen, and two Ladies,

in

in the Coach, about 18 Pounds in Money, a
Gold Watch, a Diamond Ring, set round
with small Brilliants, and a large Brilliant on
the Top, one Hoop Ring, set round with
Rubies, and Diamonds, one Ring set round
with Rubies only, one Ring,-with a large
Red Stone on the Top, and one plain Gold
Ring, which made me very sorry I did not
leave it with the Lady, according to her Request, which she earnestly begg'd : The
Gentleman from whom the Watch was taken,
would have given me his Gold Headed Cane,
but I refus'd it, by reason we had a good
Booty out of the Coach, and I believ'd he
might want his Cane to support him, so we
rode off : However, I believe, when I am
at my Liberty, it may be in my Power to
help him to his Watch again.

About Three, or Four Days after, we
rode to *Finchly-Common*, and there kept on 'till
we came to *Whetstone*, and drinking without
Door, at a publick House, a Gentleman pass'd
by us in an open Chaise, and a Pair of Horses,
who was Reading some Papers. We took
him for a *South-Sea* Man, and it was at that
Time that all the World were robbing One
another, some for Want, and some for Lucre;
the Former of which, was my unhappy
Circumstance. We pass'd the Gentleman,
and stopp'd his Chaise, but it so happen'd,
that his Loss, was a great deal more than
our Gain ; for by the Impudence of the
Coachman, who would neither obey our

E 5   Commands,

Commands, nor his Mafter's Orders, who bid him ftop, but he would not, whereby we got but one Guinea, and a Half, fo we fevere-ly lick'd the Coachman, as he did well deferve, and fhot both his Mafter's Horfes, which made, as abovefaid, his Lofs, more than our Gain: Which Exploit happen'd on a *Saturday,* when we were clofely purfu'd by the Country, but neverthelefs we got off, and rode fafe to *London.*

The *Wednefday* following, being the 16th of *June,* we rode to *Epping,* where we robb'd two Gentlemens Coaches, the Firft on the Forrefts, with two Ladies in it, and took from them about two Pounds in Money, with a Tooth-Pick-Cafe ; and then overtaking the other Coach at the Bottom, by the *Brick-Kiln,* this Side *Woodford,* behind which was a Footman, and in it a Gentleman, and a young Woman ; we took 40 Shillings from him, but fhe faying fhe was but a Servant, we took nothing from her. A Man at the fame Time coming by, alarm'd the Country, but I, and my Companions, riding into a Wood, we ftaid there 'till Night came on, and then made the Beft of our Way to *London.* When we came to the *Green-Man,* juft off the Forreft, Three, or Four Horfe-Men ftruck into our Company, and judging it the fafeft Way to keep them Company, that they might have no Sufpicion of us, they prov'd our greateft Enemies, for the nearer we got to-wards *Stratford* by *Bow,* more Horfe-Men came
into

to our Company, 'till we got juſt by the Watch-Houſe at *Stratford*, which was lined with Men, and Arms, and then the Word was given, *Stop Highwaymen* ; ſo that on a ſudden there were about 20 Horſe-Men, and abundance of Men on Foot upon us, which oblig'd us to turn back, and take *Rumford* Road, being purſu'd for about four Miles, when I was forc'd to quit my Horſe, and with a great deal of Difficulty, I got ſafe to *London* a Foot, and my Friends as ſafe thither on Horſe-Back:

About the latter End of the ſame Month, being the 27th of *June*, I was taken upon the Information of one *Pocock*, on Suſpicion of Robbing a Stage-Coach upon *Epping-Forreſt* ; my Apprehending was by *Pocock*'s two Bro-thers, with an Intent of making a Diſcovery of my Brother, they not knowing the Place of his Abode, nor where to find him: They told me, if I would tell them where he was, it would be of great Service to me ; but telling them I could not, they carry'd me before the late Sir *William Withers*, who committed me to the *Poultry-Compter* ; notwithſtanding thoſe Robberies I committed before, no Man had a better Character than my ſelf, in my Station, for no one Living, but theſe three Perſons whom I was concern'd with, knew any Thing of my going Abroad ; nei-ther had I ever committed any Robbery, when *Pocock* made this Information of me. After 14 Days Confinement, the Seſſions

came

came on at *Juſtice-Hall* in the *Old-Baily*,
when a little before the ſaid *Pocock* was
brought from *Reading*-Goal, it being then
alſo Aſſize-Time : I expected to have been
carry'd to *Burntwood*, where the Aſſizes was
kept this Year, for that County ; but contrary to my Expectation, I was carry'd to
the *Old-Baily*, the firſt Day of Seſſions, and
forthwith arraign'd for robbing 'Squire *Had-*
dock at *Mile-End*, on the 22d of *November*
1719, which was full two Months before I
had ever committed any Fact of that Nature ;
however, I took my Tryal for the ſame, and
acquitted, tho' *Pocock* brought ſeveral Perſons
to ſwear againſt me, beſides himſelf, when I
knew none of 'em ; moreover, One of the
Women whom he brought to be a Witneſs
againſt me, declar'd, ſhe never ſaw me in all
her Life before : Again, there was one *Oliver*
Taylor, who kept Horſes in *Finsbury*, depos'd
on my Tryal, that I uſed frequently to hire
Horſes of him Three, or Four Days in a
Week ; but I ſolemnly declare, before God,
and the World, I never hir'd a Horſe of him
in the whole Courſe of my Life, nor ever
committed any Robbery with *Pocock*, tho'
he declar'd at his Death, that I was Guilty
of the Fact for which I was Try'd ; but before I was out of Trouble, he was Executed
at *Ailesbury*, in the County of *Bucks*.

Obtaining my Liberty about the Beginning
of *October* 1720, I, and my Brother, ſet
out for *Holland* from *Harwich*, whither we
went

went a-Foot, and then fet over in the Pacquet-Boat : My Brother continu'd there for a Month, and my felf for nine Weeks. As to what *Ralph Wilfon,* pretends to affert in his erroneous Book, faying, we carry'd with us to the Value of 50 Pounds, of *Wright's* Goods, is falfe, for he had but Part of one Gold Repeating - Watch, which was pawn'd at *Amfterdam,* and the Ring, which he fays in the fame Book was fold for 40 Pounds, when I had but 30 Pounds for it, as aforefaid. But it is a Cord, not a Lye, will choak him, as may be feen by his faying we both return'd in the Beginning of *Auguft,* when I did not return 'till the Beginning of *December* following, neither did I commit any Robbery with this Fellow 'till after *Chriftmas.*

The firft Exploit I ever committed with *Ralph Wilfon,* was betwixt *Hackney,* and *London,* which was in *January* 1721-22, my Brother being then in Company, we took a fmall Silver Watch, a large Silver Tobacco-Box, mark'd *J. H.* and about 15 Shillings in Money ; but it is admirable to me, how *Wilfon* can charge me with Cowardice in this Action, when Fear would never permit him to come near the Coach ; however, we gave our Booty into his Cuftody, which he deliver'd again to my Brother, as being indebted to him then in a greater Sum than it came to, befides owing me 30 Shillings to this Day, which contradicts his lending us Money (as before Noted) to buy us Horfes ; neither had he at this Time fold his Eftate.   The

The second (which was also the last) Exploit I committed with *Wilson*, none then being together but us Two, was near the Halfway-House in *Hampstead* Road, where stopping a Coach, we took from the People therein Six Shillings in Money, Three Silver Spoons, a Pepper-Box, and Salt-Seller; which *Wilson* not thinking Booty enough, the great Hero *Wilson*, sometime after I had robb'd the People, came up to the other Side of the Coach, and like a valiant Man, most couragiously took from a Woman Two round-ear'd Caps, and Three-Half-pence in *Ready-Rhino*. These are all the Actions I ever committed with him; but at this Time, as we were riding off together, I stopt a Coach in *Fig-Lane*, when he rode off, as not daring to venture to my Assistance; so I did not see him 'till I came to the Turn-pike, where asking him the Reason of not coming to my Assistance he made Answer, he saw a Man coming along the Fields.

'Tis true, I was once more in Company with *Wilson*, and my Brother, in *Hide Park* a-Foot, with an Intent to rob the Coaches; here we stopt One, and *Wilson* (as is taken Notice of before) shot himself thro' the Hand; but there was no Horse shot, neither was the Coach attack'd belonging to Mr. *Green* the Brewer, for there was a Man of that Gentleman's with me, since *Wilson's* putting out his lying Book, in the *Gate-House*, and told me Mr. *Green*, had never any Attempt made of robbing him but once, and that was behind *Buckingham-House*; and that too, was since my Confinement.   After

After *Lent* Affizes were over at *Kingston* upon *Thames*, when *Wright* was continu'd to the Affizes in *Auguft* 1721, I, and my Brother, return'd to *London*, and going together for about the Space of two Months, committed feveral Robberies in that Time, betwixt *London*, and *Hampftead*, *Cambridge-Heath*, and in *Dog-Row*, at which laft Place meeting a Gentleman in a Coach, we took from him a Silver Watch, about 20 Shillings in ready Cafh, and three Pocket-Books, in which were feveral Notes: Juft as I was going off, I felt in his Pocket a Tobacco-Box, in which he faying there was 10 Guineas, and a Half Bread-Piece, begg'd heartily I would not take them, becaufe they were not his own, but not believing the Story, we carry'd off the Prize: However, finding by his Pocket-Books, he was of a dangerous Profeffion, (as being a Rope-Maker by Trade) we were neverthelefs fo Civil as to fend his Pocket-Books, and Notes, to a Coffee-Houfe in *Lombard-Street*, but withal writing to him, that the Favour of returning them was more than he deferv'd, unlefs he would for the future forfwear his Trade.

The next remarkable Thing we did was on a *Saturday* Night, when meeting a Coach in *White-Crofs-Street*, as we were going Home, my Friend faying there was a Gentleman in it, whom he fancy'd was going to *Hoxton*, we rid back and ftopt him by the *Common Hunt*'s in *Bunhill-Fields*, and took from him about
14 Pounds,

14 Pounds, which Loſs we ſuppos'd was more
than he knew of, for we believ'd he was one
of our Fraternity, and ſo had not Time to
tell his Money ; beſides, we took from him
a Pair of Pocket-Piſtols, loaded with Powder
and Ball, a Silver-Hilted Sword, and a very
nice Half-Hunting Whip : And as for the
Money we took from him, it was in an old
greaſy Leather Pocket, freſh torn out of ſome
Man's Breeches, and for this Reaſon we believe him to be One of us.

The next Exploit we did was under *Buckingham-Wall*, where we ſtopt a Gentleman,
and Lady, in their Coach, and took from
them a Gold Watch, a Gold Snuff-Box, a
Pair of Diamond Ear-Rings ; but the Lady
(I believe) ſunk her Watch in ſome more
ſecret Place, than the Gentleman had ſecur'd
his, for we could not find it high, nor low ;
but however, by Way of Reprizal for that
Loſs, we took from them 18 Pounds more.

The next Companion I went with, was
the unhappy *George Sympſon* ; and the firſt
Action we enter'd into, my Brother being
alſo With us, was upon the Counteſs Dowager
of *Strafford*, in *Richmond-Lane*, taking from
her Ladyſhip, about ſix Pounds in Money,
a Gold Ring, a Croſs, and a Ticket ·for the
King's-Evil ; (*Sympſon* then liv'd with one
Mr. *Green*, in *Mark-Lane*, being on a Grey-
Horſe of his Maſter's) and when we were in
the Middle of our Exploit, *Sympſon* riding up
to the Side of the Coach where my Brother
was,

was, his Horfe turning fhort, flung him, and ran to the *Feathers-Inn* at *Richmond* : I alighting from my Horfe, flung the Bridle over my Arm, whilft I rifled the Lady in her Coach, and was ftepping out again, in order to remount, my Horfe had flipt his Bridle, and ran away alfo. *Sympfon* rid immediately after my Brother's Horfe ; in the mean Time we kept the Lady in her Coach, and my Brother talking very good *French* to her, fhe feem'd pleas'd to ftay during our Pleafure. At laft *Sympfon* brings my Brother's Horfe, but did not fee mine ; however, they being both mounted, we releas'd the Lady, and her Attendance, and went to the *Red-Lyon* in *Richmond*, where I had fet up my Horfe before, and thither he was got again, without his Rider ; but they telling the Hoftler he had flung the Gentleman, gave him a Shilling, and brought him to me in *Richmond-Lane*, where they had left me behind ; then being all mounted, we rid fafe to *London* ; and in about a Week *Sympfon* gave his Mafter Warning, and quitted his Service.

The next Exploit that *George Sympfon*, and we did, was on the *Cirencefter* Stage-Coach, betwixt *Knight's-Bridge*, and *Kenfington*, taking from the Paffengers about [Nine Pounds in Money, Two Mourning Rings, and a Silver-Hilted Sword. The Gentleman begg'd very heartily, that we would not take the Sword, fwearing by his Maker feveral Times, it was only a Brafs Mounting ; but when I came
Home,

Home, I found it, to my great Satisfaction, to be of a better Sort of Metal.

The next Enterprize we, and *Sympson* did, was under *Buckingham-Wall*, where we stopt a Gentleman's Coach, and four Horses ; but had we known as we llbefore, as we did afterwards, we would have sav'd ourselves the Trouble of making that Attempt, for we met with a very small Booty, only one Guinea, about 14, or 15 Shillings in Silver, and a Piece of Queen *Anne*'s Gold for the Evil : Had there been more current Coin among it, I would not have taken the Evil-Piece, or at least-wise had sent it back again ; but coming Home, and finding in a Purse, some old Shillings of *Oliver Cromwell*'s, it made us suspect, they were some of his damnable Crew, and so we retain'd it.

The *Bury* Stage-Coaches, we robb'd Five, or Six Times, and the *Huntington* Coach also, in which we were pretty Successful ; for if they had no Money in their Purses, we made it good in their Boxes, or Portmanteaus ; especially by one Lady, and her Maid, in the *Bury* Coach, from whom we took both their Boxes, in which they said was no Money ; whereupon we gave them our Word, and Honour, that if there was no Money in them, we would return them again ; but finding in them Three small Pieces of Plate, with some Chocolate, and Tea, we kept them ; but nevertheless sent 'em back Apparel of much greater Value, which the

Lady's

Lady's Woman receiv'd that very Night, at the *Green-Dragon-Inn,* in *Bishopsgate-Street.*

Next, in *July* 1721, we meeting with a Couple of Coaches in *Fig-Lane,* which we took for Gentlemen's, becaufe cover'd in Mourning, we attack'd them ; but when all came to all, they were only five People in each, returning from a Funeral, from whom we took about 40 Shillings, and a Cypher Ring ; but the Woman that own'd the Ring, crying fhe was a very poor Body, that fold Tripes, and Trullibubs in *Field-Lane,* I return'd it her again ; which was the laft Robbery I ever committed in Company with my Brother, and *Sympfon,* who then went into *Lincolnfhire.*

Then I pickt up *Butler Fox,* with whom I became acquainted at the *Poultry-Compter,* when I was Prifoner there, about two Years ago; and the firft Robbery we went upon, was on the 27th of laft *July,* when we robb'd the *Huntington* Stage-Coach, by *Mount-Mill,* near *Iflington,* in which was one Gentleman, and five Women, from whom we took about Five, or Six Pounds in Money, a Silver Watch, and Silver-Hilted Sword ; and for this Robbery Juftice *Cooms,* fent a Commitment againft *Butler Fox,* to *Newgate* ; but the Profecutors being then out of Town, he was not Try'd for that Faft.

The next Robbery *Butler Fox,* and I committed, was on *Putney Common,* where ftopping a Coach, and Four Horfes, in which
was

was the Honourable Colonel *Archibald Hamilton*, and two Ladies, and his Servant, at some little Diftance from it on Horfe-Back, upon whom Seizing firft, we took from him a rifled Barrel Gun, and attack'd the Perfons in the Coach ; we took from them about fix Pounds in Money, a Silver-Hilted Sword, a Tortoife-Shell Box, with Silver Bottom, and Sides, within the Lid three Mad's Heads, a fix-corner'd Box, Mother of Pearl at Top, with King *Charles*'s Head cut thereon, and a Piece of Flower'd *French* Silk ; then we made the Coachman get down, and turn out his Pockets, as fuppofing he might have had the Colonel's Watch, but we judg'd of the wrong Perfon, for his Footman had it, fo we mifs'd of it. Since my Confinement at the *Gate-Houfe*, the Honourable Col. *Archibald Hamilton*, was with me there, and amongft Seven, or Eight Men, he pofitively pitch'd upon me, to be One of the Perfons that had Robb'd him. This Robbery was committed upon the 15th of laft *Auguft*, between the Hours of Seven, and Eight at Night, and for it *Butler Fox*, was Executed laft *March* at *Croyden*, in the County of *Sarry*.

The next Expedition the abovefaid *Butler Fox*, and I went upon, was on the 2d of *September* following, when we Robb'd the *Cirencefter* Stage-Coach, about One in the Morning, between *Knight's-Bridge*, and *Kenfington*, taking from the Paffengers about 25 Shillings, as being prevented by two Men

on

on Horse-Back, behind the Coach, and the
Patrole upon the Road, from Rummaging them
any farther; so we rid off, and Robb'd the
Huntington Coach the same Morning about
Three, at *Mount-Mill* by *Islington*, taking
from the Right Worshipful Sir *Edward Lawrence*, a Green Purse, in which was a Guinea
and a Half, his Pocket-Book, in which were
Notes of great Value, his Cloak-Bag, in
which were five *Holland* Shirts, two White
Wastecoat, a Tye-Wig, a new Piece of
Fustain, a Piece of new Blue Cloth, a Piece
of new Shalloon, a Piece of new Muslin,
several Neckcloths, and Turnovers, a Plad-
Gown, lin'd with Red Calimanco, six Pounds
of Chocolate, a Canister of Tea, and several
other Things. For this Robbery I was taken,
and committed to the *Gate-House*, on the 4th
of *November* 1721; and since my Confinement I return'd that worthy Gentleman his
Pocket-Book, and Notes, with (I think) all
his other Things, excepting a Piece of new
Muslin.

For these Two last Robberies *Butler Fox*,
was Try'd at the *Old Baily*; and tho' the
greatest Proof was made against him as ever
was known in that Court, by a great Chyrum,
or Cloud of Persons, corroborating my Evidence, yet was he acquitted; but own'd himself Guilty of the said Facts, when he suffer'd
Death at *Croyden:* I leave the the World to
judge whether that Criminal dy'd wrongfully
upon my Information.

By

By the Way, it is farther to be obſerv'd, that when my Brother, and I, were in *Holland*, we purpos'd to rob upon the Highway in that Country, but finding the Roads all along to be Dyk'd, or Damn'd, on both Sides, our Purpoſe was aitogether Impracticable on Horſe-Back ; however, we attempted one Night a-Foot to rob a *Dutchman* between *Vlaerding*, and *Schierlam*, taking from him 14 Ducatoons, ſix Shillings, and about 10, or 12 Stivers in Money ; for which, he gave us as many Curſes, in his own Language ; yet we could not blame the poor *Lanceman*, becauſe, according to the old Proverb, *You muſt always give the Looſer Leave to ſpeak.*

Alſo when we were in *France*, we intended to rob there on the Highway, and in order thereto, we reſolv'd to enter ourſelves into the Gang of *Cartouche*, and *Pilliceir*, the greateſt Robbers of this Age, before they were Broke upon the Wheel; but conſidering again, that they, and their Gang, ſcarce committed a Robbery without a Murder, the Horror of ſhedding ſo much Blood, deterr'd us from entering into that ſanguine Fraternity. However, my Brother, and I, committed ſome Robberies in that Country, and particularly once near St. *Germain en lape*, where meeting a Couple of Coaches, with ſix Horſes each, fill'd with Noblemen, and Ladies, of the Firſt Rank ; after the ſcaring Words of *Stand, and Deliver*, were pronounc'd to them in *French* by my Brother,

for

for he could speak that Tongue very well; I alighted, and plunder'd the Quality of eight Gold Watches, and as many Purses of Piftoles, with fome Diamond Rings, and Bobs, fo that our Booty we made to be 800 Pounds Sterling, and Better.

Hence making the Beft of our Way for *Rhoan* in *Normandy,* we there contracted with a Merchant for as many Pieces of Silk, Velvets, and Damasks, as came to 123 Piftoles, giving him 20 Piftoles in Part of Payment, with Orders to fend 'em forthwith to our Lodging, becaufe we were to go on Ship-board the next Morning by Break of Day. It being then about 10 of the Clock at Night, the Merchant fent a Porter with the Goods, whom we attacking in the Street, my Brother, and I being both Mask'd, we took them from him, went ftrait to our Inn, which the Merchant did not know, for we had told him a wrong Place, and pretending earneft Bufinefs requir'd us into the Country that Night, our Horfes were immediately Sadled, and we then made the Beft of our Way for *Calice,* and there taking Shipping, we both of us fafely arriv'd in *England.*

Proceeding from *Dover* towards *London,* my Brother, and I, overtook a Carrier betwixt *Canterbury,* and *Sittingborn,* who, as we had certain Intelligence given us by the Chamberlain of an Inn, had a Pack on One of his Horfes, containing a confiderable Value, we attack'd the Carrier, and driving

the

the Horfe which carry'd it into a By-Lane, we prefently flung off the Pack, and cutting it open, took thereout in Money, fine Laces, and other Things of light Carriage, to the Value of Four Hundred and Fifty Pounds.

The fame Day we overtook a Waggoner, within a Mile of *Dartford*, and feeing fome goodly Boxes in his Waggon, we made bold to make Seizure of One of 'em, tho' there were 15 or 16 Paffengers in it ; but they being moft Women, we got our Prey with a very little Refiftance ; in which, we found ten Guineas in a Gold Snuff-Box, a Pearl Necklace, with a Gold Crofs ty'd to it, a Silver Watch, and a Silver Caudle-Cup gilt with Gold, and then rode away ftrait to *London*.

But before I come to an End, I am oblig'd to take Notice of a Falfe, and Scurrilous Paper, put out by Mr. S-----p a Printer, lately Convicted at *Guild Hall*, in *London*, for Printing a moft Scandalous, and Vile Pamphlet, highly Reflecting on the prefent Government ; and for which, having been before committed to *Newgate*, he infinuates, that there he became acquainted with my Brother, and *George Sympfon*, and that they fhould confefs to him that *Wright* the Barber, and *Butler Fox*, were wrongfully Hang'd by my Information, for they were not with me in thofe Robberies for which they fuf-fer'd Death, but in Company only with them Two ; which is a moft notorious Falf-
hood

hood, for *Sympfon* never had any perfonal
Knowledge of *Wright*, and *Fox*, fo they could
not Rob with him ; neither was my Brother (but *Wright*, and *Fox*, only with me)
in thofe capital Crimes for which they died :
Therefore, I am very well affur'd, that he made
a better Preparation for his latter End, than
that of Hazarding the Salvation of his Soul,
by departing the World with a Lye in his
Mouth, as S———p above-mention'd, has
bafely publifh'd.

Furthermore, we will give this Account
about Mr. *Wright* the Barber, in the *Old-Baily*,
that before he went upon the Highway, he
took to very petty Things, as privately Robbing his Neighbours ; and they thinking him
an honeft Fellow, had the leaft Sufpicion of
him ; and tho' they could not tell abfolutely
how the Robbery was committed, yet it is
fo far detefted fince, that when *Wright* found
the Sweetnefs of thofe Silver Tankards, he
would prefume then to go upon the Highway,
and accidentally he was taken upon that Account ; and the Perfon concern'd with him,
was oblig'd to be an Evidence againft him ;
and upon my Information was convifted by
Law : And farthermore, to prove this Faft
true, they were melted down by *Harry D*---
in *Fofter Lane*, Brother to *John D*-------,
Try'd about three Years ago for Coining, but
acquitted.

N. B. The Tankards above-mention'd,
were Stoln from one Mr. *Price*, a *Welfhman*,

that

that keeps the *Bell* Ale-Houfe in the *Great Old-Baily*: Farthermore, one *G——* being acquainted with *Wright*, advis'd him to *D——* to be melted down, with the Perfon abovementioned, and by the fame Token he had been Robbing on the Highway with my Brother, *D——*, and *G——* .

N. B. *I defire, as I am under Confinement, that Mr.* Purney, *Ordinary of* Newgate, *will be modeftly pleafed to juftify what he has fo falfely inferted in his* Dying-Speeches, *about my Brother* John Hawkins, *to be Truth, of Robbing the* Briftol-Mail, *who (as he faid) was put out to be a Plaifterer by my Father, which, let the World judge, whether my Father could put him to that Trade, when my Father was dead eight Months before he was Born.*

But to conclude, I have here given a full, and impartial Account of all irregular Tranfactions, which I have been concern'd in upon the Highway, to which I never had an Inclination, had not I been addicted too much to Gaming, which prompted me to fupport my felf in fuch vicious Courfes; but tho' I have very highly Offended againft the Laws of my Country, yet, as Providence has fo much took me into its Protection, as to prolong my Life to a longer date, I hope in God I fhall make fuch good Ufe of that Mercy, and Favour, which I have found under the Afflictions of a long Confinement, that as foon as I obtain my Liberty, I will endeavour, thro' God's Grace, to procure, by living an honeft fober Life, the Love, and Efteem, of all Mankind.   *James*

JAMES BARTON, *a Highwayman.*

JAMES BARTON, was descended of very good Parents, his Father having a very good Estate in *Hampshire,* and he being the only Child they had living, he was put at about 12 Years of Age to *Winchester*-School, his Parents designing to bring him up for a Divine, or a Lawyer. But he was from his meer Infancy very untoward, and as his Years increas'd, so did his Archness, which was not Harmless, but very Mischievous, and Roguish, so that he had not the least Inclination for Literature.

His Parents finding the Aversion their Son had for Learning, they took him Home; and though they had enough to leave him, for his Maintenance after their Decease, yet seeing how much he indulg'd himself to idleness, and keeping loose disorderly Persons Company; to break him of those Vices which too early began to be riveted in him, by such wicked Conversation, they put him Apprentice to a Goldsmith in *Portsmouth*: But First of all he was to be a Month upon liking, but before a Fortnight was expir'd, he gave such eminent and signal Proofs of his Unluckiness, that his Master sent him Home to his

F 2   Friends

Friends again. The chief Occafion of this Exile from *Portfmouth* was this : One Day *Johnny Gibfon*, the Governour of this Garrifon, being fitting as ufual, on a Bench by the Guard-Houfe, on the Parade, and taking a little Nap, this *Barton* found an Opportunity of tying a fmall Cord about his Legs, and at the fame Time, ty'd a dead Rat to the Bottom of his Wig behind. Prefently after, a Man of War coming into the Harbour, and firing her Guns, *Johnny Gibfon* ftarted out of his Nap, and rifing up haftily, as going towards the Guard-Houfe, down he fell on his Face, which much bruis'd it, and broke his Nofe : Several Soldiers came to his Affiftance, and helping him up, Quoth he, *Lods, Ife believe they are going to tye me Neck, and Heels, for Slauping on my Poft. The muckle Deel ftap Hemp in his Guts, and blaw his Bladder full of Pebble Stones, whoever the Loon was. May the Deel brauk my Craig, but that Ife would, if Ife had him here, cut off both his Lugs, or elfe as fmall as Herbs to the Pot.* But when *Johnny* found the Rat ty'd to the Tail of his Wig, he fwooned away, he having as great an Antipathy againft that Sort of Vermin, as *Bob Burnbam*, the Book-Binder in *Little-Britain*, had againft Mice. But when he was recover'd again, and having found out the Spark that thus ferv'd his Governourfhip, he had him fent to the Houfe of Correction, where he was well flogg'd three Days fucceffively, and then recommended to his Parents again,

again, with the Character of being a very
unlucky Rogue.

With what kind Reception he met with
at Home, it is easily judg'd; but in some
short Time after, he was sent upon liking
again, to another Master, who was a Linnen-
Draper at *Southampton.* Here he had not been
a Week, but observing a Woman at the next
Door to his Master, never miss'd washing a
White Earthen Chamber-Pot every Morning,
and left it in the Yard 'till Night, it lying by
the Pales within *Barton*'s Reach, he lays hold
on it one Day, and bor'd a Hole through the
Centre of the Bottom of it; at Night the
Woman fetches it in as usual, and having Occasion to make Use of it after she was in Bed,
as fast as she fill'd the Pot at Top, it found
an Evacuation through the Hole at Bottom:
Quoth her Husband, *What a Plague is not the
Pot wide enough, but you must piss besides?*
she says, *Indeed, my Dear, I don't, for I hold
it exactly over the Pot.* The Husband replies,
*Hold it over the Devil don't you, I tell you,
you do piss beside. I don't,* says she again.
Quoth he, *Pox on you, you do, for I am all
wringing wet.* Quoth she, *I suppose the Tap's
loose, and the Drink runs about.* Up starts the
Husband, swearing, and cursing like any
Dragoon; strikes a Light, runs to the Bar-
rel, and swears a great Oath, that both Tap,
and Spiggot too was fast. Then making an
Examination about the Bed, it was all in a
Float; looking next into the Chamber-Pot,

without

without taking it from the Floor, and feeing
not a Drop of Urine in it, Quoth he to his
Wife, *Look'e here you d---mn'd B----h, did not
I tell you how it was? You held your curfed,
confounded Water-Gap exactly over it, have you
not? See what a fweet Pickle my Shirt is in; I
reckon I fhall have all the Dogs in Town, follow
me to fmell Pifs, and pifs upon me to boot:
Look upon the Sheets, and Bed-Cloaths, as wet
as if they had been juft taken out of a Bucking-
Tub.* Says fhe, *Indeed, my Dear, I was never
fo much miftaken in my Life, I could almoft
have fworn I held it exactly over the Pot; but
the Beft may be miftaken fometimes.* So then
fhe rofe, and with her Husband, was forc'd
to take up their Quarters in another Bed 'till
next Morning: When rifing, and rinfing the
Pot in the Yard, the Water running then out
at the Bottom, fhe found that fhe was not in
the Fault, but that the Member-Mug had
Sprung a Leak; of which acquainting her
Husband, and he finding out the Engineer,
that Sprung the Mine, under the Earthen
Machine, he acquainted his Mafter of it,
who forthwith fent him Home to his
Father.

His Father, and Mother, being oblig'd to
give their unlucky Son *James* Entertainment
again, whom they then intended to put Apprentice to a Grocer at *Petersfield*, where
before he was Bound, he was alfo to be fome
Time upon liking: It happen'd one Day,
that the Mafter being from Home, the Maid
busy

busy above Stairs, and this their 'Prentice in the Yard, a Customer in the Shop knocking, the Mistress, who then was drawing some Cyder, which had been but Tapt that Day, went and serv'd the Person, *James* observing this Motion, goes and drinks heartily of the Cyder himself, lets all the rest of it run about, which was upwards of Thirty Four Gallons, and privately conveys the Spiggot into his Mistress's Pocket.

At Dinner, the Maid was order'd to bring a Tankard of Cyder to the Table: She goes into the Cellar, where she was up to the Ancles in Cyder, ready drawn to her Hands, and star'd like a dead Pig, to find no Spiggot in the Cask. She returns with the melancholy News of the Cyder being flung over Board; the Master Swears like an Emperour, at the Carelessness of, who he could not yet tell; and the Mistress Fretting, and Fuming, said she was there last, and drew the last Cyder, but vow'd and protested she had wrung the Spiggot fast in. All Three then went into the Cellar, with a Hue and Cry after the Spiggot, which could not be found high, nor low; 'till upon some Occasion the Mistress happening to put her Hand into her Pocket, and finding it there, quoth she, in a great Surprize, *Dear me! here it is, see here it is, alas! how may One be mistaken; I could really have taken my Oath, before a Justice of Peace, that I had certainly left it in the Barrel: But a Customer knocking very earnestly in the Shop,*

F 4 *and*

*and no Body there to serve her, for you know,
my Dear, you was out this Morning, the Maid
at the same Time, was up Stairs about her Business, the Boy was at the necessary House, and
being then drawing my self Half a Pint of Cyder, I went hastily into the Shop, and in this
Hastiness, without any Thought of what I was
about, I have put the Spiggot into my Pocket,
and have let the Value of Ten Shillings run to
waste.* The Grocer finding it was his Wife's
Fault, put it off with a Laugh, and said no
more of the Matter. Here *James* might have
come clean off of this unlucky Frolick, but
Glorying in his Unluckiness, and telling the
Maid the Truth of the Story, he and she
shortly after fell out, and then came out the
Murder, for she told her Master, and Mistress, how the Cyder came to be let about the
Cellar; for which the Father was forc'd to
pay, and take his Son Home again.

However, his Parents were resolv'd to try
him once more, to make him a Tradesman,
but *James* thinking that being a Mechanick
would spoil his Gentility, he had the Relish
of being a Gentleman altogether, as his Father. But yet, contrary to his Will and
Inclination, he was put, and bound Apprentice to a Mercer, for Seven Years, at *Rumsey*
in *Hampshire.* He had not been here a Quarter of a Year, before he began to play his
Freaks in the Family, beating the Children,
fighting with the Maids, sh--tt--g in his
Mistress's Shoes, and picking his Master's

Money-

Money-Box ; infomuch, that they were already weary of him. But quickly he became acquainted with one *Keele,* another Apprentice in the fame Town, who was a Brother to one *Richard Keele,* that was Hang'd in *December* 1713, with one *William Lowther,* for willful Murder. For this *Richard Keele,* who was Born, and Bred in *Rumfey,* and *William Lowther,* having committed a felonious Fact, they were apprehended, and committed to *Newgate* ; and being Try'd for Theft at *Juſtice-Hall* in the *Old-Baily,* and found Guilty by the Jury, they were both Burnt in the Hand, and order'd to hard Labour for a Twelve-Month, and a Day, in *Clerkenwell-Bridewell.* Accordingly they were both carried thither Hand-Cuff'd, in Company of another Thief, nam'd *Charles Houghton,* and when *William Seymour,* then Turn-Key of the Common-Side of *Newgate,* had deliver'd them up to one *Perry,* the Overseer of *Bridewell,* they refusing to have Irons put on them, and to beat Hemp, a bloody Fight enfu'd, in which *Charles Houghton,* One of the abovesaid Criminals, was Shot through the Heart, and dropt down dead upon the Spot : *Richard Keele,* had his Right Eye Shot out ; and *William Lowther,* was most dangerously Wounded in several Places in the Back : However, they made shift to ftab *Perry,* the Overseer of *Bridewell,* fo that he prefently died of his Wounds ; and they had made their Escape, had not Juftice *Fuller*

come with a ftrong Affiftance to the Jayl,
from whence he committed them back to
Newgate again for Murder, where *Keele*, and
Lowther both recover'd of their Wounds.
When Seffions came again, *Keele* being afraid
to ftand his Tryal, threw himfelf into a Salivation, fo that *Lowther* could not then be Try'd
without him, as being both Principals in One,
and the fame Fact; but the Seffions following,
they were both brought to the Bar, Arraign'd,
Try'd, Convicted, and Condemn'd for willful
Murder. Being now under Sentence of
Death, they made all the Intereft they could
for a Pardon, but to no Purpofe; for they
were both Hang'd upon *Clerkenwell Green*,
and their Bodies convey'd to *Holloway*, within
Two Miles of *London*, where they both
Hang'd in Chains, 'till they rotted, and
dropped away by Piece-Meal.

But to return to *James Barton* again, when
he became intimately acquainted with One
of the Brothers of the abovefaid *Richard
Keele*, he then became as infolent, and as
mifchievous to his Neighbours Abroad, as he
was to the Family at Home; infomuch that
his Mafter, and Miftrefs, were never at Reft;
for the continual Complaints, that were Daily, and Hourly made againft him; whereupon it being moft abominably Unfufferable,
that his Mafter, who had 60 Pounds with
him, gave him his Indentures, and returning
Barton's Father Half the Money, for the other
Half he ftopt for Victuals, and Drink, he
had.

had in the Year and Half, he had been with him, and 14 Pounds, which he could positively Swear he had wrong'd him of; so he got rid of this notorious Rascal, who contriv'd all the Ways and Means to bring nothing but Scandal and Disgrace on his Father and Mother, who have a very fair Character all over *Hampshire.*

Now *Barton* being at Home with his Parents again, he still ran as fast as he could to his own Destruction; for heeding neither God, nor Man, he had no Regard to Religion, at which he made a meer Scoff, as also the Clergy, or any that belong'd to the Church. For at the Church at *Farum,* within Seven Miles of *Gosport,* the Clerk thereof pitching very often upon One particular Psalm, which he admir'd above all the Rest, *James Barton,* cuts off the first four Lines in the Ballad of *Chivy-Chace,* and pasted it over the first Verse of this Clerk's belov'd Psalm. The *Sunday* following the Clerk happening to pitch upon the same Psalm, he began with,

God prosper long our noble King,

So far it went well, without the Clerk's finding out that they were no Words of a Divine *Psalmist.*

Our Lives, and Safeties all;

The

The Clerk thought this was all Good still, and so proceeds.

A woful Hunting once there did
In Chivy-Chace *befal.*

The Clerk here finding this was more than what he had ever Read before in the *Psalms,* *Egad,* quoth he, *this is the first Time I ever knew that the Devil kept a Pack of Hounds :* And so chooses another Psalm. But he had lik'd to have lost his Place by it, but that it was found out to be an Imposition upon his Clerkship.

So another Time, a certain Parson of another Church in *Hampshire,* who had also the Benefit of being Master of a Free-School, because his Vicarage was but a small Maintenance ; the old Man would take his Scholars to Church with him every Day, when School was broke up in the Afternoon, and always Read to them the Fifteenth Chapter of the First Epistle of St. *Paul* to the *Corinthians,* which Treats on the Resurrection. *Barton* knowing this, he one Day finely erases out with a Pen-Knife, the Letter *C*, that is in the Word *Changed,* in the Fifty Second Verse, where it says, *We shall all be Changed in the Twinckling of an Eye.* Now when the old Parson was come to these Words, and missing the *C* out of the Word *Chang'd,* he hums, and ha's at it, pores, and puts his Eyes close to the Bible, and still wanting the *C*, he pulls his
Spectacles

Spectacles out of his Pocket, puts 'em on, and falls a Hunting after *C* again ; which not finding, quoth he, *Well Children, I know not how it is, but I believe St.* Paul *is turn'd* Jew, *again, and going to Persecute the* Chri-stians *at* Damascus, *for he says, That we shall be all Hang'd in the Twinkling of an Eye.* And so dismisses his Scholars, without making an End of the Chapter.

This Fellow was so much addicted to Swearing, that when he light on any Profligates, as wicked as himself, he would Swear, and Curse, with 'em for a Wager, and has too often won the Bet, that at last he would lay Two and Three to One upon his own Head, without letting any Body have the Chance of being Part'ners, by going Halves with him. He was a great Prophaner of the *Sabbath-Day,* and would be more Wicked thereon (if it was possible) than upon any other Day.

He was very disobedient to his Parents; but I know not of any Murder, he was Guil-ty of, unless we may lay this to his Charge. About three Years ago, when several Persons in a very riotous Manner, gether'd together, and Blacking their Faces, and other Ways disguising themselves, they were call'd the *Blacks* of *Waltham,* from their first Appear-ing in great Bodies thereabouts in *Hampshire* : This *James Barton* was One of those Rioters, going along, and helping, aiding, abetting, assisting, and comforting them, in their seve-ral

ral villainous Enterprizes of Robbing Gentlemens Parks, Killing their Deer; Rooting up Trees, Extorting Money from them with Menaces of Firing their Houses, and sometimes committing Murder. But at last a Proclamation being issued out for suppressing them, with Promise of a Pardon, to such as should discover their Accomplices, *James Barton*, made himself an Evidence, and Hang'd Three, or Four of them, upon his Information, by which Means he escap'd the Gallows this Time.

Adultery, and Fornication, were his darling Sins, having had Two, or Three Bastards at a Time laid at his Father's Door, whereupon his Father then turn'd him out of Doors for good and all. But tho' he was thus abandon d to the wide World, being rejected by his Parents, slighted by his Relations, scorn'd by his Friends, and hated by all others that knew him, yet did not this reclaim him ; he still pursu'd his wicked Courses to a higher Degree. He cheated every Body he came near, so that no Body would have any Dealings with him, upon any Account whatever: Then he took to Thieving, was seldom Sober, and addicted much to Gaming, and all other Vices.

When I was at the *Lent* Assizes held at *Winchester*, in *March* 1724-5, I happen'd to lodge at the Inn, where this *James Barton* had but lately been, and fell into Cards there with some Company; the Game he play'd at was *All-Fours*; and at any Time when he
turn'd

turn'd up *Jack*, he would cry, *There's travelling Charges.* This Saying became a common
Expreſſion among all People afterwards,
when they play'd at *All-Fours*; and the Occaſion of it was (as I was there inform'd) upon
this Account. About a Fortnight before my
being there, *James Barton*, being one Night
(as above noted) at the ſame Houſe, playing
at *All-Fours*, and calling *Jack*, when he turn'd
it up, *Travelling Charges*, it became a common
Name there, upon *Travelling Charges*'s Diſaſter:
For having loſt about four Shillings, and aſk-
ing for a Bed there, the Inn-Keeper knowing
what a vile Raſcal he was, would not let him
lie there; whereupon *Barton* goes out of
Doors, and took up his Lodging in the Fields
all Night; next Morning early he Robb'd a
Woman upon *Buſſelton-Common*, of twelve
Shillings odd Money, for a Breakfaſt; at
Noon, being Apprehended, a Conſtable gave
him his Dinner; and by Night, he ſafely
Arriv'd at *Wincheſter* Goal, for his Supper.

Shortly after the Aſſizes coming on at *Wincheſter*, he was Indicted, and Try'd, for this
ſame Robbery, which he confidently deny'd,
altho' the Money, and Purſe, in which it
was, was found in his Pocket, with the very
Deſcription the Woman had given, of what
the Purſe was made, and the Marks thereon,
and what Money was in it, in their various
Species of Shillings, Six-Pences, Half-Crowns,
and Half-Pence. The Matter of Fact was
plainly prov'd againſt him, and the Priſoner
pro-

producing not one Person to fpeak in his behalf, and making no other Defence for himfelf,
than alleging, that the Woman who Profecuted him, was not One of a good Character ;
the Jury brought in their Verdict Guilty ;
and accordingly Sentence of Death was pafs'd
upon *Travelling Charges* : As alfo at the fame
Time upon another Perfon, for Robbing
his Mafter, 'Squire *Abonethy* of *Stone* ; upon
two Brothers, who made not above 41 Years
of Age betwixt 'em, for Robbing on the
Highway ; and upon one Mr. *Cook*, an Apothecary of *Alton*, and his Maid-Servant, for
the Murder of their Male Baftard Infant.

Before the Judge went away, he repriev'd
all the condemn'd Criminals, excepting the
Eldeft of the two Brothers, and this *James
Barton*, altho' his Father made great Intereft
to fave his Life, tho' he was to be Tranfported
for ever, fo he was not Hang'd, to bring an
indelible Scandal, and Difgrace on the Family.
The fatal Day of Execution being come, the
other Prifoner appointed for Death, and he,
were convey'd by the Sheriff, and his Officers,
to the Foot of the Hill, on which the Gallows is erected : Here alighting, they went
up to the Tree, to which their Halters being
ty'd, *James Barton*, fpoke to the numerous
Spectators as follows.

Gentlemen,

Gentlemen, and others,

*I AM this Day come justly to suffer an ignomi-
nious, and most shameful Death, for a Crime
of which I own my self Guilty: I need not tell you
of what good Parents I am Descended, because
they be as conspicuously Noted all over this Country
(in which I First drew my unhappy Breath) for
their Vertues, as I am for my manifold, and
most enormous Vices. I am not so much concern'd at the Fear of Death, as the Manner
of the Death I am to die, because it will be a
most cutting Thing to my most indulgent Parents, whose good Advice, and Councel, had I
but follow'd, I had avoided this untimely Fate :
But I hope no Body, who has but the least Christian Charity, Pity, and Compassion in 'em,
will Reflect my Misfortune on them, or any of
my Relations ; since my unfortunate Condition,
is only owing to my self. I return my Father,
and Mother, most hearty Thanks, for the Intercession they made, to save the Life of an
unhappy Son, which is not worth saving ; for
tho' I am but a young Man, not exceeding
Three and Twenty Years of Age, yet have I
deserv'd the utmost Severity of Justice before
now. I heartily beg Pardon of all People whom
I have at any Time wrong'd in Thought, Word,
or Deed ; especially she, who hath justly cut me
off in the very Prime of my Youth: As I forgive all my Enemies, and die in Charity with
all Mankind, I hope my shameful End, may be
an Expiation for those Offences, which have*
given

*given People an Occasion of Loathing, and De-
testing my very Name and Memory. I was
in my Infancy most Strictly and Religiously
bred up in the Doctrine and Principles of the
Church of England, as it is now Establish'd by
the Laws of the Land; and though I am a very
unworthy Member of it, yet do I die in that
Communion; hoping, that my most Heavenly
Father, through the Intercession of his only beloved Son, and my blessed Saviour, who by a
most painful Crucifixion, did shed his most precious Blood, not only for me, but for the Sins
of the whole World, will vouchsafe to look upon
me with Eyes of Pity and Compassion, in
this my great Hour of Distress; I most humbly
implore, he will be most graciously pleased,
when I am gone hence, and no more seen, to
take my poor Sin-Sick Soul, into the cælestial
Mensions of his eternal Rest.*

He, and his Fellow-Sufferer, joyn'd very
fervently in Prayers, and singing Psalms,
with the two Divines that attended them at
the Place of Execution; after which having
some few Minutes allow'd them, for their
more private Devotions, they were then
turn'd off the Ladder, whilst uttering these,
or the like Ejaculations; *Lord have Mercy
upon us! Christ be Merciful to our poor Souls!
Sweet Jesus! let us this Night Sup with thee
in* Paradice.

His Body, after Execution, was deliver'd
to his Friends, who privately Buried it, with
a Stone

a Stone over his Grave, but no Inſcription ; whereupon ſome Body, for good, or ill Will, wrote upon it, in Chalk, the following Epitaph.

James Barton *lies here,*
But don't ſhed a Tear ;
 Becauſe he did Cheat us too long.
For long did we Hope,
He wou'd leave us by Rope ;
 But Hope for ſix Years he did wrong.

ELEONOR SYMPSON, *a Shoplifter.*

ELEONOR SYMPSON, was Born of very honeſt Parents, at *Henley* upon *Thames,* in *Oxfordſhire* ; her Father being a Farmer, to whom ſhe laid a Baſtard, got on her by the Clerk of the Pariſh, for which Piece of Impudence, being turn'd out of Doors, ſhe came up to *London,* and turn'd common Whore. Whilſt ſhe continued this wicked Courſe of Life, ſhe pickt up late one Night a Linnen-Draper, to whom pretending ſo great Modeſty, and Baſhfulneſs, that ſhe was aſham'd to go with a Man into a Tavern, or an Ale-Houſe ; they at laſt agreed to go
into

into a dark Ally, where whilſt the Cully was
feeling what Gender ſhe was of, ſhe in the
mean Time was feeling for his Watch, which
privately drawing half-way out of his Fob,
quoth ſhe, *The Watch is coming, Sir* : He being eager on his Game of *High Gammer-Cook*,
cry'd, *D---n the Watch, I don't value the
Watch of a Farthing*. At laſt, when ſhe had
got the Watch out of his Fob indeed, and
tranſported it into her own Pocket, ſhe ſaid
again, *Pray, dear Sir, make haſte, for I vow
the Watch is juſt here* : He ſtill not apprehending her Meaning, reply'd again, *D---n
the Watch, I tell you I don't value the Watch
of a Farthing*. So the Sport being over, they
parted, but he had not gone far, when beginning to have a Thought about him, he
felt for his Watch, and finding it out of its
Precinčts, he made all the Haſte he could
after his Miſtreſs, and overtaking her in St.
Martin's-Lane, charg'd her with a Conſtable,
who committed her to the *Round-Houſe* all
Night. Next Morning the Linnen-Draper
appear'd againſt her at St. *Martin*'s Veſtry,
where charging her upon Oath, before the
Juſtices, of her Robbing him of his Watch:
Quoth One of the old *Mumpſimuſſes, Well,
Mrs.* Jelliver, *what have you to ſay for your
ſelf now ? you ſee the Fačt is ſworn poſſitively
againſt you*. Mrs. *Jelliver*, as he call'd her,
dropping a very fine Courtſy, and looking as
demure as a Whore at a Chriſtening, ſaid in
her Defence ; *That going Home laſt Night to*
my

my *Lodging, that Gentleman there, who is my Accuser,* did *so far prevail with me as to be Naught with him in a dark Ally, and whilst he was jumbling me up against a Wall, Sirs, to pass the Time away, I play'd with his Watch, which being half-way out of his Fob, I told him, let him deny it if he can, that the Watch was coming, whereupon he reply'd, D——n the Watch, he did not value the Watch of a Farthing ; nay, when I had the Watch quite out of his Fob, and put it into my own Pocket, at the same Time pointing to it, I plainly told him, the Watch was here ; but still he was so eager at his Work, that he said again, D——n the Watch, I tell you I don't value it of a Farthing ; so thinking it of more Consequence than that comes to, I was carrying it Home for my own Use, but since he requires it again, here it is Gentlemen, and I freely return it him with all my Heart.* At this Confeſſion, the Juſtices were all ready to ſplit their Sides with Laughing ; and making the Complainant give his Miſtreſs a Guinea for his Folly, he had his Watch again, and ſhe being diſcharg'd, went about her Buſineſs.

Another Time *Nell Sympson,* being pickt up by a Couple of Captains in the *Coldſtream,* or Second Regiment of *Foot Guards,* they carry'd her to *Rigby*'s Ordinary, at the *Roe-Buck* in *Suffolk-Street,* where having a good Supper, and being alſo much elevated with Wine, they began to Act ſeveral Beaſtialities upon her ; but ſhe made them pay for their Frolick

Frolick in the End ; for having drank them to
fuch a Pitch, that they both fell into a found
Sleep upon the Floor, when honeft *Nell*
began to dive into their Fobs, and Pockets,
whence fhe took a Couple of Gold Watches,
2 Purfes of Guineas, fome Silver, 2 Gold
Snuff-Boxes, 2 Diamond Rings off their Fingers, broke the Silver Hilts off their Swords,
then fh--t—g in both their Perrukes, which
fhe clapt on their Heads again, went off without faying fo much as a Word to any Body.
When they awoke, and found their Lofs,
what Vollies of Oaths, and Curfes, flew
about the Room, like Peals of great Ordnance!
there was ftriving betwixt them, who fhould
Swear the fafteft, but all to no Purpofe, the
Whore being gone they knew not whether,
they were forc'd to be contented with their
Calamity ; and what was Worfe too, to pay
a Reckoning of 4 Pounds, into the Bargain.

One Time *Nell* meeting a Butcher's Son
of *Clare-Market*, who is now a *Juft-Afs* in
the fame County, he being difpos'd to have
a Game at *Tricke-Tracke* with her, for you
muft know, that by his Father's Trade, he
was given to the Flefh, fhe takes him into
Piffing-Ally in *Holywell-Street*, otherwife call'd
the Backfide of St. *Clement*'s in the *Strand*,
fo eminently Noted for Taylors felling there
their *Cabbage* ; no fooner were they arriv'd
into that dark Hole, fo fit for Fornication,
and Adultery, but as he was lugging out his
Dagger, to whip her through the Beard, fhe

at the same Time lugg'd out his Silver-Hilted
Sword from his Side, which he never paid
for to this Day, and cry'd, *Pray, Sir, don't
play the* Spaniard *upon me, to use both Spado,
and Rapier, upon me at once, I shall never be
able to bear it.* The *Just-Ass,* who's a Man
of no great Metal at the Best, reply'd, *My
Dear, I'll use you gently ;* and in that he was
as good as his Word, for being Dead-Drunk,
he fell down on his Arse, and cry'd out
Thieves ; whereupon *Nell* having a great
Presence of Mind, takes up her Coats, stops
his Mouth with her *T——y-M——y,* pisses
down his Throat, which he really taking for
Aqua Mirabilis, said he was very well
satisfied, and would pay the Reckoning next
Day to a Farthing; but *Nell* carrying off
his Sword, Wig, and Hat, into the Bargain,
never came again to ask him for it. While
he was wallowing there in Sir *Reverence,
Urine,* and other Nastiness, who should come
by but a *Lion,* with his *Jackals* before him,
to seek for a Prey, for the Bearer of the
painted Staff; so joyning Heads together
about dividing it, they then began to lift up
the puny Carcass, but finding who it was,
they were all struck in a Heap, the Booty
was not so good as they expected, they carried him to the Place of his Birth, laid him
upon a Butcher's Block, and left him to shift
for himself. Now it happening to be about
One of the Clock on the *Saturday* Morning,
the Butcher who own'd the Block, was
                                        Drinking

Drinking at an adjacent Ale-House, whilſt he
was there, a Calf newly kill'd, but not
dreſt, was ſtoln from before his Shop, which
miſſing, he fell a Swearing, and Staring, like
a Devil for his Loſs, call'd out to the Man
that was then putting out the Stands, and
Sheds, againſt the Market-People came, and
ask'd him if he knew any Thing of his Calf.
D --n me (reply'd the Fellow) *can't you ſee ?*
Why, it lies upon your Block there. By G---
(quoth he) *ſo it does*; *well*, Jack, *I beg your*
Pardon, for I did not ſee it 'till you told me.
So taking out his Knife, and whetting it on
his Steel, quoth he, *Prithee* Jack *come hither,*
and lend me a Hand to lift him on One of the
Hooks, to flay him. In the mean Time he
was briskly whetting his Knife ſtill, and
fluſtrated with Liquor, did not mind what
his Calf was made of, 'till *Jack* coming to
aſſiſt him, finding it was ſomewhat of a Man,
ſaid to him, *Maſter, this is* Juſt-Aſs *ſuch a*
One, 'tis no Calf, but yet, Sir, as his Fleſh
may be a Novelty, I don't know but it may fetch
a Penny in the Pound more than the beſt Mut-
ton in the Market, conſidering he has fed him-
ſelf a long Time upon lac'd Mutton, and will
to his dying Day, if he can have it Gratis, *for*
he never lov'd to pay for any Thing in his Life,
unleſs needs muſt, when the Divel drives. The
Butcher ſeeing his miſtake, kicks him off of
the Block, but was bound over for it next
Day, and had he not have made up his Loſs
by *Nell,* would certainly have Proſecuted
him for the Robbery.   But

But a little after this Eploit, *Nell* finding that
her Tail brought her not the Comings in she
expected, though she was a tolerable hand-
some Woman enough, and a good *Tongue-Pad,*
she was resolv'd to try what her Hands could
do ; accordingly she turns *Shoplift,* and privately Stole with a great deal of Judgment
upon Stratagem; for the first Experiment she
made this Way, was at a certain Mercer's on
Ludgate-Hill, whither going in a Chair very
well drest, with a Couple of sham Footmen
attending her, in good Liveries ; when she
came into the Shop, she call'd for several
Pieces of Silk to look on, in the mean Time
an Apple-Pasty coming in for the Family, she
seem'd on a sudden to be taken very Ill, and
withd ew from the Place where she was, to
the farther End of the Shop, and fate at the
End of a Counter, under which was a great
deal of rich Silks : Her Footmen taking the
Hint of her Illness, told the Journey-Man,
there happening then to be none but him, that
they believ'd their Lady (who past for the
Countess of *Colrain*) being newly Married,
long'd for some of the Apple-Pasty just then
come in, for she was mighty apt to long of
late, for any Thing that was Good. The
Journey-Man pitying her Condition, presently ran up Stairs, and acquainted his Master,
and Mistress of the Matter, they were
mightily concern'd at it, but before they
came down, she gave her 2 Footmen 6 whole
Pieces of Silk, who put it into the Chair,

G   the

the Chairmen not fuppofing any otherwife
than that the fuppos'd Lady (whom they did
not know too) had bought it. When the
Mercer, and his Wife came down, they invited her up Stairs, which Kindnef-, after
fome feeming Reluctancy, fhe accepted of,
Eat very heartily of it, as fhe might of other
Varieties too which were there, but fhe refus'd
them. When fhe had done, fhe return'd 'em
many Thanks, invited 'em to her Lodgings in
St *James's-Square*, and for their extraordinary
Civility, promis'd to lay out 5, or 600 Pounds
with 'em, before fhe, and her Lord, went to
Ireland. When fhe came down Stairs, fhe
laid out 4, or 5 Guineas, pitch'd upon other
Silks, to the Value of 120 Pounds, which
ordering to be brought to her Houfe as aforefaid, in the Evening, becaufe fhe was going
then to pay a Vifit to the Dutchefs of *Somer-
fet*, at *Northumberland-Houfe* at *Charing-Crofs*,
fhe then took Chair, and went off: But within a few Hours afterwards, the Silks fhe had
Stoln being mifs'd, there was a great Outcry,
the Mercer fwearing that the longing Lady,
had long'd for more than fhe could Eat ;
which was as he faid, for going to enquire
after her in St. *James's-Square*, there was no
finding the Lady *Colrain*, nor any Thing like
it.

Another Time fhe went to a Linnen-Draper's Shop in *Cornhill*, attended with a Couple
of Footmen behind a hir'd Chariot, who
knocking at the Door with an Authority,
for

for 'twas then about 8 or 9 at Night, in Winter-Time; the Journey-Man open'd it, and g ve Admiſſion to this ſuppos'd Perſon of Q iality, and her Attendants, whom ſhe pretended to ſend to a Couple of Merchants by the *Eaſt-India-Houſe*, and being ſhew'd ſeveral Parcels of the fineſt Muſlins, ſhe pitch'd upon as much as came to 80 Pounds, when pulling out a Purſe, in which ſhe had not above 20 Guineas, and perhaps moſt of 'em Counters, quoth ſhe, *Upon my Word, Sir, I have leſs Money about me than I thought for, ſo I cannot pay what I have agreed for, therefore I beg the Favour of you to let your young Man, your 'Prentice here, juſt ſtep to Mr. ſuch a One, my Banker in* Lumbard-Street, *and telling him you are come from the Counteſs of* Co rain, *deſire him to pay you* 100 *Pounds upon Sight of this Note.* Away goes the 'Prentice with the Note, and in came her 2 Footmen, who preſently knocking down the Journey-Man, ſtunn'd him to that Degree, that they carried off above 200 Pounds of Muſlin into the Chariot, and went off with it, before the other could recover himſelf, which was for above a Quarter of an Hour, when calling down his Maſter, told him of the Diſaſter, and wondering the 'Prentice did not come back in above an Hour's Time, a Meſſenger was ſent for him to the Banker, where they found him charg'd with a Conſtable, for bringing a forg'd Note; but when the Maſter came in his Behalf, and told how the

Matter

Matter was, to his Lofs of above 200 Pounds, he was difcharg'd.

But not long after this notorious Robbery, *Nell Sympfon*, was taken in the Act of Shop-Lifting at *Sturbridge-Fair*, and was committed to *Cambridge-Goal*, and the Affizes following being Try'd, receiv'd Sentence of Death, whereupon fhe pleaded her Belly, and a Jury of Matrons being impannell'd, as is ufual upon fuch Occafions, fhe was brought in quick with Child, and was really fo, for fhe was brought to Bed of a Girl, before the Affizes following, when being call'd down to her former Judgment, and accordingly Hang'd at *Cambridge*, upon *Saturday* the 19th of *July* 1714, aged 28 Years.

WILLIAM CADY, *a Highwayman, and Murderer.*

THIS unhappy Gentleman, *William Cady*, was Born at *Thetford*, in the County of *Norfolk*, and was the Son of a very eminent Surgeon, who beftowing upon him good Learning, he was fent to the Univerfity of *Cambridge*, where he was a Servitor to the Father of the prefent Right Honourable the Lord Vifcount *Townfhend*, and then a Student at *Trinity-College*, and in Time became a Batchel-lor

lor of Arts. Afterwards withdrawing himfelf from the *Mufes*, upon the Death of his
Father, who being a great Spendthrift, had
left his Son, and one Daughter nothing to fubfift
on, he came up to *London*, where he profefs'd
Phyfick ; and an Uncle of his lying danger-
oufly Ill of an Impofthume, fending for him
to have his Advice, he went to vifit him, and
being introduced into his Chamber, the firft
Thing he did was to find out how his Uncle's
Stomach ftood affected, that he might pre-
fcribe Medicines accordingly. In order to
this Scrutiny, he views well the Table, and
Windows, to fee if no foul Difhes, or Plates
lay there, and obferv'd whether there were
no Bones of Chickens, or other Poultry were
flung under the Chairs ; but at laft looking
under the Bed, and feeing an old Saddle lying
there, quoth he, *Uncle, your Cafe is very def-*
perate. How fo (reply'd the old Man) *I hope*
I am not paft Recovery. Heavens knows that
beft, fays the Nephew ; *but, however, I tell you*
this, that you have got a moft violent Surfeit ;
which if not Timely remov'd, will prove Mortal.
No, Nephew (quoth the Uncle) *you are out*
there ; 'tis an Impofthume I am afflicted with.
An Impofthume ! (reply'd the Nephew) *a*
Devil arn't you ; I fay 'tis a violent Surfeit, for
by G--- looking under your Bed here, I find you
have Eat a whole Horfe, and have left nothing
but the Saddle and Stirrups for Orts. At
which Saying, the old Uncle fell into fuch a
violent Fit of Laughter, that the Impofthume

prefently

broke, and he became a well Man again in less than a Fortnight. And truly it is not impossible that Imposthumes have been cur'd by violent Fits of Laughter, occasion'd by unusual Actions, or Sayings: For we Read of a certain Cardinal at *Padua*, who lying at the Point of Death with this Disease, his Servants fell to rifling his House, pulling down even the very Hangings in his Bed-Chamber, where at the same Time being an Ape, and finding an old Cap, he secures that for himself, and putting it on his Head; the Cardinal at his apish Tricks was seiz'd with an excessive Fit of Laughter, which breaking the Imposthume, he recover'd his Health, and Goods too. So likewise a Lady at *Orleans* in *France*, lying very Ill of an Imposthume, her Maid being a Sleep on a Pallet-Bed by her, with her Posteriours all bare, and letting a rousing F----t, a Monkey in the Room, being sensible from what Part the Noise came, went presently smelling, and making ugly Faces, and chattering about the Place, which gave the Report, which Exercise of Pug's so pleased the Lady, that not forbearing to laugh more than ordinary, it broke the Imposthume, and gave her speedy Ease and Health.

But whether Mr. *Cady*'s taking his Uncle's Imposthume for a Surfeit, proceeded out of Ignorance, or knowing otherwise, but only said so with a Design it might have the Effect it produc'd, we leave our Readers to judge ; but let it be as it will, his Uncle, for so unex-

pected

pected a Cure, gave him 50 Guineas, which
he confum'd, as taking after his Father for
Extravagancy, in lefs than a Month ; and being weary with the Study of Phyfick, he bid
adieu to *Galen*, and *Hippocrates*, and betook
himfelf to the Highway for a Livelihood.
His firft Exploit in this pernicious Way was
perform'd on *Hounflow-Heath*, where meeting
with Monfieur *Shavalier*, Captain of the
Grenadiers, in the firft Regiment of Foot-
Guards, kill'd in the Weft of *England*, when
he went againft the Duke of *Monmouth*, and
another Gentleman, he rid boldly up to them,
enquiring, as being a Stranger, which was the
Road to *Stanes* ; they courteoufly told him,
that they were going thither themfelves, fo
that if he would be pleas'd to bear them Company, he fhould be welcome : *Cady* thank'd
'em for their Civility, and rid talking along
with 'em for about a Mile, when feeing the
Coaft clear, he fuddenly Shot one of his Guides
thro' the Head; then riding up to *Shavalier*,
told him, that he muft deliver his Money, or
otherwife fuffer the fame Fate as his Comrade:
Quoth Monfieur, *Vat you mean, Shir ? vat,
give you my L' ayent ? no Shir, me be one Captain in de Guards, derefore me vil Fight vid
you, before me vil part vid any Ting.* Cady reply'd, *If you pretend to be a Soldier, you ought
to know it is your Duty to obey the Word of Command, or otherwife I fhall prefently tye you Neck
and Heels, or make you run the Gantlet.* Quoth
Monfieur, *Begar, dat vil be pretty, vat tye an*

Officer

Officer Neck and Heels, and make him run de Gantlet, no, dat vas never known. Come, come, Sir, (reply'd Cady) *dally no longer, or may I be double d---mn'd, if I do not immediately lay you sprawling, by that burstened Belly Son of a Bitch there.* Begar, (quoth Monsieur) *you be one unconscionable Son of a Bitch, to demand Money of me, ven me owe you none.* Sir, (said Cady) *there's not a Man Travels the Road but what owes me Money, if he has it about him; therefore as you are one of my Debtors, you shall pay me before we part; so make no longer delay, but open your Purse-Strings, you* French *Son of a Whore, or by Hell and Furies, your Blood shall satisfy the Debt this Moment; If you are a Man Fight, if not, deliver what you have this Moment.* Hereupon Monsieur *Shavalier* exchang'd a Shot or Two with his Antagonist, who Shooting his Adversary's Horse, he surrender'd his Gold Watch, a Diamond Ring, and a Purse of 26 Guineas; after which, tying him Neck and Heels, and Nailing the two hind Lappets to a Tree, he rid off with his Booty, in quest of another Prey.

His next Progress was to *Bagshot-Heath*, where meeting with the Viscount *Dundee*, (who was kill'd at the Fight of *Gillycranky* in *Scotland*, after the late Revolution in King *William*'s Time) attended by only a couple of Footmen on Horse-Back, with their Lord, who was also very well mounted; he comes riding up to them full speed, enquiring, if they did not see a single Man ride that Way
harder

harder than ordinary, who, he faid, had Robb'd
and Undone him, in taking 20 Pounds from
him, which he was going to pay to his Landlord for Rent. Now there was a Man juft
before rid by his Lordfhip, as if he had been
upon Life and Death, which was *Cady's* Comrade, and defcribing his Cloaths too, they
told him there was fuch a Perfon paft by about
half an Hour ago ; whereupon *Dundee* in
Commiferation to the honeft Man, as he took
the Complainant to be, ordered his Footmen
to rid after the Rogue, faying, they were
enough to take one Man : And in the mean
Time the Servants was in purfuit of one Villain, the other Villain Robs their Mafter of
60 Guineas, and a Gold Watch, and Snuff-
Box ; and to prevent his Lordfhip's riding
after him too, Shot his Horfe. Now he follows the Footmen, whom he found a Mile off,
bringing his Comrade Prifoner, and ordering
them to let him loofe, they deny'd it, as fuppofing them to be both Rogues, and that in
their Abfence, he had taken the Advantage of
Robbing their Mafter ; whereupon a bloody
Engagement enfu'd on both Sides, One to obtain their Liberty, and the Other to apprehend what they juftly fufpected to be no better
than Highwaymen ; but in the Skirmifh, *Cady* killing One of their Oppofers, the Other
made a running Fight of it, and rid up with
all fpeed to the Relief of his Lord, whom
he found a-Foot, and Robb'd of above 100
Pounds.

His Lordſhip complaining of this Robbery at Court, when he came to Town, an Order was put into the *London* Gazettee, promiſing the Reward of 50 Pounds, to any that ſhould apprehend *Cady*, and his Comrade, ſo that they were convicted thereof. Hereupon *Cady* made the Beſt of his Way beyond Sea, and Travelling to *Doway* in *Flanders*, he went to the *Engliſh* Seminary there, and turning *Roman-Catholick*, was admitted, upon the Superior's Examination, and finding him to be a good Scholar, into holy Orders, of the Fraternity of the *Benedictine* Fryers. In this Station he behaved himſelf with ſuch ſeeming Devotion, and Piety, that he had more Penitentiaries came to confeſs their Sins to him, than any Two again of his Brethren ; but *Cady* not fancying this Monaſtick Life, and that his Hypocriſy would at laſt be found out, for he could not confine himſelf to the Vows of Poverty, and Chaſtity, he was reſolved to try his Fortune again in his native Country, rather chooſing to live a merry Life, tho' but a ſhort One, than under the Strictneſs of ecclesiaſtical Obedience. Now his Mind is put upon the Rack of Invention how to get Money, ſo feigning himſelf indiſpos'd he kept his Chamber, where ſeveral Perſons coming to Confeſſion, among them were a Couple of young Gentlewomen, both Rich, and Handſome, whom firſt Confeſſing, he very piouſly Confeſſes himſelf to them, telling them how he was in great want of Money, and if they
did

did not supply him, they should never go
thence alive; at the same Time holding a
Couple of Pistols to their Breasts, and swearing if he presently died for it, he would Shoot
'em both if they made but the least Noise.
Upon this terrifying Threat'ning from their
Father Confessor, they fell a Trembling like
Aspin Leaves, and immediately making an
Enquiry into their Pockets, found 'em lin'd
with about 50 Pistoles, which they freely
made an Offering of to their ghostly, I mean
diabolical Father, which he very favourably
took, as an Attonement of their Transgressions, and their two Diamond Rings into the
Bargain: Then laying them on their Backs to
give them a Taste of his Manhood, he Robb'd
'em of their Virginity as well as their Money;
next he Gagg'd and Ty'd them Neck and
Heels; and pretending to his Brethren of the
Convent, that he would go out to take the
Air a little, instead of going back again, he
went farther a Field, chang'd his cannonical
Habit, and made the Best of his Way for
England.

Cady being now arriv'd in his own Country
again, out of which he had been about two
Years, he continued to be as great a Rogue as
ever he was, for in his Journey from *Dover*
to *London*, meeting on *Black-Heath* with one
Sandal, a great Hop-Merchant, living at *Waringbury* in *Kent*, and his Wife, both on one
Horse, he demanded their Money, which *Sandal* refusing to give, stood in his own Defence,
and

and oppos'd him, by firing two Piſtols; but
miſſing his Aim, he was oblig'd to lie at the
Mercy of his Enemy, who preſently made
them diſmount, when the firſt Thing he did
was killing their Horſe, then ſearching Mr.
Sandal found about 28 Pounds, which he converted to his own Uſe; then he fell to exami-
ning his Wife's Pockets, in which finding
but Half a Crown, *Oh! you bloody B----ch*
(cries *Cady*) *is this all the Money you have
about you? Come, come, off with that Ring from
your Finger, for I muſt not ſpend my Time in
Vain about you.* She earneſtly begg'd he wou'd
not take that from her, becauſe it was her
Wedding-Ring, and would not be willing to
looſe it for twice the Money he had taken
from her Husband, as having had it 20 Years
and better. *You whindling B----ch* (quoth
he again) *don't tell me of its being your Wedding-Ring, Marriage be d----nd, and you too, I
don't know what any of your Sex has to do to Marry
at all, when they may have Children enough without that fooliſh chargeable Ceremony; but be Poxt
to you, yon muſt be Married too, to be a Whore by
Licence; come, come, let's ſee the Ring I ſay,
for otherwiſe I ſhall make bold, for quicker Diſ-
patch, to cut your Finger off for it.* The good
Woman finding it was in vain to uſe any
Words with him, tho' ever ſo good, pull'd it
off her Finger, but inſtead of giving it to him,
put it into her Mouth, and ſwallow'd it; at
which *Cady* fell a Swearing, and Stamping,
as if he would have Sworn the Earth into
Atoms,

Atoms, crying out, *Ob! you cheating B----cb, have you chous'd me fo ?* But by G---- *you fhall carry it neither to Heaven*, nor Hell *with your* So Shooting her thro' the Head, he ript her open, aud took the Ring out of her Body, faying at the fame Time to her Husband, whofe Heart to be fure relented to fee fuch a tragical, nay more barbarous than inhuman Action, *Your Wife's a Bite I fee, but I think now I have Bit the Biter.* So remounting his Horfe, he rid away as faft as he could, leaving the forrowful Widower to attend the bloody Corpfe, 'till fome Paffengers came by, to affift him in carrying it to the next Inn they came to.

The fame Night *Cady* came ftrait to *London*, but fearing (as well he might) that it would be to hot too hold him, to avoid being apprehended by a *Hue* and *Cry*, he did not ftay above an Hour before he rid as faft as he could for *Scotland*, where tarrying about a Month, he made towards *England* again, and betwixt *Ferribridge* and *Doncafter*, in *Yorkfhire*, meeting with one Dr. *Moreton*, a Prebandary of *Durham*, he faluted him with the melancholy Tone of *Stand and Deliver, or d----n him he was a dead Man.* The Clergyman never having been us'd perhaps with fuch ill Language before, or if he had, he was not willing to comply with his unlawful Demands, refus'd to part with what he had, and began to exhort him with grave Advice, and good Councel, to refrain from fuch ill Courfes; withal, telling the Danger that both his Body,

and

and Soul too were in, by committing such
Crimes which were forbidden both by the
Laws of God, and Man ; but all his Preach-
ing was in vain, for *Cady* looking as terrible
as Death's Head on a Mop-Stick, swore and
rav'd like a mad Man for Money, and told
the reverend Gentleman, that he might as
well sing Psalms to a dead Horse as him, for
he heeded him no more than the Pope of *Rome*;
therefore he must deliver his *Mammon*, or
otherwise prepare himself for Death, for he
had but a short Time to live in this World,
unless he presently answer'd his Expectation.
Whilst *Cady* was uttering these Words, a
Stone Horse in an adjacent Field smelling his
Mare, came Snorting and Neighing like a
mad Creature, and presently covering her,
Mr. *Highwayman* was forc'd to dismount to
save himself from Mischief; which seasonable
Adventure giving the Parson the favourable
Opportunity of riding away, he fell a swearing as if he would rend the Skies with his
loud Peals, and whole Vollies of Oaths, dif-
charging them by Wholesale, and cursing and
damning all Whoring, if Horses must Whore
too as well as Men ; but, quoth he, I'll spoil
your Game Mr. *Stallion*, before its out ; so
pulling a Pistol out of his Pocket, Shot him
thro' the Head, then presently remounting his
Mare, he gallop'd full speed after the Pre-
bendary, and overtaking him before he had
got three Quarters of a Mile, he said, *You
unconscionable Dog, how could you have the hard
Heart*

Heart to leave me, without leaving me some-
what to defray my Charges on the Road? So
forthwith searching him, and finding not a
Farthing about him, for he had in the Interim
he had rid away, hid his Money in a Hedge,
which *Cady* supposing too, because he knew
a Man in his Circumstances would not be so
far from Home, as 30, or 40 Miles, without
some Money in his Breeches, swore he should
never go Home alive, if he did not shew him
where it was, which the other refusing, he
made no more to do but Shot him through
the Heart; for he valu'd no more killing a
Man, than he did to Eat, or Drink.

He then pursu'd his Journey cross the Country towards *Norfolk*, with an Intent to see
his Friends, and Acquaintance at *Thetford*;
but within 2 or 3 Miles of the Town meeting a Coach, in which were 3 Gentlemen,
and a Gentlewoman, he made up towards it,
and being Mask'd, they stood upon their
Guard, and were resolv'd to dispute a Point
with him; so being within Pistol-Shot of his
Prey, One of 'em Shot off a Blunderbus,
which had the Misfortune of missing, without
doing him any other Damage than having One
of the Bullets grazed on his left Arm, which
only tore his Coat, Wastcoat, and Shirt, and
just rais'd the Skin; whereupon he rid up in a
great Passion to the Coach, Robbing them all
of about 130 Pounds; and as for the Person
that Shot him, swearing that the Loss of his
Money should not intitle him to any Quarters,
he

he Shot him dead in the Coach, and then cutting the Reins, and Braces, of the Horses, went off, without seeing any of his Relations, or others, whom he knew at *Thetford.*

Now he steers his Course towards *London* as fast as he could, and coming over *Finchley-Common*, he attacks a Lady, who was riding there on Horse-Back for the Air, with only one Footman to attend her, whom bidding to *Stand*, he fell very Rustically upon her, pulling a Diamond Ring off her Finger, a Gold Watch from her Side, and taking a Purse of 80 Guineas out of her Pocket, which barbarous Usage her Footman resenting, in calling him Thieving Rogue, Villain, Rascal, and other Names, suitable to his Character, he presently stopt his Mouth, by sending a Brace of Balls through his Head ; then cutting the Girts of the Lady's Horse, he was going off with his Booty, but was intercepted by a Couple of Gentlemen, who saw his Transaction at some Distance: With these he engages for his Liberty, firing as fast as he could, and they on the other Side firing at him again, 'till in the Skirmish they Shot his Horse under him, so he was oblig'd to continue the Fight on Foot, which he maintain'd 'till he had discharg'd all his Pistols ; when being apprehended, they carry'd him before a Justice of Peace at *Highgate*, where after a long Examination, being charg'd with a Murder, and Robbery, he was committed under a strong Guard to *Newgate*, where he still continu'd

a meer Reprobate, without any Remorſe of
Conſcience at all, for the Blood he had ſhed,
within the ſmall Space of 4 Years. At length
his Tryal came on at the Seſſions-Houſe in
the *Old-Baily*, where he behav'd himſelf very
Impudently to the Bench, telling the Lord
Mayor, and the Recorder, that they were a
Couple of old *Alms-Women*, and knew no
more of Law than they did of Goſpel, which
was nothing at all; but the Matter of Fact,
of which he ſtood Indicted, being plainly
prov'd againſt him, he receiv'd Sentence of
Death, and being then put into the condemn'd
Hold. This Place of Horror, and Darkneſs,
did not yet make any Alteration in his Manners, for he wou d ſtill Swear, and Curſe, Damn,
and Sink, Sing, and Roar, and get Drunk;
being in great Hopes of a Reprieve from King
James the Second, and which too (as having
great Friends at Court) he had undoubtedly
obtain'd, had he not waſh'd his Hands in
Blood; ſo his Day of Execution being come,
and the Cart ſtoping as uſual under St. *Sepul-
cher*'s Wall, whilſt the Bellman rang his Bell,
and repeated his exhortatory Lines to him,
to put him in Remembrance of preparing
himſelf for his latter End, he fell a Swearing
at the Sheriff's Officers, asking what they
detain'd him there for to hear an old Puppy
chatter Nonſence; ſo being convey'd to *Tybourn*,
he was there Hang'd in 1687, Aged 25 Years,
without ſo much as converſing with the Ordinary, ſaying Prayers to himſelf, or making
any Speech at all. *Sawney*

SAWNEY BEANE, *a Robber, Murderer, and Cannibal.*

IN all Ages paſt, and preſent, 'tis impoſſible for Hiſtory to parallize, or the Age to come, for ſuch unheard of Cruelties, and Robberies, that were committed by one *Sawney Beane*, a *Scotchman*, in the Reign of King *James* the Firſt, before he came to the Crown of *England*, by the Demiſe of Queen *Elizabeth*.

The aboveſaid *Scotch* Robber was Born about 8 or 9 Miles Eaſtward of the City of *Edinburgh*, in the County of *Eaſt-Lothian*, of Parents who went a Hedging and Ditching, for their daily Bread, and brought up this their Bloody-Minded Child to the ſame Occupation for his Livelyhood ; but as he grew up, his Diſpoſition to Idleneſs not permitting him to follow an honeſt Employment, he left his Father, and Mother, and ran into the Country, where following a moſt wicked Courſe of Life, and taking up with a Woman as Vicious as himſelf, inſtead of Living in any City, Town, or Village, they took up their Lodgin a Rock by the Sea-Side, on the Shore of Shire *Galloway*, where they Liv'd for upwards of 25 Years, having both Children, and Grand-Children,

Children, in that Time, and brought up fo
Heathenifhly, Wicked, and Cruel, that they
never feparated, kept no other Company but
themfelves, and had nothing to be fupported
by, but only Robbing, and which was Worfe,
they never committed any Robbery without
a Murder.

For Living fo Retired, and Private, as they
did from the World, no Body whenever they
met, or faw 'em, knew who they were, or
from whence they came; neither did they
ever frequent any Market, for any Sort of
Provifion; but as foon as they had Robb'd,
and Murder'd, any Man, Woman, or Child,
they left not any Carcafe behind 'em, but
carried it to their Den, where cutting it into
Quarters, would Pickle them, and Live upon
human Flefh, 'till they got another Prey of
the fame Kind. But they had generally Su-
perfluity, infomuch, that they oftentimes in
the Night-Time, but at a great Diftance from
their fanguine Manfion, throw Legs, and Arms,
of fome they had kill'd, into the Sea, which
the Tide has caft up at feveral Parts of the
Country, to the great Aftonifhment of the
Beholders. Perfons that have gone about their
lawful Occafions, fell fo often into the Hands of
thefe mercilefs *Cannibals*, that never returning Home again, it made a general Outcry,
among their Friends, and Relations; infomuch,
that the whole Country being Alarm'd at
fuch a common Lofs of People, which frequently happen'd in Travelling into the Weft
of

of *Scotland*, private Spies were fent out into
all thofe Parts, to find out, if poffible, the
Manner how thefe melancholy Matters happen'd.

But their ftricteft Search, and Enquiry,
into the Lofs of the King's Subjects were to
no Purpofe ; however, feveral honeft Travellers
were taken up upon Sufpicion, and wrongfully Hang'd, upon bare Circumftances ; befides
feveral innocent Inn-keepers that were Executed, for no other Reafon, but that Perfons
that had been thus Loft, were known to have
lain in their Houfes, and fuppos'd to have been
Murder'd, and Robb'd by them, and their
Bodies privately buried in obfcure Places, to
prevent a Difcovery. Indeed Juftice (tho'
wrong plac'd) was Executed with the greateft
Severity, in Hopes of deterring thefe frequent
Murders, whereupon feveral Inn-Keepers on
the Weftern-Road of *Scotland*, left off their
Bufinefs, for fear of being made the like Examples, and follow'd other Employments ;
fo that Travellers on the other Side again,
were put to many Inconveniencies when they
went Abroad, for want of Accommodation
for themfelves and Horfes, when they were
difpos'd to bait, or put up for Lodging at
Night.

It was the Admiration how thefe Villanies
could be carried on at this Rate, and not the
Villains be found out ; fo that when feveral
had been Executed, and not any One at the
Gallows, made any other Confeffion, than that
they

they were Innocent for what they Died ; this rigorous Way of proceeding was left off, and the finding out of the Murderers left wholly to God to bring to light, in the due Time he was pleas'd to think fitting.

Sawney Beane, with his Wife, Children, and Grand-Children, still pursue their barbarous Actions with Impunity, and being somewhat Numerous, they would Attack 4, 5, or 6 Men together, if they were on Foot ; as for Horse-Men, Two were the Most they would ever set on, and with such Caution, that an Ambuscado was laid to secure them, ride which Way they would, provided one, or both, made their Escape from the first Assailents ; thus whose Fortune soever it was to fall into their barbarous Hands, he, or she, never came off with their Lives. The Place was solitary where they Inhabited, and when the Tide came up, the Water went for near 200 Yards into their subterraneous Habitation, which reach'd almost a Mile under Ground, so that if they were ever seen thereabouts by any Person, 'twas in the least Suppos'd that any Thing Human, would reside in such a dismal Place of perpetual Horrour, and Darkness.

The People they had kill'd were not exactly known, but yet it was reckon'd, that in the 25 Years they had Reign'd in these inhuman Slaughters, that they had wash'd their Hands in the Blood of above 1000 Men, Women, and Children ; and the Discovery of these *Cannibals* was thus made at last.

A Man,

A Man, and his Wife, behind him on the same Horfe, coming one Evening from a Fair, and falling into the Ambufcade of thefe mercilefs Wretches, they fell upon 'em in a moft furious Manner; the Man to fave himfelf as well as he could, fought it bravely againft them with Sword, and Piftol, riding fome of 'em down by main Force of his Horfe, from which his Wife, in the Conflict fell off, and was prefently Murder'd before the Husband's Face; for the Female *Cannibals* forthwith cut her Throat, fucking her blood with as great a Guft as if it had been Wine, ript up her Belly, and pull'd out all her Intrails; which unparellel'd Barbarity, made the poor Man make the more obftinate Refiftance, as expecting the fame Fate, if he fell into their impious Hands; and fo far it pleas'd Providence, that 20, or 30 Paffengers, riding that Way from the fame Fair he had been at, *Sawney Beane*, and his Blood Thifty Clan withdrew, and made the Beft of their Way thro' a thick folitary Wood, and fo retir'd to their Den.

The Man, who was the Firft that ever came off alive, that fell into their Hands, told 'em what happen'd, and fhew'd them the bloody Spectacle of his Wife, whom the Murderers had dragg'd fome Diftance off, which ftruck 'em all with Stupefaction and Amazement; fo they carried him with them to *Glafgow*, and relating the Matter to the Provoft of that City, he immediately fent to the King about it, who in 3 or 4 Days, came

in

in Perfon himfelf thither, as being defirous to fee the Apprehending of this Villain, who for fo many Years had been Pernicious to the Weftern Part of his Kingdom.

A Body of about 400 Men, well Arm'd, fet out on Horfe-Back, with the King, who had feveral Blood-Hounds with 'em, and came with the Man to the Wood by which he was Attack'd, but found no Sign of any Habitation all over it. They then went thro' it, which led down to the Sea-Side, when the Tide being out, and going all along the Shore, they pafs'd by this Cave of *Sawney Beane's*, without taking any Notice of it as a Place of Habitation, 'till fome of the Blood-Hounds running into it, and fetting up a moft hideous Barking, Howling, and Yelping, the King, and his Attendants came back, and look'd into it, but feeing nothing for Darknefs, they could not tell what to think of it, but neverthelefs imagin'd fomewhat more than Ordinary by the Blood-Hounds making fuch a Noife there, going quite out of Sight, and would not come out.: Torches were fent for, and a great many Men ventur'd into it, and tho' there were feveral intricate Turnings, and Windings, in this private Recefs from Mankind, yet they at laft came to the Apartments of *Sawney Beane*, where to their great Surprize, they found the Legs, Arms, Thighs, Hands, and Feet, of Men, Women, and Children, hung up like dry'd Beef, and fome Limbs lying in Pickle ; a great Mafs of Money, both Gold, Silver, Watches,

Watches, Rings, Swords, Piftols, and a great Quantity of Cloaths, both Linnen, and Wuollen, and infinite other Things, which they had taken from them they had Murder'd.

These they all Seiz'd, took what human Flesh they found there, and Buried in the Sands, and brought out Prifoners, *Sawney Beane*, and his murdering Family, which, befides himfelf confifted of his Wife, 8 Sons, 6 Daughters, 18 Grand-Sons, and 14 Grand-Daughters, begotten in Inceft. They were prefently all Pinion'd, and carried to *Edinburgh*, all the Country, as they pafs'd along, flocking in Multitudes to fee this curs'd Tribe, who were no fooner come to their Journey's-End, but they were put into the *Talbooth* for one Night, whence the next Day, being conducted under a ftrong Guard to *Leith*, the Men, without Procefs, or any Manner of Tryal, had their privy Members cut off, and flung into a Fire before their Faces, then their Hands, and Legs, were cut off, by which Amputation they Bled in fome Hours to Death : All this Torture being juftly inflicted upon them in Sight of the Wife, Daughters, and Grand Children ; they were then all Burnt in 3 feveral Fires, all Dying like the Men too, without Repentance, but Curfing, and Venting, dire Imprecations, to the laft Gafp of Life.

Captain

Captain ZACHARY HOWARD, Murderer, and Highwayman.

THIS unhappy Perſon was a Gentleman Born, and Bred, and coming to an Eſtate of 1400 Pounds *per Annum*, left him by his Father in *Gloucesterſhire*, juſt about the breaking out of the *Civil-Wars* in *Forty-One*, a true Sincerity to Allegiance, and Loyalty, inſpiring him with the Gallantry of Fighting for his King and Country, he mortgag'd his Eſtate for 20000 Pounds, with which he rais'd a Troop of Horſe, for the Service of *Charles* the Firſt ; and the Command of it being given to him by that unfortunate Monarch, he remain'd in the Army 'till the Republican Party becoming ſole Conquerors, over Religion and Monarchy, he was then oblig'd, among many other *Cavaliers*, to go into Exile ; from which he not long after return'd, with King *Charles* the Second, and attended on him in the Fight at *Worceſter*, where he perform'd Wonders, to retrieve the Honour and Glory of his lawful Sovereign, who being entirely Routed by the *Parliamentarians*, did, with much difficulty, Eſcape the Enemy, by hiding himſelf in an OAK, in *Warwickſhire* ; and

H   after

after 6 Weeks wandering up and down, *In-cognito*, here in *England*, he at length found a Paſſage for *France*, and in Foreign Countries paſs'd away 12 Years, when he was RE-STOR'D again to the Throne of his Anceſtors, by a general Conſent of the greateſt Part of the Nation.

In the mean Time the aboveſaid *Zachary Howard*, remain'd in *England*, and being out of all Employment, and his Eſtate out of his Poſſeſſion, he had no other Way of ſupporting himſelf, but by going on the Highway ; Swearing to be Reveng'd on all Perſons that were againſt the Intereſt of his Royal Maſter. Accordingly he attack'd all whom he met, and knew to be of that Party : The Firſt whom he aſſaulted on the Road, was the Earl of *Eſſex*, who had been General of the Parliament's Forces ; and tho' he had 5, or 6 in Retinue, as he was riding over *Bagſhot-Heath*, he nevertheleſs rode up to his Coach, and Cammanding the Driver to *Stand*, he next gave the *Word of Command*, for his Lordſhip to *Deliver*, upon fair Terms, or otherwiſe he, and his Servants, muſt expect no Quarters, for had he, and they, as many Lives each of 'em as the Counteſs of *Zealand* had Children, when ſhe was deliver'd of 365 at one Birth, he would Sacrifice them all to his juſt Reſentment, for not only being Diſloyal to their lawful Sovereign, but for their Impudence too, of denying him 1200 Pounds, he had then in the Coach, and which he ſuppos'd,

was

was fqueez'd out of Forfeited Eftates, Church-
I ands, and Sequeftrations ; but his Lordfhip
being unwilling to venture his Life for fuch a
Trifle, deliver'd his Money to the bold Robber,
who told him, that fince the Stages were voted
down, the only Play-Houfe being at *Weftminfter,* he might go, and Act his Part again,
there for more Coyn, againft he met him another Time, at fome other Place, convenient
for ftripping a *Round-Head* of his facrilegi-
ous Wealth.

Another Time overtaking on *Newmarket-
Heath,* the E----l of P--------, fo much celebrated, for making comical Speeches to the
Houfe of Commons, and attended only but with
one Footman, he held fome Difcourfe with
his Honour for about half a Mile, when coming to a convenient Place, which was proper
for his Defign, the Word of Command, *Stand,
and Deliver,* was prefently given to his Lordfhip, tagg'd at the End with twenty *G------
d------mes,* that he would Shoot him on the
Spot, if he did not immediately furrender
what Money he had. Quoth the E----l, *By
your terrible Oaths, Sir, you appear to me a
ranting Cavalier ; have you taken a Leafe of
your Life, that you durft to venture it fo againft
two Men ? Howard* reply'd, *I durft to venture
it againft Two more, with your Idol* Oliver
Cromwell, *at the Head of you, for all he's a
Bird of Prey, for the moft of his Trophies are
in a Church-Window ; and if he deals with Men,
'tis when he takes 'em Napping in an old Monu-*

ment, then down goes *Dust*, and *Ashes*, as not being able to resist his sacrilegious *Villany*. Oh! (quoth *P------*) he's a precious *Man*; a Man of great *Courage*, who has Fought the Lord's *Battles* with *Success*. He, and his *Rebels*, (reply'd *Howard*) are nought but Mars his *Petitoes*; such sniveling *Cowards*, that 'tis a *Favour* to call them so: But this *Talk* delays *Time*, and *Delays*, you know, breed *Dangers*, therefore, out with your *Purse*, Sir, or I shall out with your *Soul* else, if you have any. So presenting his Pistol, he dismounted his Lordship, by Shooting his Horse under him, then taking from him a Purse of Broad-Pieces of Gold, and a rich Diamond Ring, he made him mount behind his Man, to him he ty'd him Back to Back, and in that Condition, with his Face towards the Horse's Tail, he rid Swearing, and Cursing, Damning, and Sinking, 'till he got into the next Town, where no small Flock of People gather'd about his Lordship, in Admiration of his riding after that preposterous Manner.

When *Fairfax* came to be General of the Parliament's Army, and lying with some Forces in the County of *Northumberland*, he took up his Quarters at *Newcastle* upon *Tine*; at the same Time *Howard* happen'd to be in the same Town, and understanding that *Fairfax* was about sending a Man to his Lady with a Parcel of Plate, which was presented to him by the Mayor, and Aldermen, of that Corporation; when the Day came that he set

out

out with the Prefent, our Highwaymay alfo
bide adieu to *Newcaftle* the fame Morning,
and overtaking the *Roundhead* on the Road,
they enter'd into a deep Difcourfe of the prefent Times, with which *Howard* feeming as
well pleas'd as the other, the *Republican* took
him for a very honeft Fellow, baited, and
din'd together, lay in the fame Bed at Night,
and fo continued in this friendly Manner,
'till the Meffenger was within a Day of his
Journey's-End. Next Morning, being the
laft they fhould be together, *Howard* thought
it was high Time then to put his Defign into
Execution; fo before Dinner, coming to a
Place very proper to act the Part of a Robber
in, he demanded the Portmanteau, in which
was the Plate, valued at 250 Pounds: The
other being a refolute Sort of a Fellow, deny'd
the Delivery of it; whereupon a Combat
enfu'd betwixt 'em, in which *Howard* had his
Horfe Shot under him, after a Difcharge of
2 or 3 Piftols on both Sides; however, the
Fray ftill continuing, he Fought on Foot, 'till
at laft he Shot his Adverfary thro' the Head,
of which Wound he immediately fell to the
Ground, and breath'd his Laft. *Howard*
nimbly mounts his Horfe, and at the Diftance
of 5 Miles off from the Place of their Rencounter, hides the Portmanteau of Plate in a
hollow Tree, and went to Dinner at the next
Town, from whence he made the Beft of his
Way to *Farringdon*, in *Berkfhire*, where *Fairfax* his Wife had a Houfe, which he reach'd

H 3   by

by Night, and deliver'd her the following Letter.

My Dear, Newcastle upon Tine, Aug. 10th, 1650.

*H*Oping you, and my Daughter Elizabeth, *are in good Health*; *these few Lines are to acquaint you, that my Company is so acceptable to the Inhabitants of* Newcastle, *that their Mayor, and Aldermen, have made me an extraordinary Present of Plate, which I have sent up to you by my Man* Thomas, *a new Servant, whom I would have you make much of, as finding him a very honest Fellow, according to the Character of those Gentlemen by whom he was recommended to my Service. I am (the Lord be prais'd) very well at present, and earnestly long for the Happiness of enjoying your good Company, which will not be long now, for I think of coming Home within this Month, or 5 Weeks at farthest; in the mean Time, I subscribe my self, your loving Husband, 'till Death,*

W. Fairfax.

By these Contents his Wife finding a Parcel of Plate was sent to her by the Bearer, as she thought, and enquiring of her suppos'd Man for it, he told her, that he was in Danger of being Robb'd of it on such a Heath, by some suspicious Persons, whom he saw riding before him, therefore for Security of so great a Charge, he put it into the Hands of and Inn-Keeper, dwelling at such a Town, from
whence

whence he could fetch it in 2 Days. This Excuse of his Carefulness pass'd over will enough with his new Mistress, who made very much of him, and pretending to be fatigu'd with his Journey, went to Bed betimes. But no sooner were the whole Family (which confisted of herself, her Daughter, a couple of Maids, and 2 Men-Servants) also gone to their Repose, but *Howard* arose, and dressing himself, went with Sword and Pistol, into the Servant's Apartments, to whom threatening present Death, if they made but the least Noise, he gagg'd, and ty'd them Hand, and Foot, with the Bed-Cords. Having secur'd them fast enough, he went into Mrs. *Fairfax's* Chamber, who was then in Bed, and first Ravishing the Daughter, he then fell on Board of the Mother, afterwards gagg'd, and ty'd them, as he had the Servants, and next made a strict Scrutiny into the Trunks, Boxes, and Chests of Drawers, from which taking about 2000 Broad-Pieces of Gold, and some Money in Silver, he made the best of his Way off with the Booty.

After his committing this Robbery, and Murder, there was a Proclamation issued out by the Commonwealth, promising 500 Pounds for the Apprehending him, whereupon to avoid being taken, he fled to *Ireland,* where he also pursu'd his Robbing on the Highway, 'till being notoriously known there, he return'd to *England* again, and Landing at *Highlake,* came to the City of *Chester.* At the same

Time

Time *Oliver Cromwell*, lay there with a Party
of Horfe, and putting up in the fame Inn
where that Ufurper had taken up his Quarters,
paſs'd for a Gentleman that was going to Tra-
vel beyond Sea for his Diverfion. He behav'd
himfelf here according to what he pretended
himfelf to be, fpent his Money with a great
deal of Liberality, and Counterfeiting himfelf
a *Round-Head,* as always fpeaking againſt the
Royal Family, and applauding the Murder of
King *Charles* the Firſt, *Oliver Cromwell* was ſo
much taken with his Converfation, that he
would feldom be out of his Company, Dining,
and Supping together, 'till about a Fortnight
after contracting this familiar Acquaintance
with each other, *Howard* paying old *Noll* an
early Vifit, one Morning in his Bed-Chamber,
which was even on the fame Floor with the
other's, he found him in a praying Pofture,
and knocking him down backwards, with the
But-End of a Piſtol, prefented it to his Breaſt,
and fwore that if he attempted to fpeak the
leaſt Word, he would prefently Shoot him
through the Head, though he was fure to be
Hang'd for it on the Sign-Poſt before the Door.
Theſe terrifying Words ſtruck the *Republican-
Hero* with fuch a *Pannick Fear,* that he permitted the Affaulter to do what he pleas'd,
even to Gagging, and Binding him Hand and
Foot ; after which he rifl'd a Couple of Trunks,
out of which taking about 1100 Jacobuſſes,
then taking the Pan out of the Clofe Stool,
which was pretty well fill'd with the nauſeous
Excrements

Excrements of this much more nauseous *Rebel,* he clapt it on his Head, and then taking his own Horse, and Portmanteau, as pretending he had some Business about 20 Miles off, and should not return 'till the next Day, he rid clean away. In the mean Time, *Oliver* thinking he was far enough off, falls a knocking and thundering, with his Legs, and Close-Stool Pan, for some Body to come and deliver him out of *Limbo,* who no sooner saw what he had upon his Noddle, suppos'd it had been his Head-Piece, 'till the Smell thereof, and the Danner running about his Ears, and Chaps, made them sensible of their Mistake, they immediately unbound him, who presently fell on his Knees to Prayers, for his great Deliverance, from the Fury of a most wicked Cavalier ; and then rising up, curst him, and his Gentility, to the Pit of Hell.

But within a Week after, *Howard* sent *Oliver* a Letter, wherein he signify'd, that he was in very good Health, that what he had done to him he apply'd to the good Use of making him Reflect, it was only an *Israelite* had spoil'd an *Egyptian,* therefore the Offence (if he thought it any) was Pardonable. When *Oliver* saw the jeering Contents of it, and from whom it came, he presently flung it into the Fire, and vow'd he would very well know what Company he kept for the Future, for Fear he should fall again into the like Disaster. However, *Howard* did not long enjoy his Liberty after this Exploit; for one Day venturing

H 5   ring

ring to attack Half a Dozen Officers of the *Republican Army*, as they were riding over *Black-Heath*, they vigorously oppos'd his Assault; and though he had Kill'd one of them, and desperately Wounded 2 others, yet he was overpower'd by the Remaining 3, and taken. By this Time several Passengers coming by, they assisted in carrying this bold Robber before a Magistrate, who forthwith committed him to *Maidstone-Goal*, whither *Oliver Cromwell*, went to see him, and insulted him with a great deal of contumelious Reproaches. When he came on his Tryal at the following Assizes, he had Evidences enough appear'd against him, to convict him, if he had had 20 Lives, for he was Sworn against not only by the Officers who took him, but also by General *Fairfax*'s Wife, and Daughter, and *Cromwell*; whereupon Sentence of Death was past upon him for 2 Robberies, 2 Rapes, and 2 Murders; when he came to the Place of Execution, Apparell'd all in White, he own'd himself Guilty of what he stood Condemn'd for, but was sorry for nothing, but the Murders he had committed; but yet considering on whom they were Acted, he thought the Crime so much the Less; and that if he was to be Pardon'd, he protested he would never leave off Robbing the *Round-Heads*, so long as One of 'em was left in *England*: And that which is more Remarkable, *Oliver Cromwell* being also in the Country, to see the Last of him, 'twas observ'd that *Howard* smil'd upon him with a

very,

very great Air of Scorn, and Contempt, and told him, that if he had had his juſt Reward, he had been Hang'd before now : So being turn'd off the Ladder in 1651-2, he Ended his Life, Aged 32 Years.

Major GEORGE STRANGWAYES, *a Murderer.*

MR. *George Strangwayes* (commonly known in the Country where he chiefly reſided, by the Name of Major *Strangwayes,* an Office which he had with much Honour and Gallantry perform'd in the *Civil-War,* in the Reign of King *CHARLES* the Firſt) was ſecond Son to Mr. *James Strangwayes,* of *Muſſen* in the County of *Dorſet,* a Gentleman of an antient, and unblemiſh'd Family, whoſe Vertues this unhappy Son of his, 'till ſullied by this raſh Act of ungovern'd Paſſion, which we are going to mention, did rather ſeem to illuſtrate by a conſtant Courſe of worthy, and manly Actions, than any Ways to degenerate from the beſt Atchievements of his moſt ſucceſsful Predeceſſors. He was a Perſon that had a brave, and generous Soul, included in a ſtout, and active Body. He was of Stature Tall, and fram'd to the moſt maſculine Proportion

portion of Man; his Conſtitution ſuch as rather fitted him for the active Employments of
buſy War, than the more quiet Affairs of
Peace, affecting Studies; yet was he not ſo
much a Stranger to thoſe Arts, which are the
adorning Qualifications of a Gentleman, but
that he had Sacrificed to *Minerva*, whilſt in
the Temple of *Mars*; and in the moſt ſerious
Conſultations, had always a Judgment as dex-
terous to Adviſe, as a Heart daring to Act.
What he appear'd moſt Unskillful in, was
Love's Polemicks, he having ſpun out the
Thread of Life, without twiſting it in Matrimony.

The Father of Mr. *Strangwayes*, dying about
ſome ten Years before the following Misfortune fell upon this unhappy Son, left him in
Poſſeſſion of the Farm of *Muſſen*; leaving
his eldeſt Daughter, Mrs. *Mabellah Strangwayes*,
afterwards Wife to Mr. *Fuſſel*, his Executrix.
The Eſtate being thus left, Mrs. *Mabellah*,
being then an antient Maid, Rents the Farm
of her Brother *George*, and Stocks it at her
own Coſt; towards the Procuring of which
Stock, ſhe engag'd herſelf in a Bond of 350
Pounds, to her Brother *George*: Who preſu-
ming on her continuance of a ſingle Life, and
by Conſequence, that her perſonal Eſtate,
might in Time return to thoſe of her then
neareſt Relations, of which himſelf had a juſt
Reaſon to expect (if not the Whole) the
greateſt Share; he not only intruſted her with
the fore-mentioned Bond, but likewiſe with
that

that Part of the Stock, and fuch Utenfils of the
Houfe, as by his Father's Will, properly belong'd to himfelf ; which he prefum'd fhe could
better fecure, paffing under the Notion of hers,
than he, whofe whole Eftate was liable to
the dangerous Hazard of Sequefteration, a
Difafter fo Epidemical, as many Thoufands
befides himfelf, by fad Experience, knew in
thofe Times, that Honefty, the common
Prefervative againft other Calamities, was the
principal Means, that made them obnoxious
to this.

His Eftate being (as he then conceiv'd) thus
in a fair Probability of Prefervation from
thofe Vultures of a Commonwealth, Seque-
ftrators, by the calm Neutrality of a difcreet
Sifter, they for fome Time liv'd happily together, he making the Farm of *Muffen* the
common Place of his Refidence. But on a
fudden the Scene alters, and fhe whom he
thought Age, and a long continued fingle Life,
had imprifon'd too faft in her Virgin-Ice, e'er
to be thaw'd with the Thoughts of a Matri-
monial Life, began to exprefs fome Inclination
of Affection towards Mr. *Fuffel,* a Gentleman
of good Efteem in the Country where he
liv'd, which was at *Blandford,* an eminent
Town in *Dorfetfhire,* and of much Repute
for his eminent Abilities in Matters of Law.

Mrs. *Mabellah Strangwayes,* now no longer
difguifing her Affections, to the abovefaid Mr.
Fuffel, being then a Widower, lets her Refo-
lutions difcover themfelves in fo publick a Way,
that

that it foon arrives to the Ear of her difcontented Brother, who, tho' not apparently for any former Hatred between them, yet (as is moft likely) doubting thofe Abilities of Mr. *Fuffel's* which (fince in relation to the Law) he with many others were pleas'd by an eafy Metaphor to term Subtilty, might, if not prejudice him in Part of his own Eftate, yet wholly deprive him of that Part of his Sifter's, which before Hope (grounded on fair Probabilities) told him he was of all Men moft likely to enjoy. To prevent this approaching Storm, he lets his Sifter know his Defguft of her intended Marriage; and being further exafperated by her unmoveable Conftancy, broke out into fuch exuberant Expreffions of Paffion, that to her Terror, he affirms, if ever fhe Married Mr. *Fuffel,* to be the Death of him, either in his Study, or elfewhere.

Now he and his Sifter are parted, at which Time (as fhe pretends) he unjuftly detain'd much of the Stock belonging to the Farm, which either by her Father's Will, or her own Purchace, was properly hers; withal fhe denies any fuch Thing as the Sealing the aforementioned Bond, pretending it only a Forgery of her Brother's. On the other Side, he complains of Injuries done to him, of no lefs Extent, than the endeavouring to defraud him of a Part of his Eftate, befides the Money due by Bond. Thefe were the Differences which firft Fomented a Rage, not to be
                                  quench'd

P. 159

quench'd but by Blood, and may be seen by what follows.

Mr. *Fuffel*, both for the better profecuting his own Suits againft his Brother *Strangwayes*, as likewife for the following of feveral Caufes for many others, he being a Man of very great Employment, being in this City one *Hilary* Term, had his Lodging one Story High, at the Sign of the *George* and *Half-Moon*, 3 Doors farther without *Temple-Bar* than the *Palfgrave's*-Head Tavern, oppofite to a Pewterer's Shop: He being retir'd to his Lodgings between 9 and 10 (not having been in it above a Quarter of an Hour before the Faft was done) he fitting Writing at his Desk, with his Face towards the Window; the Curtains belonging to it being fo near drawn, that there was only left Room enough to difcern him, 2 Bullets Shot from a Carbine, ftruck him, the One through the Forehead, and the Other in about his Mouth; the third Bullet, or Slug, ftruck in the lower Part of the Timber of the Window. The Paffage where the other two came in (fince in the Corner of the Window) being fo narrow, that little more than an Inch over, or under, had fav'd his Life, by obftrufting their Paffage. In that *Punftillo* of Time, wherein the Bullets ftruck him, e'er giving Warning by a dying Groan, and the Swiftnefs of the Aftion, not giving Warning to his Clerk, though then in the Room, to affift his murder'd Mafter, 'till preceiving him to lean his Head on the

Desk,

Desk, and knowing him not apt to fall afleep
as he Wrote, conceiving that fome more than
ordinary Diftemper was the Caufe of it, he
draws near to affift him ; but being fuddenly
terrified with the unexpected Sight of Blood,
fuch an amazing Horror Seizes him, that for
the Prefent he is in a dreadful Extafy loft to
Action ; but fpeedily recollecting himfelf, he
with an hafty Summons calls up fome of the
Houfhold, by whofe Affiftance he difcovers
what a fad Difafter had bereav'd him of his
Mafter ; they fpeedily make down into the
Street, but found there nothing that might
Light them with the leaft Beam of Information, all (as if directed by thofe evil Angels
that Favour fuck black Defigns) appearing, as
they conceiv'd, more filent, and ftill, than is
ufual in his populous City, at that Time of
Night. Officers are rais'd, and Mr. *Fuffel's*
Son acquainted with the fad News; who, e'er
he could fpare Time to mourn his Father's
unexpected Death, muft with more active
Paffion (as near as thofe dark Sufpicions,
which only directed them, could give leave)
profecute his Revenge : Several Places are
troubl'd with a fruitlefs Search ; the Firft that
was apprehended, being a Barber, whofe
Lodging being in the fame Houfe with Mr.
Fuffel's, and he that Night abfent, gave them
very pregnant Caufes of Sufpicion.

Having yet apprehended none that they
had on former Differences, any important
Reafon to fufpect; young *Fuffel* calling to
Mind

Mind thofe irreconcileable Quarrels, which had of long Time been between his Father, and his Uncle *Strangwayes*, he propounds to the Officers the Apprehending of him; which Motion finding a general Aprobation, is fuddenly profecuted, and he apprehended between 2 and 3 in the Morning, being then in Bed, at his Lodging in the *Strand*, over againft *Ivy Bridge*, at one Mr. *Pym*'s a Taylor, a Door on this Side the *Black-Bull*-Inn, which is now *Bull-Inn-Court*. He being now in the Cuftody of the Officers, is had before Juftice *Blake*, by whom, altho' with an undaunted Confidence, denying the Act, he is committed to *Newgate*; where remaining 'till the next Morning, he is then by a Guard convey'd to the Place where Mr. *Fuffel*'s Body lay, where before the Coroner's Jury, he is commanded to take his Dead Brother-in-Law by the Hand, and to touch his Wounds, a Way of Difcovery, which the Defenders of Sympathy highly applaud.

But there having been nothing difcoverable by this Experiment, he is return'd back to Prifon, and the Jury (tho' but with little Hopes of Satisfaction) continue their Inqueft. Several Ways are prepounded by the Foreman of the Jury, for the Difcovery of the Murderer, one of which was this: That all the Gun-Smiths Shops in *London*, and the adjacent Places, fhould be examin'd what Guns they had either Sold, or Lent that Day; this being a Matter in the Apprehenfion of moft of the

Jury

Jury, fo near approaching to an Impoffibility, as not without much Difficulty to be done ; one Mr. *Holloway*, a Gun-Smith living in the *Strand*, then one of the Jury, faid, it was a Task in his Opinion, who knew how nume- rous Men of that Profeffion were, in and about the City, not to be done; withal al- leging, that for his own Part he let One, and made no Queftion but feveral others had done the like : This Saying of his being by the ap- prehenfive Foreman, fpeedily took notice of, he is demanded for the Satisfaction of the Reft of the Jury, to declare to whom he lent the Gun ; he after fome fmall Recollection, anfwers to one Mr. *Thompfon,* living in *Long- Acre,* formerly a Major in the King's Army, and now Married to a Daughter of Sir *James Afton's.* Upon this, a fpeedy Search is made after Major *Thompfon,* who being abroad, his Wife is took in Hold, who, tho' clearing herfelf from the Knowledge of any fuch Thing as the Borrowing of the Gun, yet is continu'd a Prifoner, 'till her Husband fhall be produc'd; who being then about fome urgent Occafions in the Country, on the firft News of her Confinement, fuddenly haftens to *London,* where being Examin'd before a Juftice of Peace, he Confeffes he borrow'd a Carbine that Day of Mr. *Holloway,* and that he bor- row'd it at the Defire of Mr. *George Strang- wayes,* who acquainted him with no farther Ufe he intended to make of it, than for the Killing of a Deer; for which Ufe he charg'd

it

it with a Leafe of Bullets, and a Slug. Being thus charg'd and prim'd, between the Hours of 7 and 8 at Night, he meets Mr. *Strangwayes* in St. *Clement's-Church-Yard*, to whom he delivers the Gun: But to give you a certain Relation who fir'd the Gun, is that which we believe no Man could ever tell except Mr. *Strangwayes*, who carry'd that great Secret with him to his Grave, denying to reveal it at the Seffions here, as referving it for the geneal Affize hereafter. Between the Hours of 10 and 11, on the Night the Murder was committed, he brought back the Gun to Major *Thompfon's* Houfe, where leaving it, he retires to his Lodging, where, in his Abfence, he had left One to Perfonate him: That Piece of Policy being thus perform'd, he comes (according to his ufual Cuftom) into his Lodging about 7 in the Evening, and going up into his Chamber, made fome fmall ftay there, from whence taking the Advantage of a Time in which he found the Employments of the Houfhold fuch as not to have leifure to take much Notice of his Actions, he fecretly conveys himfelf down Stairs, and having a private Way of opening the Door, conveys himfelf out, and his difguis'd Friend in, who, by thofe of the Family being oft heard walking about the Chamber, occafions that miftaken Depofition of theirs, concerning his being in the Houfe.

Having now concluded that Act of Darknefs he went about, he is once more return'd

turn'd to his Lodging, and secretly discharges
his disguis'd Friend, hasting to Bed, he lay
there (tho' in all Probability with no very
quiet Night's Rest) 'till 3 in the Morning, at
which Time the Officers (as aforesaid) enter'd
the House, and apprehended him. On *Monday* following, being the 21st of *February,*
1657-8, Major *Thompson,* to hasten the En-
largment of his imprison'd Wife, return'd to
London, and made *Affidavit* before Justice
La Wright, of his borrowing a Gun for Major *Strangwayes,* but knew not that it was
upon any Design of Murder ; which striking
the Murderer in an amaz'd Terror, after some
few Minutes of a deep, and considerate Silence, in a most pathetical Manner, he ac-
knowledges the immediate Hand of God, to
be in this most wonderful Detection.

On the 24th of *February,* he is brought to
his Tryal at the Sessions-House in the *Old-
Baily,* where being demanded to plead, he
Answers. That if it might, on his being Try'd,
be admitted to him to die by that Manner of
Death, by which his Brother fell, he would
plead ; if not, by refusing to plead, both pre-
serve an Estate, to bestow on such Friends,
for whom he had most Affection ; and withal,
free himself from the ignominious Death of
a publick Gibbet. Many Arguments were
us'd by the Lord Chief Justice *Glyn,* and the
Rest of the Bench, to induce him to plead,
as laying before him the Sin he committed in
refusing to submit to the ordinary Course of
                                             the

the Law, and the Terror of the Death his obstinate Silence would inforce them to inflict upon him. These, with many other Motives were us'd, but all invalid, he remains impenetrable, refusing either to plead, or to discover who it was that fir'd the Gun ; only affirms (which he continued to his Death) that whoever fir'd it, it was done by his Directions.

'Tis said his haughty Spirit, had often on the Sight of the Deceas'd, rais'd in him impetuous Storms of Rage ; such that often broke out into Intemperance, as both by Word, and Letter, he several Times challenges him ; and in Consideration of his being something more impair'd by Age than himself, offers him what odds in Length of Weapon, he could with Reason, and Honour demand. This encountring nought but a silent and slighting Repulse, he one Day meeting him in *Westminster-Hall,* accosts him with this Compliment.

Brother Fussel, it argues not Descretion in us, of either Side, we being both Cavaliers, *to submit our Causes to this present Course of Law, where the Most of our Judges are such as were formerly our Enemies ;* Calice-Sands *were a fitter Place for our Dispute, than* Westminster-Hall.

But Mr. *Fussel* not only refus'd that Way of deciding the Quarrel, but also Indicts his Brother *Strangwayes,* as a Challenger, which adding more Fuel to his former Rage, put him upon this dangerous Way of Satisfying his vindicative Passion.

But

But not to inguſt too far in Cenſuring the
Act, we preceed to declare the Demeanor of
the Actor, who perſiſting on his firſt Reſolution not to plead, hears from the offended
Court, this dreadful Sentence.

THAT the Priſoner be ſent to the Place
*   from whence he came, and that he be put*
into a mean Houſe, ſtopt from any Light ; and
that he be laid upon his Back, with his Body
bare, ſaving ſomething to cover his privy Parts:
That his Arms ſhall be ſtretched forth with a
Cord, the One to one Side of the Priſon, the
Other to the other Side of the Priſon ; and in
like Manner ſhall his Legs be us'd: And that
upon his Body ſhall be laid as much Iron and
Stone, as he can bear, and more ; and the firſt
Day ſhall he have 3 Morſels of Barley Bread, and
the next Day, ſhall he Drink Thrice of the
Water in the next Channel to the Priſon-Door,
but no Spring, or Fountain Water: And this
ſhall be his Puniſhment 'till he Dies.

This Sentence being paſt upon him, he
was remanded back to *Newgate.* This being
One of the laſt Scenes he was to Act on the
Stage of Mortality, he had the frequent Aſſiſtance of ſeveral Divines ; namly, Dr. *Wilde,*
Dr. *Warmſtrey,* Mr. *Jenkins,* Mr. *Watſon,*
and Mr. *Norton,* 'till *Monday* the Laſt of
February ; when about 11 of the Clock in
the Fore-Noon, the Sheriffs of *London* and
Middleſex, accompanied with divers Officers,
came

came to the *Press-Yard*, where after a short
Time of stay, Major *Strangwayes* was guarded
down, cloathed all in White, Waftcoat,
Stockings, Drawers, and Cap, over which
was caft a long Mourning Cloak.— From
hence he is guarded to the Dungeon, the fad
and difmal Place of Execution, being accompany'd with fome few of his Friends, amongft
whom was the Reverend Dr. *Warmftrey*, to
whom turning, he faid, *Sir, will you be pleas'd to
affift me with your Prayers?* The Doctor Anfwer'd, *Yes, Major, I come to officiate that
Christian Work, and the Lord strengthen your
Faith, and give you Confidence, and Affurance,
in the Merits of Jesus Chrift.* After they had
fpent fome short Time in Prayers, then applying himself to the Company, in General,
with a Voice fomething more elevated than
Ordinary, fpeaks thefe Words,

*For my Religion (I thank my God) I never
had a Thought in my Heart to doubt it. I die
in the* Christian *Religion, and am affur'd of my
Intereft in Chrift Jesus, by whofe Merits I
queftion not but my Soul fhall e'er long Triumph,
over the prefent Afflictions in Eternity of Glory,
being reconcil'd to the Mercies of my God,
thro' my Saviour Jesus Chrift, into whofe Bo-
fome I hope to be gather'd, there to enjoy that
eternal, infinite, and boundlefs Happinefs,
wherewith he Rewards all the Elect; fo the
Lord blefs you all, blefs you in this World, 'till
he brings you to a World ever bl-ffed, and
blefs*

bleſs me in this laſt, and dreadful Tryal ; ſo
let us all pray, *Jeſus*, *Jeſus*, have *Mercy* on me.

Having ſaid this, he takes his ſolemn, and
laſt Leave, of all his lamenting Friends, and
now prepares for that dreadful Aſſault of
Death, he was ſpeedily to encounter ; his
Friends plac'd themſelves at the Corners of
the Preſs, whom he deſir'd, when he gave
the Words, to lay on the Weights; his Hands
and Legs are extended, in which Action, he
cries out, *Thus were the ſacred Limbs of my
ever bleſſed Saviour ſtretch'd forth on the Croſs,
when ſuffering to free the Sin-Polluted World
from an eternal Curſe.* Then crying out with
a clear and ſprightful Voice, *Lord Jeſus, receive my Soul,* which was the promis'd Signal ;
thoſe ſad Aſſiſtants perform their dreadful
Task, and laid on at firſt Weight, which
finding too light, for a ſudden Execution,
many of thoſe ſtanding by, added their Bur-
thens to disburthen him of his Pain; which
notwithſtanding, for the Time of its continuance, as it was to him a dreadful Sufferance,
ſo was it to them a horrid Spectacle, his dying
Groans filling the uncouth Dungeon with the
Voice of Terror; but this diſmal Scene ſoon
finds a quiet Cataſtrophe, for in the ſpace of
8 or 10 Minutes, at the moſt, his unfetter'd
Soul left her tortur'd Manſion, and he from
that violent Paroxiſm falls into the quiet
Sleep of Death. His Body having lain ſome
Time in the Preſs, he was brought forth, in
which

which Action, e'er Coffin'd, it was so much expos'd to the publick View, that many Standers by beheld the Bruises made by the Press, whose triangular Form, being plac'd with the Acute about the Region of the Heart, did soon deprive that Fountain of Life of its necessary Motion, tho' he was prohibited that usual Terror in that kind, to have a sharp Piece of Timber laid under his Back, to accelerate its Penetration. The Body appear'd void of Scars, and not deform'd with Blood, but where the Eminences of the Press touch'd on the middle Parts of the Breast, and upper of the Belly; his Face was Bloody, but as it appear'd to the most inquisitive Spectators, not from any external Injury, but the Violent forcing of the Blood from the larger Vessels into the Veins of the Nose and Eyes: And now committed to that sable Cabinet his Coffin, he is in a Cart that attended at the Prison-Door, convey'd to *Christ's-Church,* where his Ashes shall Sleep, 'till Time herself be dissolved to Eternity.

After his dreadful Sentence was pass'd upon him, and he remanded back to *Newgate,* he Writ the following Letter to his Brother-in-Law Major *Dewey,* a Member of Parliament, and a Gentleman that had Married another of his Sisters.

I   Dear

Dear Brother,

*I Hope these Lines, and pressing Death, will
so far expiate my Crime, as to procure your,
and my other Friends, Forgiveness; for my Conscience bears me Witness, I was provok'd by
many of my Brother-in-Law's insufferable
Wrongs. After divers Parles, finding his inveterate Spleen so implacable, as to indict and
inform against me at the open Bench, my Flesh
and Blood, held no longer Patience, but sought
to usurp the revengeful Attribute, which God
appropriates to himself, when he would not answer me in single Combate, tho' I gave him advantage in length of Weapon; yet this I will
assure you, that I did not intend his Death, but
by the discharging the Piece, to have only terrify'd his Heart from practising dangerous Suits,
and thereby to let him know, that he was at my
Mercy, if he contemn'd the same: In a Word,
each hath his Death, I by this untimely Fall: The
one to my Revenge, the other to the Law; which
invokes me to pay the one willingly, being confident that the other is cancelled by the All-seeing
Eye of divine Mercy and Justice; these in
short are the last Words of your dying Brother,*

From the *Press-Yard*
  in *Newgate, Feb.*   George Strangwayes.
  23d 1657-8

S T E P H E N

STEPHEN EATON, GEORGE ROADES, *and* SARAH SWIFT, *Murderers and Robbers.*

THE abovesaid *Stephen Eaton*, a Confectioner, *George Roades*, a Broker, and *Sarah Swift*, were 3 most wicked profligate Wretches, who, in Company of one *Henry Prichard*, a Taylor, and 3 other Men; among the many Villanies they Daily committed, were resolv'd to act another villainous Action upon Mr. *John Talbot*, a Minister, a Gentleman who had been Chaplain to one of King *Charles* the Second's Regiments in *Portugal*, where he continu'd in the Discharge of his Office, 'till the Recalling of the said Regiment; and arriving at *London*, he Preach'd 3 Months at St. *Alphage* in the *Wall*. Afterwards he was Curate at a Town call'd *Laindon* in *Essex*; whence coming to *London*, upon the Account of a Law-Suit between him and some Persons of that Parish, he apply'd himself to his Lawyer, and had some Intimation that his Adversaries design'd to Arrest him; hereupon he was shy whither he went, and with whom he convers'd; but soon after he took Notice of

I 2   6 Men,

6 Men, and one Woman, that dogg'd him whither foever he went ; after many fhiftings from Place to Place, in order to his Avoidance of them, he betook himfelf to *Gray's-Inn*, whither fome, or all of thefe Perfons follow'd him ; fo that he took full and accurate Notice of them. Whence he fent by the Hands of 2 Gentlemen belonging to that Inn of Court, one or two Letters, requefting fome of his Acquaintance, and Friends to come to his Affiftance, all this while he only fufpecting an Arreft.

They failing, he apply'd himfelf to a Gentleman's Chamber at *Gray's-Inn*, where ftaying 'till he fuppos'd all Caufe of Danger was over, after a fhort Refrefhment, fteer'd his Courfe the back Way thro' *Old-Street*, over the Fields towards *Shoreditch* ; not long after he came into the Fields, he preceiv'd the fame Perfons which before dogg'd him to purfue him ; whereupon in this ftraight, it being late, near 11 of the Clock, he fought to make his Efcape by breaking thro' a Reed-Hedge, to a Garden-Houfe ; but before he could reach his defign'd Shelter, one, or more feiz'd him, and firft pickt his Pockets, where they found about 20 Shillings, and his Knife, with which one attempted to kill him ; the Cut in the Coller of his Doublet fignifies, that they endeavour'd to cut his Throat before they ftript him, but the Wound feems to inform, that they Firft pull'd off his Coat and Doublet, and then executing their fo long waited

for

for Intention on him. As to the Manner and
Form of his Wound, whether it was becauſe
the Knife was broad pointed (and ſo it was
judg'd) that it might not by ſtabs do full Execution, or that theſe pretended to an exquiſite
Skill in Butchering Men, they Firſt cut out a
Piece of his Throat about the Breadth of a
Crown-Piece, but miſt the Wind-Pipe; then
in the dependant Part of the Orifice, they
ſtabb'd him with the Knife, the Point whereof
reach'd near unto the Lungs; but ſo Providence did order their Cruelty, that they miſt
the recurrent Nerves, by which he had been
ſilenc'd, as alſo the jugular Veins, and Ar-
teires, by the opening of which, he had re-
midileſs bled to Death, and poſſibly no ſuch
Diſcovery had been made of the Murder.

It muſt not be omitted, that whilſt they
ſtrove, and this barbarous Fact was committed at *Dame Annis ſo Cleer*, on *Friday* Night,
the 2d of *July*, 1669, that the Dogs in the
Garden open'd much, and by their fierce
Barking awaken'd ſome Perſons, who in regard of the Light, ſuppoſing it Day-Break,
came down to look after their Marketing;
whereupon the Murderers left their Prey,
and Mr. *Talbot*, altho' mortally wounded, crept
after them, through the ſame Breach he had
made at his Entrance into the Garden, fearing leaſt he might not be found, and Periſh
for want of Help, if he continu'd there; he
went not far before he fell down in the Place
where he was found lying. Beſides the Bar-

king

king of the Dogs, he obferv'd, that the Beafts
did very much Bellow, as if God had caus'd
this Cruelty of the Dogs, to be fome kind of
Occafion of Mercy to the wounded Man, and
to reproach the more deftructive Fierceneſs
of thefe Murderers; and had open'd wide the
Mouths of the Beafts of the Field, to amaze
and afright them from this Slaughter of an
Innocent; but becaufe the Voice of thefe
Creatures feem'd not loud enough to deter
thefe Affailants from profecuting their Bloody
Attempt. Soon after the Heavens fpake
terribly in Thunder, which poffibly did fo
aftonifh thefe Wretches, that they efcap'd
not far from the Place where they did this
horrid Exploit. And as if thefe Occurences
were not fufficient to the End for which they
were appointed, a great Shower of Rain fell,
which drew the Brick-Makers out of their
Huts and Lodgings, to fave their Bricks from
the Rain, by covering them with Straw. By
fome of thefe Mr. *Talbot* was efpy'd, lying in
his Shirt and Drawers Bloody : Notice hereupon was given to the Reft, and when they
came to him, he being rais'd up, and cherifh'd
with a little Strong-Water, immediately
pointed which Way the Murderers went.
The Watch near *Shoreditch*, having Notice
of the Murder, fome Perfons of them went
out, as well to take care of the wounded
Gentleman, as alfo to find out, and apprehend the Offenders : One of thefe fearing
alfo an Arreft, kept in the Search a loof off,
and

and he firſt diſcover'd a Man lying amongſt the Nettles, whom he ſuppos'd likewiſe to be kill'd; but calling his Companions, the Perſon appear'd by the bloody Knife lying on one Side of him, and the Miniſter's Doublet on the other, to be Guilty of the Murder, and accordingly he was ſeiz'd; at Firſt he ſeign'd himſelf aſleep, but being well awaken'd, he attempted to make his Eſcape; a Pewter-Pot being found near him, the Mark newly ſcrap'd out, one of his Guard broke his Head with it, and ſo he became more quiet and tractable. In the mean Time Mr. *Talbot*, by the great Care of the Officers, and the People Watching that Night, was convey'd to the *Star-Inn* at *Shoreditch Church*, and put to Bed, and a Chyrurgeon immediately ſent for to dreſs him.

When this *Eaton* was brought before him, he ſtraitways knew him, and by Writing declar'd, he was the Perſon that cut his Throat, and that 5 more, and a bloody Woman, were his Aſſociates. He being (upon his Requeſt) a ſecond Time brought before him, then continu'd his former Accuſation, whereupon he was carry'd before Juſtice *Pitfield*, and by him after Examination committed to *Newgate*: It was not long before the Woman was found, pretending herſelf likewiſe to be aſleep, and when the Officers brought her before Mr. *Talbot*, he preſently knew her, and enquir'd of the Conſtable whether her Name was not *Sarah*, for he had

heard

heard One of her Comrades fay in *Holbourn,*
Shall we have a Coach Sarah ? She being ask'd
her Name, and not fufpecting the Reafon,
faid her Name was *Sarah*: Shortly after another Perfon was taken, whom likewife he
knew, and a Fourth, who were committed
to *Newgate*.

The true Copy of a Letter which the abovefaid Mr. *Talbot* fent to a Perfon of Quality,
on the *Wednefday* following.

SIR,

ON Friday *laft walking in* Holbourn, *a*
Gentleman, a very Stranger to me, bid me
look to my felf, for I was dogg'd by Knaves,
and fo God knows it prov'd to my Sorrow, yet
know I not for what Caufe I was purfu'd ; I
mov'd to Gray's-Inn, *'till I thought this Malice*
might have been over ; after this I was ftill pur-
fu'd, and God knoweth that I knew none of their
Faces ; Houfes, Streets, Highways, all was one ;
thus for above 7 *Hours I was dogg'd, 'till I was*
almoft Dead with Wearinefs ; at laft, ftriving
to get to my Inn, I went a new Way, thinking
to efcape them, but could not ; for at 11 *of the*
Clock that Night, 6 *Men, and one bloody Wo-*
man, firft cut my Throat, and then ftabb'd me
in the Throat. I was found and brought by the
Officers of the Parifh of Shoreditch, *where I*
am carefully provided for ; an able Doctor, Dr.
Hodges, *and a Chyrurgeon, one Mr.* Lichfield,
takes Care of me. I can Eat nothing, neither
                                                can

can I speak any Thing but Ay and No. There are 4 of my bloody Enemies in Newgate, *at* Hick's-Hall *these* 4 *are cast; to Day they are to be at the* Old-Baily

Your humble Servant,

From the *Star-Inn* in Shore-ditch, *July* 7th, 1669.   **J. Talbot.**

Mr. *John Talbot*'s Account of his wandering from one Place to another, when he was dogg'd by several Persons.

THE Reason why I could not escape them was this, into what Place, House, Alley, or Corner soever I came, I was watch'd and dogg'd, by several Persons; I took Sanctuary in Councellor Prichard's *Chambers in* Gray's-Inn; *a certain Time; out of his Chamber I had Liberty to go into the Walks, in the very Walks I was dogg'd; I return'd again into the aboresaid Chamber, afterwards I walk'd in the upper Gallery there, 'till I thought all was well; then it was past* 3 *of the Clock in the After-Noon, then I went into the Lane; I thought the People had been Mad, they pursu'd me Bloodily; at* 5 *of the Clock I Housed, and got a Cup of Beer, but immediately I was forc'd to fly; then I was pursu'd 'till I was stabb'd by* 6 *Men, and one bloody Woman. I am so Sick, I can Write no more.*

I 5   **Several**

Several Atteftations was made before the
Juftice of Peace, relating to this Gentleman's
being dogg'd and ftabb'd, by Mr. *James Ky-
noin*, Mr. *John Savil*, Headborough, Mr. *Thomas Hutchins*, Weaver, of *Holloway-Lane* in
Shoreditch, Mr. *Edward Banifter* Headborough,
living at the *Red Lyon* in *Holloway-Lane*, Mr.
John Chapman, Headborough of *Shoreditch*,
and Mr. *Went*, Conftable of *Shoreditch* Parifh;
which laft attefted, that as he was coming
out of the Garden where Mr. *Talbot* had been
wounded, he efpy'd over the Highway a
Shed-Door open'd, and a Woman coming out
with an old Pair of Bodice in her Hand,
whom he queftioning, and finding it to be her
Trade to gather Rags, let her pafs, demand-
ing of her, if any other Perfon was in the
Shed ? to which fhe anfwer'd, There was a
Woman, upon which he going in, found her
Snorting, either being, or pretending to be
afleep ; whom he with his Guard, foon rous'd
up, and finding her fomewhat Sufpicious,
brought her to the wounded Man, whom he
had gotten to Bed, and was by that Time very
much reviv'd with Neceffaries he had likewife
procur'd for him ; and therefore taking the
Woman into the Room to him, he did by
Writing demand of him, if that was the
bloody Woman, that he had before wrote of
to him in feveral Papers ? To which he prefently wrote fhe was; being fo pityful a fcrubb'd
loufy Creature, that any Man would loath to
come near to her; fo he foon carry'd her to
                                          her

her Companions, with whom fhe us'd much of the canting Language, faying, *Take Coach, take Horfe*, and *mill the Gruntling*, by which fhe was meant, *Cut a Throat, take a Purfe, and fteal a Pig.*

The laft Note Mr. *Talbot* Writ, which was the Night before he Dyed.

Mr. *Wem*,

P R A Y get fome to fpeak to the Ordinary, to enquire of Eaton *who employ'd him, or bir'd him. If fo, let Eaton get their Names: Or whether any of* Laindon *People did abett, confent, or contribute to his bloody Faft.*

Whereupon Mr. *Went*, upon Execution-Day, repair'd to *Newgate*, and attain'd the following Atteftation from a *Chaplain* that was prefent with the Prifoner, not meeting with the *Ordinary*.

The *Chaplain* attefted, that before that Time, he had fome Conference with *Eaton*, and went again with the Note I had of Mr. *Talbot*, queftioning *Eaton* about it, who utterly deny'd it, as he fhould utter it before an eternal Judge, and that he is altogether Clear and Innocent of the Crime laid againft him; and that he never faw the Face of Mr. *Talbot*, 'till he was on *Saturday* Morning brought before him; which faid Gentleman likewife queftioning *Sarah Swift*, the Day before Execution,

cution, concerning her being Guilty, and urging her to confeſs the bloody Fact, ſhe anſwer'd, ſhe would Burn in Hell, before ſhe would confeſs any Thing.

When the Priſoners were brought to the Bar, a bloody Knife was produc'd; they all deny'd that they ever ſaw it, and that they knew the Perſon wounded, or any Thing of the ſaid Murder, or Robbery; but many Witneſſes were call'd who were at the taking of theſe Offenders, but eſpecially one Perſon, who was the Firſt that found the wounded Man, Mr. *Talbot*, did declare theſe Words, or Words to the like Effect, That firſt finding of the ſaid wounded Man, he view'd him, and found that his Throat was cut, whereupon he call'd for Help, and then walking about the Place where he lay, he eſpy'd a bloody Doublet, and approaching near to it, he ſaw a Man lying as it were aſleep between the ſaid Doublet, and the ſaid bloody Knife, but calling to the Man, he awak'd and roſe up, thereupon he laid hold on him, and endeavouring to eſcape, he gave him a knock over the Head, and broke the Skin, whereby did iſſue forth a little Blood; and afterwards ſearching the Pockets of the ſaid Perſon, whoſe Name was *Stephen Eaton*, he found 4 Pieces of Tape, One of which ſaid Pieces of Tape was Bloody, beſides ſome Money and other Things, which being ask'd how he came by them, could not at preſent give any poſitive Anſwer; but at the Seſſions-Houſe being ask'd how that Tape came

came Bloody, anſwer'd, it was occaſion'd by his bloody Head ; but the Witneſs ſwore it was impoſſible, there being not ſo much Blood as would wet his Hair. But the main Evidence againſt the ſaid Offenders were the Subſcriptions of the ſaid Mr. *Talbot* ; for when any of them were brought before him, he writ down that ſuch a one had Robb'd him ; and alſo in his Writing much exclaiming againſt one *Sarah*, mentioning her to be the bloody Woman, that cry'd, *Kill the Dog.*

The Offenders Names (as aforeſaid) were *Stephen Eaton*, a Confectioner, *Sarah Swift*, *George Roads*, a Broker, and *Henry Prichard*, a Taylor ; who being all Perſons of a looſe Life, and not able to give any good Account of their Habitations and Behaviour, were by the Jury brought in Guilty of the ſaid Robbery, and intended Murder, of the ſaid Mr. *Talbot*, for they could not prove where they were after 6 of the Clock the Night before the ſaid Fact was committed.

Midd. ſſ. The Information of *Thomas Lichfield*, of the Pariſh of St. *Botolph*'s *Biſhopſgate*, *London*, Chyrurgeon, taken, and acknowledged, the 13th Day of *July*, in the one and twentieth Year of the Reign of our Sovereign Lord King *C H A R L E S* the Second, *Annoq. Dom.* 1669.

*T*HIS *Informant ſaith, that he being ſent for, as a Chyrurgeon, to take care of one* John Talbot, *who was Wounded in his Throat :*
This

*This Informant at his coming, searched his
Throat, and found a Wound therein of the
Depth of 3 Inches, and of the Breadth of 2
Inches, which penetrated into his Lungs, which
as this Informant verily conceives was done with
a Knife, he this Informant apply'd several Medicines for the Cure thereof, but found the same
to be Mortal. And the said* John Talbot *died
on* Monday *the* 12th *Day of* July *instant,
about One of the Clock in the Morning, and
farther saith not*

John Cowper, *Coroner.*   Thomas Lichfield.

The Attestation of the *Ordinary* of *Newgate.*

I Was in the Cart at the Executing of 3 (Henry Prichard *having the Favour of a Reprive*)
*of those Persons Condemn'd for the Murder of
Mr.* Talbot, *and intending to examine them
about it, I was told and assur'd, by two Mini-
sters then present, that they would confess nothing
of it, and therefore I thought it not needful farther to enquire, but presently went to Prayer.*

Henry Gerard, *Minister of* Cree-
Church, *and* Ordinary *Instituted.*

As the Care of Mr. *Talbot's* Wounds was
committed to Mr. *Lichfield,* an able Chyrurgeon, he diligently attended him, and skilfully
manag'd his Business; and that nothing might
be omitted, which might conduce to his Recovery,

covery, a Physician was likewise call'd, namely, Dr. *Hodges*, who was One of the two Physicians employ'd by the City, during the Time of the dreadful Visitation in 1665; and at the Request of Dr. *Thiscross*, Minister to the *Charter-House*, Dr *Ridgely* sometimes met there, by whose joynt Direction he seem'd in a hopeful Way of Cure. From *Monday* Morning to the *Sabbath* following, no ill Symptoms appearing, either upon Account of the Wound, or otherwise; for altho' he was taken up very wet, and lay in the open Air some Hours, yet thro' their experienc'd Abilities, he was secur'd from a Fever: Several Chyrurgeons, namely, Alderman *Arris*, Mr. *Pierce*, and others, did freely and chearfully afford their Assistance: About Noon on *Sabbath Day* he was drest, the Wound well Condition'd, a very laudable Digestion appear'd, and he seem'd more chearful than formerly; but so it pleas'd Providence, within 2 or 3 Hours after, a violent Fit of Coughing seizing him, a Branch of the Jugular broke, if not the Jugular it self, and in a short Space, before any One could come in to his Assistance, the Effusion of Blood was so great, that he Fainted, and his extream Parts were cold; after the Flux was stopt, upon Coughing, he Bled again, 'till his Condition became deplorable; about 1 or 2 that Morning, he sent for Dr. *Atfield*, Minister of *Shoreditch*; and whereas before, he said little else than *Ay*, or *No*, being requested by his Physicians, and

Chy-

Chyrurgeons, not to put thofe Parts upon a
great Relation, but rather to write his Mind,
he fpake freely to the Doctor, who defir'd
him to declare his Judgment, in relation to
Juftification, which he freely did, faying,
That he hop'd to be Sav'd by the Merits of Je-
fus Chrift only ; and the Doctor preffing him
to fignify whether he was fully fatisfy'd to
his Accufation of the Perfons condemn'd, he
readily anfwer'd, that he was well affur'd,
that he was not miftaken in what he had
done, relating to that Bufinefs ; being then
enquir'd of, whether he could freely forgive
them, he reply'd, that he pray'd for the
Welfare of their Souls, but defir'd the Law
might pafs on their Bodies: In fhort, he fub-
mitted to that Difpenfation of Providence
towards him, and refign'd himfelf up, when
the Doctor pray'd for him, and within 2
Hours expir'd, being under his great Languifh-
ment very much compos'd, and feem'd de-
vout to the Laft.

On the *Wednefday* following the Deceafe of
this unhappy Gentleman, being the 14th of
July 1669, *Stephen Eaton*, *George Roades*, and
Sarah Swift, were convey'd in a Cart to *Ty-*
bourn, where, before they were caft off, the
2 Men confefs'd the Murder; the Woman
(to ufe the common Word of the Reverend
Paul Lorrain, late *Ordinary* of *Newgate*) died
obftinate, making no Confeffion at all.

The

The *History of the Murder of* JOAN
NORKOTT, *in the County of*
Hertford, *by her Husband, Grand-
Mother, and Aunt.*

*Found amongst the Papers of that eminent
Lawyer, Sir* John Maynard, *late one of
the Lords Commissioners of the great Seal
of* ENGLAND.

First Printed in the Year 1699.

THE Cafe, or rather Hiftory of a Cafe,
that happened in the County of *Hertford*,
I thought good to report here, tho' it happen'd
in the fourth Year of King *CHARLES*
the Firft, that the Memory of it may not be
loft, by Mifcarriage of my Papers, or otherwife. I wrote the Evidence that was given,
which I, and many others did hear, and I wrote
it exactly according to what was depofed at
the Tryal, at the Bar of the *King's-Bench*, *viz.*

Joan Norkott, Wife of *Arthur Norkott*,
being Murdered, the Queftion was, How fhe
came

came by her Death? The Coroner's Inqueſt
on View of the Body, and Depoſitions of
Mary Norkott, John Okeman, and *Agnes* his
Wife, inclin'd to find *Joan Norkott, Felon de
ſe.* For they inform'd the Coroner and Jury,
that ſhe was found Dead in her Bed, the Knife
ſticking in the Floor, and her Throat cut.
That the Night before we went to Bed with
her Child.

Plantiff. In this Appeal, her Huſband being
abſent, and that no other Perſon after ſuch
Time as ſhe was gone to Bed, came into the
Houſe, the Examinants lying in the outer
Room, and they muſt needs have ſeen or known,
if any Stranger had come in : ----- Whereupon
the Jury gave up to the Coroner their Verdict,
that ſhe was *Felon de ſe* ; But afterwards upon
Rumour among the Neighbourhood, and
their Obſervation of divers Circumſtances,
which manifeſted, that ſhe did not, nor according to thoſe Circumſtances could poſſibly
Murther herſelf; thereupon the Jury, whoſe
Verdict was not yet drawn into Form by the
Coroner, deſired the Coroner, that the Body
which was Buried, might be taken up out of
the Grave, which the Coroner aſſented to,
and 30 Days after her Death, ſhe was taken
up, in the Preſence of the Jury, and a great
Number of the People; whereupon the Jury
chang'd their Verdict; the Perſons being
Try'd at *Hertford* Aſſizes were accquitted.
But ſo much againſt the Evidence, that Judge
Harvey let fall his Opinion, that it were better

ter an Appeal were brought, than fo foul a
Murder efcape unpunifh'd; and *Pafeba 4 Car.*
They were Try'd on the Appeal, which was
brought by the young Child againft his Father,
Grand-Mother, and Aunt, and her Husband
Okeman; and becaufe the Evidence was fo
ftrange, I took exict, and particular Notice,
and it was as follows.

After the Matters above-mentioned related,
an Antient and Grave Perfon, Minifter to the
Parifh where the Fact was committed (being
Sworn to give Evidence according to Cuftom)
depos'd, that the Body being taken up out of
the Grave, 30 Days after the Party's Death,
and lying upon the Grafs, and the four Defendants prefs'd, they were requir'd each of them
to touch the dead Body; *Okeman*'s Wife fell
upon her Knees, and pray'd God to fhew
Token of her Innocency, or to fome fuch
Purpofe; her very Words I have forgot.
The Appellees did touch the dead Body,
whereupon the Brow of the Dead, which
was before a Livid and Carrion Colour, (that
was the verbal Expreffion in Terminis of the
Witnefs) began to have a Dew, or gentle
Sweat arife on it, which increas'd by Degrees,
'till the Sweat ran down in Drops on the Face,
the Brow turn'd and chang'd to a lively and
frefh Colour, and the Dead open'd One of
her Eyes, and fhut it again; and this opening
the Eye was done three feveral Times; fhe
likewife thruft out the Ring, or Marriage
Finger 3 Times, and pull'd it in again, and
the

the Finger dropped Blood from it on the Grass.

Sir *Nich. Hide*, Chief Juſtice, ſeeming to doubt the Evidence, ask'd the Witneſs, *Who ſaw this beſides you?*

Witneſs. I cannot Swear what others ſaw, but My Lord (ſaith he) I do believe the whole Company ſaw it ; and if it had been thought a Doubt, Proof would have been made of it, and many would have Atteſted with me. Then the Witneſs obſerving ſome Admiration in the Auditors, he ſpake farther,

My Lord, I am Miniſter of the Pariſh, and have long known all the Parties, but never had any Occaſion of Diſpleaſure againſt any of them, nor had to do with them, or they with me, but as I was Miniſter. The Thing was Wonderful to me, but I have no Intereſt in the Matter, but as call'd upon to teſtify the Truth, and that I have done.

This Witneſs was a very Reverend Perſon, as I gueſs'd was about 70 Years of Age : His Teſtimony was delivered Gravely, and Temperately, but to the great Admiration of the Auditory ; whereupon applying himſelf to the Chief Juſtice, he ſaid,

My Lord, my Brother, here preſent, is Miniſter of the next Pariſh adjacent, and I am aſſur'd ſaw all done that I have affirm'd ; therefore that Perſon was alſo Sworn to give Evidence, and did depoſe in every Point, *viz.* The Sweating of the Brow, the Change of its Colour, the Opening of the Eye, and the
                                                    thrice

thrice Motion of the Finger, and drawing it
in again ; only the firſt Witneſs added, that
he himſelf dipp'd his Finger in the Blood
which came from the dead Body to examine
it, and he Sware he believed it was Blood :
I conferr'd afterwards with Sir *Edmund Powell*,
Barriſter at Law, and others, who all con-
curr'd in the Obſervation ; and for my ſelf,
if I were upon my Oath, can depoſe that
theſe Depoſitions, eſpecially the firſt Witneſs,
are truly reported in Subſtance.

The other Evidence was given againſt the
Priſoners, *viz.* The Grand-Mother of the
Plantiff, and againſt *Okeman* and his Wife,
that they confeſt they lay in the next Room
to the dead Perſon that Night, and that none
came into the Houſe 'till they found her dead
the next Morning.

Therefore if ſhe did not Murder herſelf,
they muſt be the Murderers : To that End
further Proof was made.

Firſt, That ſhe lay in a compos'd Manner in her Bed, the Bed-Cloaths nothing
at all diſturb'd, and her Child by her in
Bed.

Secondly, And if ſhe firſt cut her Throat,
ſhe could not break her Neck in the Bed, nor
contra.

Thirdly, There was no Blood in the Bed,
ſaving there was a Tincture of Blood onɪh e
Bolſter whereon her Head lay, but no Subſtance of Blood at all.

Fourthly,

Fourthly, From the Bed's-Head there was a Stream of Blood on the Floor, which run along 'till it Ponded in the bending of the Floor to a very great Quantity ; and there was also another Stream of Blood on the Floor at the Bed's-Feet, which Ponded also on the Floor to another great Quantity, but no continuance, or communication of Blood at either of these two Places, from one to the other, neither upon the Bed ; so that she bled in two Places severally, and it was depos'd, turning up the Matt of the Bed, there was Clotts of conjealed Blood in the Straw of the Matt underneath.

Fistly, The bloody Knife was found in the Morning, sticking in the Floor, a good distance from the Bed, but the Point of the Knife as it stuck was towards the Bed, and the Haft from the Bed.

Lastly, There was a print of a Thumb and four Fingers of a left Hand. Sir *Nich. Hide* Chief Justice, said to the Witness, How can you know the Print of a left Hand from the Print of a right Hand, in such a Case?

Witness. My Lord, it is hard to describe, but if it please that Honourable Judge to put his left Hand upon your left Hand, you cannot possibly place your right Hand in the same Posture: Which being done, and appearing so, the Defendants had Time to make their Defence, but gave no Evidence to any Purpose: The Jury departed from the Court, and returning, acquitted *Okeman,* and found
the

the other three Guilty, who being feverally demanded what they could fay, why Judgment fhould not be Pronounc'd, faid nothing but each of them faid, *I did not do it, I did not do it.*

Judgment was given, and the Grand-Mother, and the Husband Executed ; but the Aunt had the Priviledge to be fpared Execution, being with Child.

I inquired if they confeft any Thing at their Execution, but did not as I was told.

Zachary Clare, *a Highwayman.*

ZACHARY CLARE, was a Baker's Son, Born at *Hackney,* within four Miles of *London,* and by his Father bred up to his Trade ; but the Blandifhments of Youth confpiring to make him unhappy in keeping bad Company, among the reft of his wicked Companions he became acquainted with one *Ned Bonnet,* who learnt him the Trade of Robbing on the Highway, which they practifed with good Succefs, for 3 or 4 Years, in the Counties only of *Hartford,* and *Cambridge* ; and became fuch a Terror to the People of the Ifle of *Ely,* that they durft hardly ftir out far from Home, unlefs they have half a Dozen, or half a Score in a Body together,

or

or elfe *Clare* and his Comrade, would be fure
to fall upon them for what they had ; but
at length *Clare* being apprehended as Robbing
one Day by himfelf, to fave his own Neck,
he made himfelf an Evidence againft *Ned
Bonnet*, who being apprehended at his Lodging in *Old-Street*, was committed to *Newgate*, from thence, after 3 or 4 Months Imprifonment, was convey'd to *Cambridge-Goal*,
and Hang'd in the *Lent* Affizes, held there in
1712-13.
    One would have thought, that untimely
End of a Companion, who had been engag'd
with him in above 100 Robberies, would
have reclaim'd him, but inftead of being reform'd, he withdrew himfelf again from under his Father's Tuition, and took to his old
Courfes, with a Refolution of never leaving
'em off 'till he was Hang'd too. But however, dreading a Halter, he was refolv'd to
Rob by Stratagem ; and accordingly one After-
Noon riding over *Bagfhot-Heath*, he falls to
blowing of a Horn, juft as if he had been a
Poft, whereupon 3 or 4 Gentlemen then on
the Road gave him the Way, as is ufual in
fuch Cafes, and being not rightly acquainted
with the Place where they were, they made
what hafte they could after him for a Guide,
promifing to give him fomewhat for con-
dudting them to fuch a Town. *Clare* accepts
of their Civility, and being come upon the
Middle of the aforefaid Heath, where was a-
lone Houfe upon the Side of the Road, pre-
                                              tending

tending to be Thirsty, he crav'd the Favour of the Gentlemen to bestow a little Drink upon him, withal saying there was a Cup of very good Liquor. They acquiesced to his Request, rid up to the House, where a Couple of his Companions being planted, ready mounted, they attack'd the Gentlemen, at Sword and Pistol, with such Fury, that after a short Resistance, they oblig'd 'em to pay their Post-Man about 230 Pounds for safely, (but rather unsafely) conducting them into their Clutches.

Another Time *Zachary Clare* appearing on the Road, after the travelling Manner of a Parson, as having on a dark-colour'd great Coat, a diminutive Band, and a black Rose-Hatband, he overtakes a wealthy Farmer and his Wife; who taking him to be a Man of G--, were very glad of his Company. All the Way he went with 'em, his Discourse was on nothing but Grace, and every Thing else that was Good; till coming upon *Dunmoore-Heath,* in *Warwickshire,* and which to this Day, is held Famous for *Guy* Earl of *Warwick's* killing there the *Dun Cow,* said to be as large as 2 or 3 Elephants; the honest Farmer, and his Wife, asking, *Whither he was bound for?* quoth *Zachary, I am going to get in my Tithes to Night, or otherwise I must be oblig'd to fast to Morrow.* They reply'd, *Oh! Dear Sir, the Day is just shutting up, and if you have far to go, you'll be belated, as well as in Danger of being Robb'd; therefore if you'll be pleas'd to ride to our mean Habitation, which is not above 2*

Miles

Miles farther, you shall be very welcome, for a Day, or Two, or a Week if you please. No (quoth *Zachary*) *I must gather in my Tithes to Night, and therefore quickly open your Purse-Strings, or otherwise, I shall forthwith send you both out of the World, without Bail or Main-prize.* Seeing his Pistols presented at them, they were both struck with a *pannick Fear*, but yet to save their *Mammon*, they mightily expostulated with him about the Incivility he was going to shew them, hoping that a Man in his Coat would not offer such Violence to People, who were forc'd to get their Bread by the Sweat of their Brows. *D------ me* (reply'd the suppos'd Parson) *a Man of my Principles and Profession cares not in what Coat he Robs; so presently deliver what you have, or I'll this Moment Shoot you both thro' the Head.* The Farmer finding Death within an *Ace* of his Life, gave him 40 Guineas, which he had receiv'd that Day at a Market for Corn ; and also taking a large Ring off his Wife's Thumb, he left the Farmer to make the best of his Way; who all along as he rid, curs'd the Taker and his Tithes too, swearing also that 'till he had made up this Loss, he would never pay Tithes to the Parson of his own Parish, unless he was oblig'd to it by the Pick-Pocket Rascals of *Doctors-Commons*.

Shortly after this Exploit, *Zachary* got a Booty in *King's-Forrest*, in *Gloucestershire*, of betwixt 5 and 600 Pounds in Gold, and going into *Bristol*, he put up at the *Swan-Inn* in

Wine-

Wine-Street, where passing for a Gentleman
of a considerable Estate in *Essex,* he made
Love to a great Drugster's Daughter in the
aforesaid City, who at the same Time was
Courted by a wealthy Apothecary's Son, her
near Neighbour ; *Clare* giving out that he was
worth 900 Pounds *per Annum* ; the young
Woman's Parents were for the Daughter's
clapping up a Match with him, tho' contrary
to her Inclination, who was deeply engag'd
to her former Suitor. However, in Compliance to her Parent's Desire she seem'd to
favour the latter ; but by the extraordinary
Civility, and Complaisance, *Clare* observ'd
her to shew to his Rival, he was so Jealous
of 'em, that he would scarce permit 'em to
talk together alone, but he would intrude
himself into their Company, would not let
them walk Abroad, either he would acquaint
his Mistress's Father and Mother thereof, or
else walk along with 'em. His Living at a very
high Rate there, made the young Woman's
Friends not to doubt but he was what he
pretended; insomuch, that a Marriage was concluded, and the Day fix'd for Solemnizing the
same. But the Evening before the appointed
Time, the young Woman going Abroad, and
being accidentally espy'd in the Street by *Clare,*
he supposing some Assignation was made betwixt her and the Apothecary's Son, dogs
her, 'till she came to the Ruins of a large
House, standing by it self at one End of the
Suburbs : In here she went, *Clare* follow'd in

a little after, where he prefently heard the
Cries of a Woman in Labour ; which being
over in an Hour fhe return'd Home. He all
this while ftood in a Place unperceiv'd, and
when fhe was gone, went to fee what God
had fent her, which was a Female Infant,
left there naked to be ftarv'd with Hunger
and Cold. *Clare* brings the Child out of the
Ruins into the Street, and telling People as
they went along, there lay an Infant dropt
ftark naked at fuch a Place : A Concourfe
prefently furrounded it, and the Overfeers
being fent for, they put it into the Cuftody
of a Parifh-Nurfe. *Clare* then went to the
Drugfters's with a Pretence to give him Notice for his Daughter to be ready in the Morning for Church ; who told him with a great
deal of Concern, that his Daughter was all
on a fudden taken fo violently Ill that
fhe's forc'd to keep her Bed. On the other
Side the defign'd Bride (tho' he knew her
Ail as well as fhe herfelf) feem'd to bemoan
her with a great deal of paffionate Sorrow
and the more as he pretended to the Banns,
which were to make him moft Happy, muft
now be put off 'till fhe was up again, which
was about 3 Weeks ; when being joyn'd in
Wedlock together, 1000 Pounds was paid down
upon the Day of Marriage, and the Remainder of her Portion, which was 1000 Pounds
more, was to be paid upon the Birth of the
firft Child. About a Week afterwards the
Bridegroom demands the other 1000 Pounds,
which they refus'd paying, becaufe fhe had
not

not a Child yet. The Husband fwore fhe had One; the Parents fwore he was mad; quoth he, *I'll be judg'd by my Wife*; *Chucky, my Chicken* (quoth he) *have not you had a Child*? *My Husband* (reply'd fhe) *is bewitch'd, or elfe got into a merry Mood by his laft Night's Intemperance*. *Well* (quoth *Clare*) *I fee I am made a Liar on both Sides, but to convince my new Father and Mother of the Truth of what I fay, as well as my intirely beloved, but much more vertuous Spoufe, I'll go and fetch the Brungin hither, if 'tis Coated yet*. Away he goes to the Overfeers, tells them the Story, makes *Affidavit* of the fame before a Juftice of Peace. Then bringing them to the Drugfter's, where the Son-in-Law repeats the whole Story again; the old People were ftruck with Confufion and Shame; and the Daughter being thus difcovered in her Lewdnefs, and threaten'd by the Overfeers, to be punifh'd as the Law directs in fuch Cafes, unlefs fhe difcover'd who was the Father of the Child; fhe fhed a great many Tears, and retir'd to her Chamber, as they fuppos'd to vent her Anguifh; but not returning for an Hour, or Two, fo that the Overfeers were in hafte to be gone; the Father, and they going up to her, found her dead upon the Bed, having Poifon'd her felf, and the following Letter lying on a Table by her, which fhe had wrote before fhe laid violent Hands on her felf.

K 3 Dear

Dear Father and Mother,

*T*HRO' *the Frailty too much Reigning in our weak Sex, I have forfeited my Honour, but it was to Mr.* Jackson, *whom I entirely Lov'd, and who again had that Veneration for me, that he would have salv'd my Reputation, by making me happy with Marriage. The Child I bore is his; and whilst it lives, I doubt not of his Generosity of Maintaining it handsomly for my Sake; who lov'd the little Finger of him, better than the whole Body of the Man whom you made me to Marry, contrary to my Inclination; this is all Truth which I relate, upon the Words of a Daughter, who by a violent End sent herself out of the World before her Time, but with dying Wishes for the Welfare of my Parents, whom I freely forgive, making me Espouse a Man against my Will.*

Upon this Information the Overseers presently went to Mr. *Jackson* the Apothecary's Son, and tho' what is here said was not upon the Deceased's Oath, therefore the Law could not oblige him to keep the Child, yet he generously own'd it to be his, took it off of the Parish, put it to Nurse, and very handsomly maintain'd it, so long as it liv'd, which was upwards of 4 Years. Presently after this Discovery, *Zachary Clare* pack'd up his Awls; and living a very riotous and wicked Course of Life, he soon consum'd his 1000 Pounds; so that he betook himself to the Highway again,

again, 'till being very well known up and
down the Country ; and having like to have
been apprehended in *Buckinghamshire*, he narrowly escap'd, and made the best of his Way
for *London* ; where he got into a Gang of
Foot-Pads ; but liking not that Way of Robbing so well as on Horse-Back, he resolv'd to
follow his old Trade again. In the mean
Time he was destitute of Money to buy him a
Horse, Pistols, and Accoutrements, fitting
for a *Gentleman-Thief*: In order then to provide himself with such Necessaries, he puts
himself into the Disguise of a Porter, with
an old Frock on his Back, Leather Breeches,
a broad Belt about his Middle, a hiving Hat
on his Head, a Knott on his Shoulders, a
small Cord (an Emblem of what would be
his Fate) at his Side, and a sham Ticket
hanging at his Girdle ; so going up and down
the Streets, to see how Fortune might favour
his roguish Designs, it was his good Luck one
Evening to go thro' *Lombard-Street*, and at a
great Banker's, there seeing a Gentleman
sealing up a Couple of Hundred Pound Bags,
he takes the Advantage thereof at a Distance,
to walk by just as the aforesaid Gentleman
came to the Door, where calling for a Porter,
he plies him ; and the Money was deliver'd
to him, to carry along with the Gentleman
to one 'Squire *Micklethwait*'s, living near
Red-Lyon-Square. But *Zachary Clare* being
tir'd of his Burden, turns up St. *Martin's-
le-Grand* and made the best of his Way to

lighten

lighten himfelf as foon as he could of his Load. The Gentleman turning about and miffing his fuppos'd Porter, ran up and down like a diftracted Lunatick broke out of *Bedlam*, out of one Street into another; in this Lane, and that Alley; this Court, and that Houfe; crying out, *Did you fee the Man that's run away with my* 200 *Pounds.* But all his Scrutiny was to no Purpofe, for *Zachary* having a light Pair of Heels, made no doubt what hafte he could to fuch Quarters where he might have a fafe Retreat from Juftice.

Clare being thus recruited, he foon Metamorphofed his Porter's Habit into that of a Gentleman's; and from a Man of Carriage, Transforms himfelf into an abfolute Highwayman again. One of his Conforts buys him a good Horfe in *Weft-Smithfield*, whilft another provides Piftols, and other Materials, requifite for a Perfon that lives by the fcaring Words *Stand and Deliver.* Being thus equip'd, he bids *London* adieu for the Prefent, but he then might for ever; having bidden it farewel, for it was the laft Time that ever he faw it. His Progrefs now was towards the Weft of *England*; where he and his Affofiates Robb'd the *Welfh* Drovers, and feveral Waggons, befides Coaches; infomuch that they were a Dread and Terror to all thofe Parts which Border upon *Wales.* But ftaying there 'till the Country was too hot for 'em, they fteer'd their Courfe into *Warwckfhire*; where they committed feveral Robberies with
very

very good Succeſs ; 'till one Day *Zachary
Clare*, and only one more in Company with
him, going to give their Horſes a Breathing
(as your Highwayman call it, when they ride
out to take a Purſe) upon *Dunmore-Heath*,
they attack'd Sir *Humphrey Jenniſon*; and his
Lady in their Coach, who had then above
1100 Pounds in the Seat of it, and being unwilling to loſe it, he came out to give them
Battel. An Engagement began betwixt the
Highwaymen, and Sir *Humphrey*, One of
whoſe 2 Footmen was wounded in the Arm,
and the other had his Horſe Shot in the But-
tock ; but ſtill Sir *Humphrey's* Courage was
not quell'd, he maintain'd the Fight more
vigorouſly with what Piſtols he had ; 'till the
Coachman diſcharging a Blunderbus, Shot
Zachary's Horſe dead on the Spot, and himſelf in the Foot ; whereupon his Comrade
ſeeing him diſmounted, and wounded into
the Bargain, he fled for Religion, as faſt as
he could ; in the mean Time *Clare* is
taken, and Sir *Humphrey* mounting his Footman's Horſe, that was not wounded, he purſu'd *James Lawrence*, the Highwayman that
had left *Clare* in the Lurch, and took him ;
then tying *Clare* behind him, with the Legs
of both of 'em under the Horſe's Belly, they
were brought into *Warwick*, and being examin'd before a Magiſtrate, he committed
them to Goal.

Now being in cloſe Confinement, they
made ſeveral Attempts to break open the

Prifon ; and in order thereto, they had Files
Chizzels, Ropes, and *Aqua Fortis*, to facili-
tate their Efcape; which being detected by
One of their Fellow-Prifoners, they were
loaded with the heavyeft Irons the Goal af-
forded, and were alfo ftapled down to the
Floor ; under which ftrict Reftraint they
continu'd for above 4 Months, when the
Affizes coming on, they were both brought
to a Tryal, having above 38 Indictments exhi-
bited againft them, to the great Surprize of
the whole Court, who would Try them but
upon 10 of them, and upon every One of
'em the Jury found them Guilty ; when being
ask'd what they had to fay for themfelves,
before Sentence of Death was paft upon 'em
according to Law, *James Lawrence* faid, *He
had always been an unfortunate Son of a Whore;
however, if his Lordſhip would be pleas'd but
to be Hang'd for him, but for one half Hour,
or ſo, it ſhould be the laſt Favour that ever he
would ask of him any more.* Being told he
was a harden'd impudent Rogue : *Zachary
Clare* was ask'd what he had to fay for himfelf, who faid, *My Lord, I have Hang'd one
Man already by ſwearing to ſave my Life; and
to ſave it once more, if your Lordſhip pleaſes,
I'll ſwear right or wrong, againſt the whole Jury,
to Hang them too; for I vow they have done me
the greateſt Diskindneſs as ever any Men did
in their Lives.* So being condemn'd, they
were remanded back to Goal again, and fe-
cur'd in a dark Dungeon under Ground ; but
instead

inſtead of preparing themſelves for their latter End, they did nothing but Sing, and
Rant, Tear, and play at Cards, Swear, and
Curſe, and get Drunk from Morning 'till
Night : So audaciouſly Wicked were they
whilſt under Condemnation, that a grave
Miniſter in the Town, coming one Day to
give them good Councel, and wholeſome Advice, they had the unaccountable Inſolence to
throw a Pot of Drink in his Face, crying out
at the ſame Time, *Begone, you old ſuffocated
Son of a Whore, do you think we have nothing
elſe to do, than to be ſurfeited with your d----n'd
Cant ?* The Day after, they were convey'd to
the Place of Execution, behaving themſelves
all the Way very Impudently ; and even at
the Place of Execution, where they would
neither Pray nor make any Confeſſion ; whereupon the Sheriff telling them if they had any
Thing to ſay, ſpeak, for he was juſt upon
giving Orders for their turning them off ;
quoth *Lawrence* to the Sheriff, *I wiſh I was
ſafe in Bed with your Wife now.* And quoth
*Clare, I wiſh, Sir, that I had the ---- of that
young Woman there* : At the ſame Time pointing to her ; whereupon the Ladder was preſently drawn from under them, and both
Hang'd in *Auguſt* 1715, the Firſt of 'em Aged
32, and the other 26 Years.

RICHARD

RICHARD SHEPHERD, *a Housebreaker and Foot-Pad.*

THIS *Richard Shepherd*, was Born of Parents of honeft Repute, in the City of *Oxford*, but they neglected to inftruct him in Writing, or Reading ; for all the Learning he had, was only the Lord's Prayer, and the Apoftles Creed. This being his Father's firft Child, he was mighty fond of it, and as foon as he return'd from the Chriftening of his little Bantling at Church, he took the Company to a Tavern, where they drank plentifully, and made good Cheer, not forgetting a Health now and then to the new made *Chriftian*. The Father was not idle, but pratled and tipled, with the Goffips, who in their turn did him Juftice. The fpiced Bowl went merily about after Dinner, and the Baby had its 'nown Father's Nofe, and as like him as if he had been fpit out of his Mouth. But as all Things in this World are inconftant, and our Joys ever attended with fome Difafter or other ; fo here had like to have been an End of all the Mirth. For the Midwife, who had taken up the Child in her Arms, to carry it Home, going over a little Bridge, which
                                                she

she was oblig'd to pass, fell into a dirty Pond (for you must know she never baulk'd her Glass, and the Fumes of the Liquor had intoxicated her Pericranium) and would have been drown'd Child and all, had not the Company come to their speedy Assistance. As soon as they came Home, they got a Kettle of warm Water, and when the Child was undress'd, flounc'd him in, and scrubb'd him soundly; and thus he was Christen'd twice on the Day he was Born.

As he grew up, he mightily improv'd himself in unluckiness, insomuch that there came every Day fresh Complaints of the whole Neighbourhood to *Shepherd's* Father and Mother, that their Son was continually playing some unlucky Trick or other. But when he came to be 10 Years Old, he grew ten Times worse, and the whole City complain'd of him. His Father one Day took him aside, and ask'd how he could be so Wicked and Malicious. *Alas!* says he, *People abuse you, and tell you a Company of Lies; for my Part, the L---d knows, I never affronted any Body in all my born Days; for let me do what I will, some People will complain, without any Rhime or Reason. Why, now Father, to shew what I say is nothing but the Truth, take me up behind you on Horse-Back, and ride along thro' the Neighbourhood, and I'll warrant you, some spiteful Folks will say something against me.* The Father did so, and every House they came by, *Dick* (who had before let down his Breeches) took up his
Shirt,

Shirt, and shew'd his naked Buttocks. *See there,*
say they, that young unlucky Rogue, he'll come
to be Hang'd you may depend upon it; a bad Be-
ginning makes a bad Ending; as the Saying is,
I Read his Diſtany, Don't you ſee Father, ſays
he, *I do no Body no Harm, and yet they cannot*
give me a good Word. Then his Father took
him before him, and *Dick* made Mouths, di-
ſtorted his Eyes, and loll'd out his Tongue, at
every Body he met, unperceiv'd by his Father. *Oh!* ſays the good Women, *he's a*
pickled Dog, there will no good come of him,
pray God keep him from the Gallows; Neighbours,
pray look at him. Which the Father hearing,
cry'd out, *Alas!* Dick, *thou wert Born in an*
unhappy Hour, for tho' you ſay nothing, yet you
ſee how every one blames thee; and tho' you do
no Harm to any Body, yet you hear what they
ſay of you. Sometime after, his Father being
wearied with the continual Complaints of the
whole Neighbourhood, againſt his unlucky
Son, went to live at a Village about 3 Miles
out of *Oxford,* where he ſoon died with Grief;
and the Mother then being reduced to great
Poverty, inſomuch that one Day ſhe complain'd grievouſly to her Son, that ſhe wanted
Bread; quoth he, *Let me alone for that, good*
Mother, only give me a Bag, and Providence
will provide I'll warrant; which ſhe gave him
accordingly. Away goes *Dick* to *Abingdon,*
and coming to a Baker's Shop, *Hark ye me,*
honeſt Friend, ſays he to the Baker, *will you*
ſend my Maſter a Dozen of quartern Loaves,
one

one half *White*, and t'other *Brown* ; and nam'd
a Man that kept an Inn in the same Town,
and bid him come along with him for the
Money. *That I will* (says the Baker) *with all
my Heart.* Now you must understand, that
Dick had purposely made a Hole in the Bag,
which he had brought for the Baker to put his
Bread in, and when he had got a good Way
from the Baker's Shop, he lets one of the white
Loaves tumble into the Dirt through the Hole :
With that he sets down the Bag on the Ground,
saying to the Baker's Man that follow'd him,
*Pox on't, what's worse than ill Luck? I dare not
carry this dirty Bread to my Master, that's certain ; here honest Lad, step Home and change
it. And all but Reason,* says the Fellow : *Ay,
do, and I'll stay here 'till you come, make haste,
d'ye hear.* But one Thing is to say, and another to do ; *Dick* knew better Things, and
flew Home to his Mother. *There Mother*
(says he) *Providence provides you see, Eat
when you have it, and Fast when you have nothing to Eat.* In the mean While, the Servant
not finding *Dick* at the Place appointed, return'd to his Master the Baker, who went
immediately to the Inn, where he found the
suppos'd Master, but not the Man ; and only
had the Satisfaction to be laugh'd at by the
Host, besides being hooted all the Way home
by the Boys ; and the poor Journeyman for
his Carelessness lost his Place.

A little after this, *Dick* went to *Faringdon*
in *Berkshire*, and there hired himself to a Baker,
but

but the next Evening when he was to boult the Meal, he wanted a Candle, but his Master told him, that was what he never allow'd his Servants, and that he must do it by the Light of the Moon. *I ll do so,* says *Dick*: Upon which his Master went to Bed. In the mean Time, *Dick* hung the Boulter out at the Window, and boulted out as much Meal as he could into the Yard by the Light of the Moon. When the Baker got up in the Morning, to make his Bread, he found his Man *Dick* hard at it at the Window. *Hey-day,* (says he) *what a Devil have we here to do ? Do you think the Meal cost nothing, thou inconsiderate Puppy, that you throw it after this Manner upon the Ground ? Well, I see some Folks are never to be pleas'd* (says *Dick*) *do what one will ; you bid me boult it by the Light of the Moon, and you may see I was resolv'd to have as much Light as I could ; but however, there's no great Harm done, I can presently take up most of it. That's not the Matter neither* (says the Master) *it is now too late to make the Dough. Why then* (says *Dick*) *I'll borrow some of our Neighbours and bring immediately. Go to the Gallows* (says the Baker) *and bring what you find there and be d——n'd.* Away goes *Dick* to the Gallows, where finding some dry Bones, Part of a Skeleton, of a Murderer that had been Hang'd there just without the Town ; he brought them to the Baker, saying, *There, Master, I've brought you what I found at the Gallows, according to your Order,*

but

but pray what Use will you put 'em to? At this his Master began to storm and swear like a mad Man, saying, *Well, there is no enduring this; get out of my House, thou Scoundrel. With all my Heart,* quoth *Dick;* and letting down his Breeches, turn'd up his naked Breech, saying, *Hark ye, Baker, if you'll bake my Bread, here's the Oven's Mouth, and so, Sir, I'm your nimble Trout, adieu, and the D——l may be your Journeyman for* Dick.

He being now about 17 Years of Age, he was by some Relations, in Respect and Charity, to his poor Mother, put an Apprentice to a Butcher, but Marrying before he had serv'd his Apprenticeship by about 3 Years, his Master claim'd 40 Shillings down, and a Bond of 28 Pounds more, for the Remainder of his Time; whereby he was irretrievably plung'd into Debt; and being unable to recover himself, his Wife added to his Expences, she having a Child the first Year: Being thus brought to Extremities, he took ill Practices, for at *Oxford* he broke open two Houses, one a Laundress's, from whom he Stole about 20 Pounds worth of fine Linnen; the other a Mercer's Shop, out of which he took Goods to the Value of 50 Pounds more. He also Robb'd in *Hertfordshire*; had sometimes taken a Purse near *London*; Robb'd on the Highway with one formerly Executed at *Guilford* in *Surry*, but luckily escap'd being taken with him; and had also Robb'd the whole Country about *Reading* in *Berkshire*, at which Assizes

in

in the laſt Year of Queen *ANNE*'s Reign, he was Condemn'd, but afterwards Pardon'd.

Now being at Liberty once again, but notoriouſly noted both in City, Town, and Country, for a great Rogue, he was reſolv'd to try his Fortune beyond Sea; and going into *Holland*, he turns *Quack-Doctor* at *Rotterdam*, and by his nauſeous Pacquets pick'd up (for there are Fools go where you will) the Pence very faſt; for in all Nations Mankind love to be deceiv'd, and too often give more Credit to Quacks and Empericks, that run about the Country, than to experienc'd Phyſicians, tho' they pay dearer for it. Here it happen'd at the Houſe where *Dick* lay that he ſaw a little Child that lay as if Sick upon the Bed. *What's the Matter of your Child, good Landlady?* (ſays our new *Quack*) *Alas!* (reply'd ſhe) *the poor Child cannot go to his little Chair, if he could do that he would be well.* Quoth *Dick*, *I know a good Remedy for that. Do you ſo?* (ſaid the Landlady) *Well, if you can but help my poor Child, I'll give you whatever you will require in Reaſon.* Pooh (quoth *Dick*) *that is but a Trifle, I'll take but a Couple of Shilling of you.* Well, when the good Woman was gone into the Garden to fetch ſomewhat to boil with ſome Meat, what does *Dick* do, but Sh----ts a huge Lump in the Pot, and ſets the Child upon the Chair; when ſhe return'd, quoth ſhe, *Who has done this?* *I did, it was I,* (ſays *Dick*) *for you ſaid he could not go to his Chair, and ſo I carry'd him.* Upon which
ſhe

she peeps in; *Ah! Heavens bless you, says she, it was this that hurt my poor Child, but he has cack'd prettily, I see, I shall be bound to pray for you as long as I live; pray teach me how you did it, for this is a rare Secret. Not now (says Dick) but next Time I come twenty to one but I may:* And so left his Landlady well satisfy'd with a Cure.

Next *Dick* rambles up to *Nuremberg* in *Germany,* where to make himself known to the Inhabitants, he puts up Bills at the Church-Doors, the Town-House, and Corners of the Streets, giving out that he was a great Physician just arriv'd from *England* and *Holland.*; and knew how to cure all Sorts of Distempers, incident to Man, Woman, or Child. Now at the same time in the Hospital there were Abundance of Sick. The Master of the Hospital, whose Interest it was to have as few Invalids in the House as possible, found out *Dick,* and told him, if he could Cure these People, he should be well paid. *Let me alone for that,* says *Dick, give me but* 100 *Florins, and I'll Cure every Soul of them, and won't have a Penny 'till they are all out of your House* ; all which pleas'd the Master and Governor, who however gave him a small Matter by Way of Earnest. Away goes *Dick* to the Hospital, and ask'd every one of the sick Men apart, what Distemper they had, and made them all Swear, that neither of them should tell any Body what he said to them, which they accordingly did. *Well then (says Dick) it is*

im-

*impoſſible I ſhould Cure you all, for, to tell you
the Truth, one of you muſt be Burnt, and
Ground to Powder, and this Powder muſt be
given to the Reſt in their Broth, with ſeveral
other Medicines, but it muſt be he that is
weakeſt that muſt be Burnt, and* Wedneſday
*next I ſhall be here with the Governor, and cry
out aloud, to give every Soul Notice to come
out, for the laſt muſt pay for all.* As ſoon as
the Day appointed came, the ſick Men every
Soul of them were ready by Day-Break, ſome
with their Breeches, ſome with their Jackets
in their Hands, waiting for the Signal, which
Dick accordingly giving, they run out of the
Hoſpital as faſt as if Wild-Fire had been in
their Ar---s ; nay thoſe that had not ſtirr'd from
their Beds for 4 or 5 Years together, ſcam-
per'd *to the Tune of the Devil take the hind-
moſt.* Upon which *Dick* demanded his Premium, which was forthwith paid him.

Now he comes into *France,* where his
Quackery failing him, he turns *Merry-Andrew*
to a *French* Mountebank, and was ſo comical
in that Way of Drollery, that the late *French*
King, *Lewis* the Fourteenth (who had at that
Time a Fool too, whom he took much delight in, becauſe he us'd to divert his Majeſty
by playing on the *Guitar,* and ſhewing his
merry Pranks) hearing of his Fame, ſent for
him to Court, where he and the *French* Fool
could never agree ; which when the King
took Notice of, he call'd them both to him
one Day in the great Hall, and, to give his
                                                    Courtiers

Courtiers fome Entertainment, that he who
fhould out-do the other in Folly, fhould have
a new Suit of Cloaths, and 20 Piftoles, but
then it muft be done in his Prefence. Accordingly the 2 Fools (if we may reckon
Dick one, who could be as much a Fool as any
one, when he pleas'd) came at the Time
appointed, and play'd over a thoufand redicu-
lous Fooleries; the King, and the whole
Court laugh'd heartily, and 'twas hard to
judge who would have the better. At laft,
Dick bethought himfelf of a Project, which
he believ'd would not fail, for he had a ftrong
Itching for the Money and Cloaths; he therefore all of a fudden, before the King, and
the whole Court, whips down his Breeches,
and dropt a fmall Pancake in the Middle of
the Hall, and pulling a Knife out of his Pocket,
divides it into equal Parts, and flips one into
his own Mouth, offering the other Half to
the King's Fool, faying, *Here, do as I do,
Sh---t you in the Middle of the Hall, and eat
half my Pancake, and I'll eat half yours. The
Devil confound you for a nafty Dog,* fays the
French Fool, *were I fure to go naked all my
Life, I would neither eat yours, nor mine.* You
may now eafily judge who got the Reward,
the King laugh'd heartily, and was as good as
his Word; and *Dick* remain'd always in his
good Graces, as long as he ftay'd at *Ver-
failles,* which was about 6 Weeks.

    Dick had alfo learnt to dance on the Ropes
in *France;* and one Day as he was dancing
upon

upon the Rope crofs a narrow Rivulet, where
was a very great Company got together, to
fee his Activity, and to hear his Drollery, at
which he was very good ; fome unlucky Boys
cut the Rope, and poor *Dick* falling into the
Rivulet, he had like to have been drown'd ;
however, as his Time was not yet come, and
relying on the old Proverb, *He that is Born
to be Hang'd will never be drown'd,* he made
a fhift to fcramble out as well as he could, but
look'd like a drowned Rat. This you muft
think gave no fmall Diverfion to the Spectators,
for generally fpeaking, the Rabble always
laugh at Mifchief. *Dick,* however, was fo cur-
ning as to hold his Peace, how vex'd foever he
might be at this unlucky Difafter, and very
gravely told them, that every Man was fub-
ject to Misfortunes, and that we were born
to Trouble. However, fays he, I fhall be
here again to Morrow, and I fhall entertain
you with fomething new, all my own Invention I do affure you Genteels. The next Day
when they were all there, *Dick* mounts the
Rope, and having danc'd a pretty while, now
quoth he to the Boys, mind what I fay, come,
my bonny Lads, give me every one of you
your right Shoe, and you fhall fee fomewhat
New and Miraculous ; fuch a Sight, I dare
fay, that the eldeft Man, or Woman here,
never faw the like in their Lives. The Fathers not one jot wifer than their Children,
even believ'd every Word he faid, and reach'd
him every one of their right Shoes, as *Dick*
had

had defir'd. Which when he had kept a long
while with him on the Rope, the Boys wanted
their Shoes again ; for you muſt know it was
very cold, being in Winter. *Z—ds* (ſays
he) *you are ſo impatient, you've ſpoil'd the fineſt
Feat in the World, there Pox on ye for a Company of ſilly hearted impatient Puppies, take
every one his own.* And at the ſame Time
throws them all in a Heap together ; this ſet
them all a ſcrambling, one pull'd his Companion by the Hair, t'other's Noſe bled, helter-
skelter they went, tumbling over one another,
kicking and cuffing, one laugh'd, t'other cry'd,
in ſhort, the Fathers took their Children's
Part, and fell to Blows, and drubb'd one another tightly ; *Dick* laugh'd heartily, but
thought it beſt to ſtay no longer there, ſo
threw himſelf from the Rope into the River;
ſwam over to the other Side, and running
Home as faſt as his Heels would carry him,
dar'd not to come into that Neig..bourhood
for a Month afterwards.

However, *Dick* making no great Matters of
all his Trades, he return'd to *England* again in
1704, when going into *Oxfordſhire*, he found
his Wife, but the Child was dead, and to
make up that Loſs, he begot two more of her ;
for ſupport of whom, he thought Thieving a
more profitable Employment, than getting
Bread for his Family honeſtly. In order
hereto, forgetting the former Mercy he had
receiv'd, he (like a Dog) returns to his Vo-
mit again, and takes to all the ill Courſes
imagi-

imaginable, daily ſtriving to bid as fair for
the Gallows as any Man living. So getting
an Acquaintance with 2 as great Rogues as himſelf, namely *John Allen,* and *William Chance,*
they committed ſeveral Burglaries in and about
the Cities of *London* and *Weſtminſter,* and the
Country adjacent, for *Bow, Hackney, Highgate, Hampſtead, Iſlington, Kenſington, Ham-
merſmith, Fulham, Chelſea, Richmond, Wandſ-
worth, Putney, Batterſea, Lambeth, Deptford,
Greenwich,* and other little Towns and Villages,
in the Counties of *Middleſex, Eſſex, Kent,*
and *Surry,* did not eſcape their villainous
Plundering in the Night-Time, 'till the Pitcher
went ſo often to the Well that it came Home
broke at laſt; for one Night having broke
open a Perruke-Maker's Shop in *King-Street,*
going up to *Guild-Hall,* the Watch coming
by as they were making out of it, with ſeveral fine Perrukes, apprehended them, and
knocking up the Man of the Houſe, who
own'd the Good to be his, they were all 3
ſecur'd in the *Roundhouſe* 'till the Morning,
when being carry'd before the Worſhipful Alderman Juſtice *Withers,* they were committed to *Newgate*; where *Dick* ſo well play'd
his Cards, that he underhand (thro' his Wife's
coming to him) made himſelf an Evidence
againſt his Comrades *Allen* and *Chance,* whom
convicting at the Seſſions-Houſe in the *Old-
Baily,* they were Hang'd at *Tybourn* in 1705.
Hereby this Villain enjoy'd his Liberty again,
by ſhedding the Blood of his Accomplices,
                                                whoſe

whose untimely End, one would have thought
might have deterr'd him from acting the like
wicked Practices again, for fear of suffering
their Fate ; but instead of being reclaim'd,
he grew rather worse than before, and soon
getting into a fresh Gang of Rogues, went
upon other villainous Exploits with them, in
going upon the *Foot-Pad* with two particular
Persons, whose Names as yet not suspected,
he would not discover, because they had reliev'd him during his last Confinement, and
hop'd they would continue their Kindness
after his Death to his Wife, and 2 poor young
Children. But whether they will, or no,
they must stand now to their Generosity ;
and all that we have further to take Notice
of is, that for Facts committed in their Company he was taken into Custody, and being
by Justice *Saulow*'s *Mitimus* sent to *Newgate*,
for Robbing one *Thomas Farlow*, of 1 Pound
5 Shillings, on the Highway betwixt *Hamp-*
stead and *Kentish-Town* ; the Matter of Fact
was plainly prov'd against him at *Justice-Hall*
in the *Old-Baily*, he receiv'd Sentence of Death
for the same ; when being put into the condemn'd Hold, he was sollicitous for nothing
so much as about his Corps after Death, as
fearing he should be Anatomiz'd ; wherefore,
in hopes of preventing his Carcass falling into
the Surgeon's Hands, who would have no
more Mercy on it than the Hangman had, he
sent his Wife the Morning he was to die to sell
the Cloaths she had upon her to buy him a

L   Coffin ;

Coffin; and on *Friday* the 29th of *January* 1719-20, he was Executed at *Tybourn*, Aged 35 Years.

JACK BLEWIT, *a Highwayman and Murderer.*

THIS notorious Fellow *Jack Blewit* was Born near *Bull-Inn-Court* in the *Strand*, when formerly it was an Inn, which tumbling down kill'd about 7 or 8 People. His Father was a Shoemaker, who bred him up to the same Trade, but dying when he had not been bound above 2 or 3 Years, he was too Headstrong for his Mother, and would not mind his Business, so that as he encreas'd in Years, he encreas'd in Vice, much addicting himself to Drinking, Swearing, Gaming, and Whoring; and to support himself in this vicious Course of Life, he thought to have mended his Fortune by changing his Religion, which was but very little, for that of the *Roman-Catholicks*, in the Reign of King *JAMES* the Second; at which Time the Earl of *Salisbury*, then living, raising a Troop of Horse for that Prince's Service against the Prince of *Orange*, he enter'd himself into it, for *Jack* lov'd riding in his very Minority, for one
Night

Night being in Bed with his Father, when he
was giving his Mother her due Benevolence,
he being awake and finding the old Man
mounted higher than ordinary, he mounts his
Father too, and getting fast hold on the Collar
of his Shirt, cries out, *Hold fast Father, she'll
fling us both ; hold fast Father, by G―― she'll
fling us else ; see how the Jade kicks.* But as
we said before, *Jack* being now a Soldier, he
would Bully and Rake, as well as the best of
'em ; but he did not long continue in this
military Station, for upon King *William's*
Accession to the Throne, this new rais'd Regiment being mostly *Papists*, it was presently
disbanded, and he put to new Shifts to get
his Bread.

Now Raking up and down the Town, and
letting his Tongue out-run his Wit, which was
very easily done, he was often taken up for
speaking disrespectful Words against the late
King *William* the Third, and his Royal Consort Queen *Mary*, for which he was several
Times committed to the *Gate-House* at *Westminster*, where he once continued above a
Year upon one Stretch, for not taking the
Oaths to their aforesaid Majesties. At length
Jack upon some humble Submission to the
Government got his Liberty, and going very
genteel with what Incomes he got by Gaming,
he got him the good Esteem of an Ale-Dra-
per's Widow, living at *Wapping*, who was
worth above 1000 Pounds, and had no Children left upon her Hands to provide for out

of

of it. This fame Madam *Nick-and-Froth* was
up to the Head and Ears in Love with *Crifpin*,
as we may properly call him, tho' he had not
ferv'd an Apprenticefhip by fome Years ; and
he was not infenfible of the fneaking
Kindnefs which this kind Hoftefs had for him,
for entertaining him both at Bed and Board
gratis, and putting Money into his Breeches
whenever he went Abroad, infomuch that
thefe extraordinary Civilities of the Woman,
won *Jack's* Heart and Affections fo much,
that altho' fhe was not Handfome, yet her
Money made her feem a beautiful Creature
in his Eye ; and in a little Time he threw
himfelf upon the Précipice of Matrimony ;
but after the nuptial Bands were ty'd fhe
prov'd fuch a Scold, that fhe reprefented in
the Play call'd the *Taming the Shrew*, or *Sawney
the Scat*, was a Fool to her ; for fhe broke
her firft Husband's Heart with her Tongue,
and this other too fhe was alfo refolv'd to fend
the fame Way of all Flefh, if it was poffible
to be done with that carnal Weapon : But
Jack was refolv'd not to part with his Wife
at fo eafy a Rate, therefore he wafh'd away
all Sorrow from his Heart with good Wine
inftead of common Slabber, ftaying all Day long
in a Tavern, and at Night coming lovingly
Home to his Wife, would exercife a Bull's
Pizzel about her Ribs, to threfh her into better Manners, which would then fet her a
Raving worfe than half a fcore Brace of *Bil-
lingfgate* Fifh-Women, but yet in the Main
fhe

she thought her dear Bit of a Groat had some
Love for her, or else wou'd never take all that
Pains as he did about her. Indeed they led
a most uncomfortable Life together, to the
great Disturbance of the Neighbourhood,
which at all Hours of the Night would be
alarm'd with her hideous Cries of Murder,
but that which broke her Heart in about 2
Years, was his keeping a Whore in the House
with him, who must always sit at Table,
whilst the other waited on them like a Servant;
so that bidding adieu to the World sooner than
she was willing, he converted his Mourning
into a gay Habit, and in less than a Month
went upon the Hunt for another Wife, which
prov'd a worse Plague to him than the First,
as you shall hear by the Sequel of what
follows.

Jack's next Courtship was to one that was
(but unknown to him) a Jilt of the Town,
who kept a House of her own, in which she
made a very good outside shew of rich Furniture, and pass'd for the Widow of an *East-
hidia* Captain, who had left her worth above
5000 Pounds, and her fine Apparel; and
tricking up with Patch and Paint, and other
Materials us'd by Strumpets, to hide those
Defects which their Irregularities make them
contract, making her appear abundantly Hand-
somer and Younger than she really was, he
became mightily enamour'd of her, but much
more without doubt for her Money; however, she seem'd mighty Coy, and kept him

at a Diſtance, upon the Pretence of under-
valuing herſelf in Caſe ſhe ſhould Marry
with a Mechanick. *Jack* finding this the only
Obſtacle that prevented the Banns betwixt
them, what does he, but one Day goes Home,
lets his Houſe for 50 Pounds good Will, beſides ſelling of all his Drink, and Houſhold
Goods for about 169 Pounds more, and then
equipping himſelf like a Gentleman, with a
long Wig, containing more Hair than Brains,
and a Sword by his Side, he comes to pay
his Miſtreſs a Viſit, who admir'd to ſee the
ſudden Transformation. *Jack* beſtow'd on
her all the Hyperbolies he could think upon in
the *Academy of Compliments*, and ſwore that
in a little Time he would make her ſenſible
of the Reſpect and Veneration which he had
for her Perſon, whom he admir'd above any
Thing on this Side Heaven. Next Day he
was as good as his Word, for bringing about
200 Pounds of Plate, and 400 Pounds in Money, threw it upon a Table by her, and ſaid,
*My deareſt Angel, all this is at your Com-
mand*. Which Saying made her ſo Complai-
ſant, as to cry, *Dear Sir, ſeeing by this Preſent, that your Affections for me are unfeigned,
I am in Point of Honour oblig'd to retaliate
your Sincerity with an equal Proportion of Love,
and therefore I am at your Command to be yours
whenever you pleaſe to appoint the Day of Marriage, 'till when my Houſe is at your Service.*
Jack knowing that Delays oftentimes breed
Dangers, he pitch'd upon the Time of Marriage

riage to be that Day Sennight, to which she
readily consented; and in the mean Time he
lay in her House, and the Day to make these
Two *One Flesh* being come, the Nuptials were
celebrated at *Stepney* Church, and kept with
a great deal of Splendour; at Night the Stock-
ing was hurl'd, to Bed they went, and without doubt *Jack* play'd his Part so well there,
that he bid fair for a Brace or Two of young
Brungins. But early in the Morning all *Jack's*
Joy was turn'd into Sorrow and Grief, for
the Bride's pretended Man coming into their
Bed-Chamber, quoth he, *Madam, have you
sent* Bridget *any where? for she is not in the
House, and what is worse, I'm afraid, by the
Litter I see about the House, that she has taken
more than her own along with her. Oh! Heavens* (reply'd the Mistress, crying and shriek-
ing out) *ruin'd and undone! I'll be Hang'd if
the Baggage has not Robb'd me.* Here scream-
ing out in a terrible Manner awoke the Bridegroom out of a found Sleep, which no question
on't he was fallen into thro' the Vigour of his
late Performances, and upon enquiring into the
Matter, being told the Maid had Robb'd
them, he jump'd out of Bed in his Shirt, and
making a Scrutiny about the House, found his
two Trunks of Plate and Money gone, there
was Swearing, and Cursing, Damning, and
Sinking himself to the Pit of Hell, in the
mean Time the Drums and Musick came
tuning their Instruments after they had wish'd
the Bridegroom and Bride, much Joy and

Hap-

Happineſs, which made him ten Times more
mad than before, bidding them begone for a
parcel of Rogues, but ſtill they play'd on,
whilſt he ſent Vollies of Oaths and Curſes
among 'em, thicker than they fly round the
Groom-Porter's Tables; at laſt he runs out
with his Sword drawn, ſtriking one and
wounding another, breaking Hautboys and
Fiddles, and ſerving the Drummers the ſame
Sauce, but they being about 6 or 8 in Number, weather'd the Storm, and went off the
Ground with ſaluting the Pioneers-March of
Round about Couckolds, come dig, come dig. In
the mean Time his Spouſe was hiding her
Imperfections by dreſſing herſelf as faſt as ſhe
could, but poor *Jack* coming in too quick upon
her, found her Head bald, which want of
Hair ſhe had hid by the kind Aſſiſtance of ſome
Tire-Woman; he falls then a calling her all
the old Bitches he could think of, and lac'd
her into the Bargain, crying out (as truly he
might) ſhe was a Cheat, but in her own Defence ſhe flew at him again, ſetting the Marks
of her Nails and Teeth in his Fleſh, which
having not, thro' too much haſte well faſten'd
in the Sockets of her Gums, ſome of 'em
hung in his Wig, which ſhe eſpying, crys out,
*Oh! ye barbarous Rogue, what do you deſign to
Murder me? See, ſee, you bloody Villain, you
have knock'd all the Teeth out of my Head.
Where, where* (quoth *Jack) you lying B----ch,
I ſee none of 'em? Yes, you Dog* (ſays ſhe) *there
they ſtick in your Wig.* At which *Jack* pulling
it

it off, and finding it sow'd with a great many Teeth, quoth he, *Oh! you toothless Whore, what, do you wear Artificial? I've got a fine Piece of superannuated Mortality to lye by!* But what was still worse, in the Scuffle her Glass-Eye fell off of the Table and was broke to pieces, which made her attack him again, with crying out, *You barbarous Devil! I see you have a Mind to make an End of me, look here you Rogue, do you design to blind me? See you have knock'd one of my Eyes out.* Whereupon *Jack* seeing a deep Concavity in her Head, and looking earnestly at his artificial Piece of Stuff, he fancy'd he had been betroth'd to some *Succubus.* In the mean Time of this Combustion in came a *Tallyman* to demand Money for the Furniture of his Wife's House, he then began to be in a more violent Passion than ever, swearing he would never pay him a Farthing, but the Bailiffs being call'd in, who stood ready planted at the Door, they arrested him in an Action of 250 Pounds, and for want of Bail he was carried to *Newgate.* Being now under close Confinement, the dear Bit of a Groat his Wife, went after her Maid, and made herself absolute Mistress of all her Husband brought her, who lay in Goal upwards of 4 Years, when the first Act for Insolvent Debtors coming out in the late Queen *ANNE*'s Reign, he got his Liberty once again, and then going in quest of his beloved Wife, whom he found had consum'd all his Substance in a short Time upon her Cronies, had often

been

been in great Want in the *Marſhalſea* and *White-Chapel* Goal, and laſt of all, died of the Pox at *Kingſland*.

Jack being now rid of two Plagues, *viz.* a ſtincking Jayl, and a bad Wife, but being Friendleſs and Moneyleſs, he was reſolv'd to try if he could better his Fortune at Sea, ſo going on Board a Ship bound for *Guinea*, ſailing to *Old-Callabar*, they enter'd the River call'd the *Croſs-River* into *Pyrates-Iſland*, where after they had taken in their *Negroes*, and were ready to ſail, the Maſter call'd up the Boatſwain, and 3 Men more, one of which was *Jack*, to look out the Copper-Bars that were left, and carry them on Shore to Sell ; the Boatſwain with his ſmall Company deſired they might have Arms, not believing the Inhabitants were ſo harmleſs a People as reported. They took with 'em 3 Muſquets and one Piſtol, and ſo row'd towards the Shore, but their Match unhappily fell into the Water, and the Ship being fallen down lower towards the Sea, and they aſham'd to go back without diſpatching their Buſineſs, *Jack* went aſhore to the firſt Houſe to light the Match, but before he was 20 Rods from the Water-Side, he was ſeiz'd on by half a Score *Blacks*, or rather *Tawney-Moors*, and by them hal'd half a Mile up into the Country, and thrown with great Violence upon his Belly, and ſo compell'd to lye 'till they ſtrip'd him ; and more Company coming, they were ſo eager for his poor Canvas Apparel, that ſome they tore off,

others

Others they cut off, and with that several
Pieces of his Flesh, to his intolerable Pain,
and with those Rags they made little Aprons
to cover their Privities, Cloathing being very
scarce there. In the mean Time his Comrades
made the best of their Way back again to
their Ship, telling the Captain what had befel
them in having *Jack* took from them by the
Savage Natives. He was sold to a Master,
who was free to Discourse, after he had learn'd
in less than 3 Months the *Tata* Language,
which is easily attain'd, being comprehended
in few Words, and all the *Negroes* speak it. After 4 Months being in the Country, his Master
presented him to the King of the *Buckaneers*,
whose Name was *Esme*, who immediately
gave him to his Daughter *Onijab*; and when
the King went Abroad, he attended him as
his Page of Honour throughout the whole
Circuit of his Dominions, which was not
above 12 Miles, yet Boasting exceedingly of
his Power and Strength, and Glorying extreamly that he had a White Man to attend
him, whom he employ'd to carry his Bows
and Arrows. During all the Time *Jack* was
a Slave, he never knew his King go Abroad
and come Home sober; but after 2 Months
Service the King of *Calanach*, call'd *Mancha*,
hearing of this *White*, courted his Neighbour
Prince to sell him, and accordingly he was sold
for a Cow and a Goat. This King was Sober,
free from the Treacheries and Mischiefs the
other was subject to, and would often enquire

quire of him concerning the Head of his Country, and whether the Kingdom he was of, was
bigger than his own, whose whole Diminions
were not above 25 Miles in Length, and 15 in
Breadth ; *Jack* told as much as was convenient,
keeping within the Bounds of Modesty, yet relating as much as possible to the Honour and
Diginity of his Queen, informing him of the
Greatness of one of her Kingdoms, the several
Shires and Counties it contain'd, with the
Number of its Cities, Towns, and Castles,
and Strength of each, the infinite Inhabitants,
and Valour of her Subjects ; which so amaz'd
this petty Prince, that he need mention no
more of her Majesty's Glory and Diginity.
It put him into such a profound Consternation,
that he resolv'd to find out some Way to tender his Respects to this mighty Princess, and
could study none more convenient, than that
if he could find a Passage he would let him
go to *England*, to inform Queen *A N N E*
of the great Favour and Respect he had for
her, which did not a little rejoyce *Jack* ; and
he also told him that he would send her a Present, which should be 2 Cabareets, or Goats,
which they value at a high Rate ; this King
having himself not above 17 or 18. Though
our Captive lived happily with this Prince,
yet his Desires and Hopes were still to return
to his native Country ; at length he promis'd
him, that the first *English* Ship which came
into the Road, should have Liberty to release,
or purchase him ; this much rejoyc'd his

Heart,

Heart ; now he thought every Day a Year, 'till he could hear or fee fome *English* Ship arrive ; and often did walk down to the Sea-Side, earneftly expecting the Winds of Providence would blow fome in thither. About 15 Days after this Promife he had his Wifh, for then fome of the *Moors* came running to the King, telling him there was a Canoe coming, for fo they call our Ships, at which *Jack* rejoyc'd, hoping to be releas'd, yet durft not fhew it, for fear of Punifhment, or Death. The Ship came in, the Commander whereof was one Captain *Royden,* who was put in there for *Negroes.* The Day after his Arrival the King lets *Jack* go, fending him in a Canoe, plac'd between a *Negroe's* Legs, with others to guide this fmall Veffel, for fear he fhould leap over Board, and fwim to the Ship. At a Diftance he haled her in *English,* to the great Surprize of thofe within her; the *Negroes* let him ftand up and fhew himfelf to the Captain, to whom he gave an Account of his Slavery ; and being redeem'd for 5 Iron Bars, he was taken on Board, where the Seamen charitably apparelled him, for he was naked, and brought him fafe to *England,* after 14 Months Slavery.

Jack being return'd Home again, was refolv'd never to venture his Carcafs again at Sea, nor vifit Infidels to carbonado and facrifice his Flefh as if he had been a Prize-Fighter, and yet how to live on Shore he could not well tell ; but again, thinking with himfelf,
that

that as he was now Born, he muſt be kept,
therefore he reſolv'd to try his Fortune on
the Highway; and in order to which, he ſtole
a Horſe out of a Field by *Mary-le-Bone*, but
wanting a Saddle, Piſtols, and other Accoutrements, he was diſpos'd to ſell the Horſe to
buy all Materials to make him a compleat
Highwayman, and Steal another; ſo to *Smith-
field* he rides, to make the beſt Market he
could, but he had ſcarce rid a Turn or Two,
before the Owner came up and challeng'd it,
ſo poor *Jack* being apprehended, and carry'd
before a Magiſtrate, he was committed to
Newgate, and when Try'd, being Condemn'd,
he moſt earneſtly begg'd the Court to ſhew
him Mercy by Tranſportation, or any other
Puniſhment beſides Death; whereupon Sir
Salathiel Lovel, then Recorder of *London*,
waking out of a little Nap, which he had
taken upon the Bench, and hearing *Jack* cry
out for Mercy, *Why you impudent Rogue, do
you want Mercy? I think you may down on your
Knees, and pray God it is no worſe with you,
for I think the Court has ſhew'd you a great deal
of Mercy; indeed, Sirrah, a great deal more
than I ſhould have extended towards you.* But
poor *Jack* thought to himſelf, that if Sentence
of Death paſſing upon him was the Recorder's
Mercy, the Devil might take him and his
Mercy too. However, as it was his firſt
Crime, and the Proſecuter had his Horſe
again, it was his good Luck to obtain a Reprieve, and to plead to a Pardon too,
within

within 3 or 4 Months after his Confinement.

Now *Jack* being at Liberty again, he was still put to his Trumps how to live, and tho' he was unsuccessful in his first Attempt at Thieving, he would yet venture a second Time, resolving now to lose the Horse, or win the Saddle; but his Thoughts not aspiring to great Matters, as they did at first, he was resolv'd to try how Fortune would smile on his Adventures on the *Foot-Pad*; so one Evening going over *Clapham-Common*, he overtook a Gentleman riding softly along, whom unawares knocking off of his Horse, by giving him an unlucky Blow under the Ear, which kill'd him, he fell to rifling him, and took from him 40 Guineas, and a Gold Watch, worth 20 Guineas more, then putting one of the Deceas'd's Feet into one of the Stirrups, the Horse dragg'd him up and down the Common an Hour or Two before he was taken up, and carried to a House, where the Coroner sitting on his Body, the Inquest brought in his Death to be occasion'd by accidentally falling off his Horse, tho' he had lost his Watch and Money, which they suppos'd were drop'd out of his Breeches, by the Position of his Head being downwards whilst dragg'd about the Common.

Thus by this complicated Piece of Villany *Jack* having lin'd his Pockets, he made the best of his Way to *Yorkshire*, where after Cloathing himself, he bought him a Horse, Sword,

Sword, and Piſtols, and then ſeek'd out for
new Adventures on the Road; and in *Hert-
fordſhire* overtaking a Farmer's Daughter, who
was a very handſome young Woman, when
he came to a Place convenient, he diſmounts
her, and having committed a Rape on her
Body, Shot her thro' the Head, and Robb'd
her of 14 Pounds odd Money, which ſhe had
that Day receiv'd for her Father. The ſame
Evening he put into an Inn at *Ware,* whither
a Hue and Cry coming ſhortly after, he was
taken up upon Suſpicion, having ſome Spots
of Blood on one of the Lappits of his Coat,
and being ſtruck then with a Remorſe of
Conſcience, he confeſs'd the Murder, and was
forthwith carry'd before a Juſtice of Peace,
who, after a long Examination, committed
him to *Hertford* Goal. Now he began to
curſe his Fate, wiſhing that he had been kin-
der to his firſt Wife, and not meddled with a
ſecond Venture; nay, he now pray'd he had
continu'd among the *Moors* ſtill, or had been
Hang'd upon his firſt Exploit of Thieving, and
then he had been Guiltleſs of 2 willful Murders.
But it was too late now for *Jack* to repent, but
however, he pull'd up a good Heart ſtill, and
was reſolv'd to make the beſt of a bad Market,
ſo to drive away Sorrow from his Heart, he
got drunk every Day 'till the Time of his
Tryal came, which was in the *Lent* Aſſizes
1713-14, when being Condemn'd for his Life,
he earneſtly begg'd of the Judge a Reprieve,
but for a Fortnight, in order that as his Crime
was

was Heinous, he might the better prepare himself for Death, by truly repenting of that, and other his manifold Sins, and then he should be very willing to die ; which Requeſt was granted him ; and indeed he did ſpend the Remainder of the few Days he had to live in a great deal of Devotion and Humility, having 2 Divines who conſtantly attended him 'till the Day he was to die, when being carried to the Place of Execution, he confeſs'd the Murder he had committed alſo on *Clapham-Common*, and after behaving himſelf with a great deal of Piety, he was turn'd off and Hang'd, in the 45th Year of his Age.

JOHN TRIPPUCK, *a Highwayman.*

JOHN TRIPPUCK, vulgarly call'd *Jack* the *Tinman*, or the *Golden Tinman*, by having ſerv'd ſomewhat of an Apprenticeſhip to that Trade, running away from his Maſter before he had ſerv'd above 4 Years of his Time, fell into all Manner of wicked Practices to ſupport him in his extravagant Courſes, for which he had been often committed to ſeveral Goals, and was once Whipt at the Cart's Tail from *Holbourn-Bars* to St. *Giles's-Pound*, for wounding a Conſtable in the Execution of his Office. His

His only Way of Living was chiefly by Robbing on the Highway, in which Fact being apprehended in *Somerfetfhire*, he was committed to *Newgate* in *Briftol*, where daubing the Jaylor in the Fift with fome Guineas, he beftow'd no Fetters upon his Prifoner, he refolv'd therefore to loofe no Time or Opportunity, nor fpare for Pains to get out of his Cage, and in order thereto founds the Privy, which he found to his Purpofe, and in the dead Time of the Night began to dive where he was almoft fmother'd in Filth; and having Travell'd fo far 'till he met with Common-Shores could not fee which Way to go, nor meet with any Soul to fhew him the Way. Many crofs Pipes and Conveyances he found, but either he could not find an Entry, or elfe the Place too narrow (tho' he was Slender) to receive his Body : However, the hardeft Invention is acquireable, and nothing fo difficult but may be accomplifh'd by Time, Patience, and Induftry. *Jack* hearing a great Noife, which he conceiv'd might be about 20 Steps behind him, and making towards the Place, it was warm Water, which he prefum'd fome had thrown down the Houfe of Office to purge it, and finding the Pipe of a fufficient Widenefs, endeavour'd to force himfelf through; after a long pinching and fqueezing of his Body, in he goes, and found it ever wider and wider, 'till he got up fo high that he could reach the Seat, where groping to find the Hole, feel'd a Pair of warm Buttocks,

tocks, which happen'd to be a Gentlewoman
who was newly fet: The Gentlewoman feel-
ling fome Body Finger her Flefh behind, and
not dreaming of our fubterranean Paffanger,
fhrieks out, and ran away in all hafte, hardly
daring to look behind her. Our Pioneer feeing her in fuch a Fright, cry'd out, *Madam,
please to excuse me, that instead of Handling
your Breasts, I have through a Mistake seiz'd
upon your Buttocks ; neither think that I come to
do you any Harm, for I am an honest Man,
and under Hopes of Privacy and Concealment,
am come to seek Protection under your Roof,
which I hope after a full hearing of my deplorable
State, your Ladyship will vouchsafe to grant
me.*

The Gentlewoman, who at firft was aftonifh'd, was content to difpence with fo much
Time as to give *Jack* a hearing, he relating
how he was an eminent Merchant in *London*,
and was upon his Journey thither, but by
fome malicious and ill-affected Perfons feiz'd
and accus'd of what he was never Guilty, and
therefore being clapt up in Prifon, was fain
to do what none would leave undone, that is
tender of his Life ; and therefore hop'd that
the Lady would neither think it ftrange,
nor take it ill, but rather pity his fad Condition. Thefe and many other Arguments per-
fuaded the Gentlewoman to Compaffion, and
to give Credit to what he faid, the more by
Reafon of his very good Habit, which was Circumftances enough for a credulous Woman to
believe

believe all he said was real, and not barely verbal. In fine, the Gentlewoman lent him a
Shirt and other Cloathing to cover himself,
leaving him by himself in the Yard, and
shew'd him the Pump, where he made himself clean, she in the mean Time looking
through the Window, and seeing his well
proportion'd Body, began to be enamour'd
with his Person, and had hardly the Patience
to wait his coming to examine him a little
further. After he had made clean his Body,
he also wash'd his Cloaths in the best Wise
he could, and hung them up to dry ; which
done, he steps into the Parlour to give the
Gentlewoman Thanks for the great Civility
she had shew'd him, which he did with so
much Grace and Eloquence, that the Gentlewoman resolv'd that Night not to go to Bed,
but to discourse him about Affairs. After he
had warm'd him a little, she took and shew'd
him all the House round, where she let him
see most costly Furniture, besides her Plate
and Cloaths ; having done above Stairs, she
brought him below to see her Shop, which
standing in the best Place of the City call'd
High-Street, was furnish'd with all Sorts of
rich Laces, and fine Muslins, Cambricks, Hol-
lands, Silks, and *Indian* Gowns ready made,
whereof she took one, and desir'd him to
put on least he should get Cold. *Madam*,
(says he) *your Courtesy is not to be parellel'd,
whereof this is a notable Instance ; your Ladyship's
gracious Favours already heap'd upon me denote*
the

the real Worth of the interiour Habit of your
Mind, as well as your angelical Countenance and
Form do Evidence the Compleatnefs and Per-
fection of your external Perfon ; but Madam,
it is not likely, or may it in any wife be deem'd
poffible that I fhould take cold fo long as I am
within the Circle of your Sun-like Beauty, where
I could be heartily content to live and die. The
Gentlewoman was not much behind him for
a Compliment, and before many Hours were
fpent they made an infubid Vow, plighted
their Troth together in the Prefence of Heaven, and fwore perpetual Fidelity and Conftancy of Mind. This rafh Promife they
ratified with many Kiffes, and mutual Embraces of each other, fhe thinking herfelf at
worft to have a perfonable Man, whether all
other Appendencies were as he had reprefented
them or no ; and he on the other Hand in
hope of bettering his Fortune, by embarking
himfelf on a firm built Bottom, and fubftan-
tial Shopkeeper, as appear'd by what he had
already feen. *Jack* feeing her fo faft link'd
to him, as well by that irrevocable and inviolable Engagement which they had reciprocally
counterchang'd, as alfo by the great Inclination he could obferve fhe had towards his
Perfon, thought it beft by degrees to declare
the naked Truth to her, rather than conceal
it any longer.

He tells her how that of his kind Nature he
had been Surety for fome of his Relations,
and upon their failing he was fain to pay

their

their Debts, and at such and such Times he
suftain'd great Loffes at Sea, and bad D btors,
infomuch that he had been frequently in Extremities, which had compell'd him to do
fome Things which his good Confcience
would not difpence with, but he doubted not
but one good Venture or Two at Sea, would
retrieve all his Misfortunes again. This can-
did Confeffion did not in the leaft ftartle his
conftant Spoufe to be, who had rather disburfe
any Sum than to break fquares with him, who
had already infinuated himfelf so far into her
Breaft, that for better or worfe, fhe was refolv'd to embark herfelf with him into what
Eafe or Trouble the Fates fhould involve him
in, and promis'd to make him a clear Man
again ; and fhortly after they enter'd into a
State of Matrimony, when in a little while
preffing hard for his Wife to leave *Briftol*,
and remove to *London*, fhe confented to his
Requeft ; but no fooner was fhe come to
fettle in the Metropolis of *England*, but he as
quickly by his extravagant Courfes caus'd her
to repent the Parfon's ever making them *One
Flefh* ; her Riches *Jack* had confum'd in lefs
than a Year, whereupon his Wife rails and
curfes the Day that ever fhe faw him, wifhing
fhe had been in her Coffin when fhe fat upon
the Houfe of Office, or that Death had feiz'd
upon her Heart when *Jack* feiz'd upon her
Breech ; and indeed often wifhing for Death,
fhe did in 15 Months after her Marriage fall
Sick, and Died.

Jack

Jack now being destitute of a Wife as well as Money, he bethought himself of raising more after the following Manner. Having half a Dozen costly Diamond Rings, which belong'd to his deceas'd Wife, he procures 6 more every Way like those both in Bigness, Weight, and Fashion, only these he caus'd to be made were of Brass, and false Stones, these he put in 2 several Boxes, the True and False each in a Box apart. These he carries forthwith to a Jeweller, to whom he proffer'd them to sale, the Jeweller having throughly view'd them prays *Jack* to set a Price upon them, which he thinking too high, bid him set a lower, and so on 'till they made a Bargain, which was for 68 Pounds. When they were come to an Agreement, the Jeweller paid him the Money, which he told himself before, and prays *Jack* to tell it after him, which he did, letting in the mean While some Crowns and Half-Crowns fall now and then, that the Jeweller out of Courtesy took up for him, and *Jack* having the Box of false Diamond Rings in his Handkerchief, clandestinely by Vertue of *Hocus-Pocus* took up the True ones, and laid the False in their Place, which the Jeweller could not so much as observe, 'till it was too late to repent.

But this Money being soon spent, *Jack* goes upon the Highway to fill his Pockets, and one Night coming into *Brainford,* he took up his Lodging at the *Red-Lyon-Inn,* where being alighted, his Gelding was put into the Stable.
There

There happening then a Colonel to lie at this
same Inn, who saw and took a singular Fancy
for *Jack*'s Horse, ask'd him if he was willing
to sell him. *Jack* seem'd unwilling, saying,
that the Duke of *Buckingham*, by recommendation of a Gentleman, had a great Mind to see
him, and therefore was not willing to part
with him, unless upon very good Conditions,
seeing he was sure to have his Price for him:
These Words made the Colonel more eager
to buy him, praying *Jack* to set a Price, and
see if they could agree. *Jack* asks 50 Pounds,
the Colonel told him, that was a Price he
thought much too high, and will'd him therefore to be more Reasonable. He prays the
Colonel, if he had a Mind to try him, he
should not think that too dear; wherefore he
orders the Ostler to ride him out, which he
did. *Now* (said *Jack*) *do you think the Price
too High? Believe me, I am sorry that I pro-
pounded not a higher; I make no Question but I
shall make more Money of him when I go to the
Duke of* Buckingham. Sir, (replies the Colonel) *I am satisfy'd as to the Horse, but as touch-
ing the Price, I think much to give so great a
Sum, and therefore, if you are not willing to
part with him for less, I presume it will be no
Bargain with us.* Well, Sir, (said *Jack*) *there's
no great Harm done, you have your Money, and
I have my Horse.* And with that bids the
Ostler set him up, rub him well, and feed
him with Corn, which he did. *Jack* returns
with the Colonel to their Inn, where after
Supper

Supper they agreed for the Horse, the Colonel pays him 45 Guineas, and was well satisfy'd with the Bargain. The next Morning so soon as the Gates were open, *Jack* goes out to the Stable, without Reckoning with his Host, or Hostess, and demands his Horse of the Ostler, which he had Sold, and already receiv'd Money for. The Ostler neither knowing, nor mistrusting any Thing to the contrary, but that it was his own Horse, delivers him without any Scruple. *Jack* being now furnish'd with Money as well as with a Horse, thought it his best Way to ride as fast as he could to *London*, where in *West-Smithfield* meeting a Gentleman to whom he sold his Horse for the same Price, he bought one of a lesser, and rid strait into the North of *England*, leaving the Gentleman and the Colonel (in case they should meet, and not unlikely, as being both near Kinsmen) to divide the Horse, or dispute their Right.

Jack being now in *Yorkshire*, where he soon exhausted what Money he had, he lifted himself into a fresh Company of Padders, having already got into Acquaintance with the Captain of the Gang, who upon his Intimation gave him free Admission, with this Proviso, that he should first shew his Proof by Way of Tryal, or *Examen*, which he essay'd with good Success after this Manner. *Jack* passing for an Esquire, under the Name of *Bennet*, went into a noted Ordinary in the City of *York*, where several young Gentlemen did

M customarily

cuſtomarily meet twice a Week; into which being come, and looking by his genteel Habit for what he pretended to be, ſat himſelf down among them, and being in a Croud, when they firſt began to take their Places, none took occaſion to queſtion how he came thither; for beſides their Civility, for the better Con-venience of the Houſe, Strangers are admitted at the Requeſt of the Landlord; every one thought he might probably be an Acquaintance of ſome one in the Company, and therefore unwilling to put any Affront upon him, not knowing whoſe Diſpleaſure they might incur by ſo doing. But to come nearer to the Mat-ter, our pretended 'Squire obſerves when the Reckoning came to be paid, that a Gentleman who ſat at his Right-Hand, had a Velvet-Purſe charg'd well with Guineas, which made his Mouth to Water, and like a Loadſtone had ſuch an attractive Virtue, that the Purſe turn'd his Eye what Way ſoever it turn'd its ſelf. Now the Company departing, *Jack* ſeeing the aforeſaid Gentleman go, whoſe Name was *Charlton*, poſts away after him, to ſee if he could bring his Purpoſe about, and accordingly cloſes up with him, ſaying, *Sir, I perceive by your Diſcourſe at Table, that you have a Deſire to buy 2 Coach-Horſes; there is an Acquaintance of mine has a Couple, which if you have a Mind to ſee, I will give him Notice of it, that he may wait upon you at what Time and Place you are pleas'd to appoint.* Mr. *Charlton* hearing him ſay ſo, made anſwer, *Sir, 'tis true, I have 4,*

or

or 3 Days enquir'd, but cannot hear of any according to my Mind, and if you can bring me to a Sight of those 2 you speak of, you will infinitely oblige me; yet believe me, Sir, I should be loath to put you to so great a Trouble; but wherein I may serve you, vouchsafe but to Command me, and your Injunction shall be obey'd. *Jack* replies, that it was no more than his Duty to serve him, the more because his suppos'd Acquaintance had desir'd him to recommend his Bargain; and so pray'd him to go along with him to a Tavern hard by, promising to send for his Friend thither. To this Mr. *Charlton* assents; where being come, *Jack* writes to his Comrades, under the Notion of Writing about what he had intimated to the Gentleman. After he had done, he stept aside to give it a Boy, who was to carry it according to his Directions; the Sense whereof was thus.

I have met with a Cully, do you therefore come as Officers, and apprehend him as a Malefactor, 'tis a fat Bird, and for our Turn; further Directions I need not give, for a Word to the Wise is enough; but what other Instructions shall be necessary, I judge it Time enough when you make your Appearance. The World is turn'd over the Moon.

Accordingly they came, one representing a Constable, the rest his Dogs, or Followers. So soon as they came in, they seiz'd the Person of Mr. *Charlton,* in presence of *Jack,* who

made as if he had been mightily aſtoniſh'd at
the Matter, and ſhew'd himſelf greatly concern'd for him, deſiring them not to be ſo un-
civil as to drag a Gentleman out of the Houſe
at that Rate. Mr. *Charlton* prays them to
tell him what was the Matter, and upon
what Account they ſeiz'd him ; withal deſiring
them to adviſe the Matter better together,
and bethink themſelves whether he was the
Perſon or no, that they came to look for.
The ſham Conſtable with a dreadful Look,
tells him, that he, and none elſe, was the
Perſon they look'd for ; *Come, come,* added
he, *you would pretend Ignorance would you? Are
not you acquainted with ſuch and ſuch Men ?*
Naming ſome of an infamous Gang, and himſelf for one. *And are you ignorant of ſuch and
ſuch a Cheat ?* Mr. *Charlton* ſwore, and proteſted, that he never was acquainted with
that Gang of Rogues, neither did he know
any Thing of thoſe Cheats. However, notwithſtanding all theſe Aſſeverations, the pretended Officer commanded his Janizaries to
tye him faſt, as they would have done, only
Jack prays them that he might have the Liberty to ſpeak a Word with him aſide, to
which the ſuppos'd Officer gave his Conſent.
Jack therefore calls him aſide, and diſcourſes
him after this Manner. *Sir, I cannot enough
condole your preſent Trouble, into which you are
fallen, but if I can be Bail for you, I will, rather than that you ſhould be carried through the
Streets, which may tend to your Diſhonour and*
                                        Diſgrace,

Diſgrace, well knowing (although my Acquaintance with you has not been long) that you are
a Perſon of ſuch Worth, as that you cannot ⁚ but
be univerſally known, only I deſire to have ſome
Security for my ſelf, which if I ſhould demand
upon ſuch an Account, I hope you will not take it
ill, ſince you have that by you which will do it:
Mr. *Charlton* thanks him for his great Civility,
withal telling him that he was content, and
pray'd him to accept of his Purſe of Gold, which
was 125 Guineas, if that would ſatisfy him.
Well (replies *Jack*) *I hope that the Matter
will not prove ſo difficult after they find it a
Miſtake, and I queſtion not, on the other Hand,
(ſince the Officer knows me) but that he will accept of my Bail:* And with that ſteps towards
him, and offer'd his Bail. At firſt he ſeems to
ſcruple, ſaying, *That he knew not whether he
might do it or not with Safety ; but* (added he)
in reſpect of you 'Squire *Bennet, I am content
to hazard this Matter, being you ſeem to have
knowledge of him.* *Jack* having promis'd upon
his Parole to make him forth-coming, the
mock Conſtable took his leave of him and
went out, leaving them two together. When
they were gone, *Jack* began to ask him what
was the Matter? To whom the Gentleman
replies, *That he knew no more what it was than
of his Death's-Day, but that he was ſure it
was a Miſtake. If I might be ſure of that*
(quoth *Jack*) *I would go my ſelf and diſcourſe
the Officer about it, for albeit I am ſatisfy'd as
to you being wrong'd, yet People you know are*

apter

apter to *suſtain and harbour a bad Opinion of*
any Man, than a good one, and the whiteſt
Walls we ſee are the ſooneſt ſtain'd. To be
brief, he deſired him to ſtay a little, and he
would go and ſpeak with him, and if he did
not return within an Hour, that he ſhould
go to another certain Tavern, and there enquire for him, which Mr. *Charlton* promis'd
to do. *Jack* in the mean Time goes to his
Comrades, and tells them, that at ſuch an
Hour the Gentleman was to bring him a great
Sum of Money for his Security, naming when
and where, praying them not to fail meeting
him, and Mr. *Charlton*. This done, *Jack*
trips off with all Speed for *Northampton*,
having Money enough now to bear his Charges
thither. Mr. *Charlton* whom he had left behind, beginning too late to diſtruſt the Cheat,
reſolves with himſelf to go out and ſee if he
could hear of Mr. *Villain-enough*, but the
Vintner ſeeing him offer to go forth, takes
him by the Shoulder, and bad him pay before
he went, which he was fain to do. Coming
to the Houſe where *Jack* had appointed him,
he enquir'd for him, but not hearing of him,
began to diſtruſt the Matter indeed ; and at
laſt makes his Mind known to the Landlady
of the Houſe, who imparted the ſame to her
Husband, and her Husband to other Friends
then in the Houſe, who all concluded it to be
a Cheat. Whilſt they were buſy in talking,
comes the Fellow that had play'd the Officer,
and 5 or 6 of the Gang with him, and ask'd
for

for 'Squire *Bennet*, alias *Jack*. The Landlady knew that was the Name of the Bail, and pray'd them to go up to him above Stairs, which they did; but entering the Room they found that they had got a wrong Sow by the Ear, and would have ran out again, but the Man of the House shut to the Street-Door, and would not suffer them, 'till having sent for an Officer, they were apprehended and committed to *York* Goal, where they remain'd 'till the Assizes, when being Try'd for Cheats, they were Convicted, and being Fined 50 Pounds a Man, and Pillory'd three Times, had their Ears also cut off, for which Punishment, tho' too light for them, they heartily curs'd *Jack*, and his 'Squireship, by Bell, Book, and Candle.

But what Money *Jack* had thus scurvily got at *York*, he as scurvily lost at *Northampton*; for picking up a Couple of Whores there at a Fair, they shew'd him Pastime enough in Bed, 'till at last falling asleep, 2 or 3 lusty Fellows came up Stairs, and immediately clap'd a Gag into his Mouth, ty'd him Hand and Foot very fast, and put him into a great Basket, which they made fast with a Padlock, being naked, and so hard pack'd up and bound, that he could not move, nor stir, and his Mouth so secur'd that he could not cry; but hearing that he breathed too strong through the Nostrils, they unlock'd the Basket and stitch'd 'em up, which being done, and the Basket made fast again, the Rogues, and Whores, divided his

Money,

Money, Watch, and Cloaths, and went their Way. However, they had first taken care to send the Basket away in a Coach to *Coventry*, that commonly went thither from *Northampton*, with the following Superscription upon it, *viz. This to be deliver'd to Madam Isabella* Mountfort, *living at her House in Coventry, in* Warwickshire.

This Gentlewoman it seems was one who had some Time before made Complaint of her House having been broke open, and therefore 'tis suppos'd she had this Present sent her, which opening, and seeing a naked Man, was mainly surpriz'd, and began to shriek out; upon which a Gentleman near a-kin to her, ran into the Room where the Basket was open'd, and seeing the strange Spectacle, knew not what to think of the Matter, the more by reason that *Jack* gave no answer; but seeing he had a Gag in his Mouth, did all he could to take it out, unty'd his Hands and Feet, and rip'd up the Stitches of his Nostrils, as a Taylor does the Folds of an old Petticoat. Which done, they take him out of the Basket, and set him before the Fire, throwing a loose Gown about his Shoulders, for it was then very cold Weather. In the mean while they lay laughing together, not knowing how, or from whence this wonderful Present came, 'till at last *Jack* recovering a little Strength, and his Speech, began to relate all the whole Matter, without any Palliation of the Truth, which made them laugh heartily. After he

had

had warm'd himself well, Madam *Mountfort*
bid her Maid fetch down an old Suit of Cloaths,
wh ch she bestow'd upon him, as also 10 Shillings to put in his Pocket ; with which he return'd to *Northampton*, to see if he could hear
any Thing of them who had serv'd him so
kindly, but all in vain, for the Birds were all
fled.

Hereupon raving at his ill Fortune, saying,
*Alas! could there ever be so much Villany transf-
acted in the World, as is now a-Days? well, at
this Rate no honest Man is safe from Home.*
He makes the best of his Way for *London*,
stealing in his Journey thither a good Horse,
and Saddle, out of a Gentleman's Stable,
which he broke open in the Night. Within
4 or 5 Miles of *London* he met a Couple of
old Butter-Women, whom attacking with a
most undaunted Bravery, and flourishing his
Sword in the midst of 20 G—— d——me's,
for at present he had no Pistols; they in a very
short Time capitulated, by giving him their
leathern Purses, in which was 3 Pounds odd
Money. With this Booty riding in Triumph
into *Old-Street*, to visit some of his roguish
Companions, and being highly flush'd with
this Success, he was resolv'd to accomplish
greater Exploits, by getting his Bread for the
future by the Sweat of his Brow on the Highway ; so he continu'd for about 2 Years in
these Courses, and was taken in *London* for a
Robbery committed on *Gad's-Hill*, for which
he was committed to *Newgate*, where he suf-

fer'd

fer'd great Hardſhips, being forc'd for a maintenance to rob his Fellow-Priſoners of their
Hats, Neckcloths, Handkerchiefs, or Perrukes,
for which he was often kick'd and thump'd
about, and ſometimes puniſh'd in the Bilboes.
In the *Lent* Aſſizes in 1718, he was by an
Habeas corpus remov'd from *Newgate* to the
Marſhalſea-Priſon in *Southwark,* and at *King-*
ſton upon *Thames* was condemn'd for his Life ;
but having the good Luck to obtain a Reprieve,
after a Year's Impriſonment, he pleaded to his
Majeſty's moſt gracious Pardon, and regain'd
his Liberty ; but not making good Uſe of the
Royal Mercy extended towards him, he fell
again to his moſt abominable and vile Practices,
in Company of one *John Conſtable,* a Cook's
Son in *Weſt-Smithfield,* who had been condemn'd with him at the ſame Time as *Trip-*
puck was at *Kingſton* : They now being both
out of Goal, went frequently upon the Highway, and at laſt were apprehended at their
Lodging in *Caſtle-Street* behind the North-Side
of *Long-Acre,* for Robbing a Barber of two
Pence Half-penny ; but as they were carrying
away in a Coach to a Magiſtrate, one of the
Piſtols which the Beadle had ſeiz'd of theirs,
accidentally going off, moſt dangerouſly
wounded *Jack* the *Tinman,* which deſerr'd his
Tryal longer than his Comrade's, who was
Try'd, Condemn'd, and Hang'd, without his
Companion ; but by the Seſſions following, *Jack*
being cur'd of his Wounds, he was Try'd,
and Condemn'd, at *Juſtice-Hall* in the *Old-*
Baily ;

Baily ; and now being under Sentence of Death, he made what Interest he could for the saving of his Life, to commit more Villanies, but all his Endeavours to procure a Pardon again proving fruitless, he was convey'd in a Cart, with some other Malefactors to *Tybourn*, in *January* 1719 20, where he was deservedly Hang'd, Aged about 32 Years.

WILLIAM CHANCE, *a Foot-Pad and House-Breaker.*

*W*ILLIAM CHANCE, was Born but of mean Parents, near *Colchester* in the County of *Essex*, by whom he had not the least Learning at all bestow'd upon him, tho' he was from his very Infancy a Child that shew'd a promising Genius and vivicity of Wit, as appears by his following pretty Answer which he made to a Gentleman that once ask'd him the Way to a certain Place, when he was not above seven Years old ; for one Day when *Will*'s Father and Mother were gone out, he was left at Home alone, when there chanced to come by that Way a Gentleman on Horseback, who seeing no Soul, rode up to the House, and bending his Body within the Door, call'd out to know if there was any
Body

Body within, *Yes,* says Will, *there's a Man and a Half, and the Head of a Horse, for you are Half of you within the House, with your Horse's Head, and I am a Man entire.* Upon this, the Gentleman ask'd where his Father and Mother were, and he reply'd, *My Father is gone to make of one bad Thing another far worse, and my Mother is for Shame, or Injury.* Says the Gentleman, *How so?* Why, says *Will, my Father out of one bad Way, makes another Worse, for he makes Ditches that no Body should come upon Peoples Grounds; and my Mother is gone to borrow a Loaf, and if she returns one less it is a Shame, and if she does not repay it all, it is an* Injury. Upon this the Gentleman ask'd him which was the best Way to such a Place? *Will.* answer'd, *Go where these Goslins go.* But as soon as the Gentleman set Spurs to his Horse, the green Geese flew into the Water. The Traveller was in doubt what Way to take, and turning back to *Will.* told him the Geese had fled away into the Water: *It may be so truly* (says our young arch One) *but I told you, you should go where they go, but not where they swim.* Whereupon the Gentleman was forc'd to ride farther a-Field to find out a better Guide.

But when *Will.* came to be about 16 Years of Age, he was put out 'Prentice by the Parish to a Weaver in *Colchester,* where he was so unlucky, and light Finger'd withal, that at 3 Years end his Master gave him his Indentures, and sent him packing to shift for himself.

Now

Now to fupport himfelf, he takes to Thieving, but was fo good a Proficient in the Art and Miftery of taking what was not his ówn, that he was not difcover'd in it, tho' People watch'd him very narrowly, and flighted his Converfation, excepting one thaťwas then Mayor of *Colchefter*, who took a great Fancy to *Will's* Archnefs, and was in fuch Favour with him, that he often din'd with him at his Table. So one Day above the reft, after Dinner, fays Mr. Mayor, Will, *I have often heard of thy Dexterity ; if thou wilt this Night fteal the Bed I lie upon out of my Chamber, I'll give you 5 Guineas ; and this I promife you on the Word of a Gentleman.* Will was very much troubled at this Propofal of the Mayor, and anfwer'd him after this Manner. *Sir, I am apt to think by what you now fay, that you take me for a Thief, but I do affure you I am no Thief, nor the Son of a Thief, but get my Living by my own proper Induftry, and the Sweat of my Brows ; but if it be your Pleafure that I fhould be brought to an untimely End, for what you would now have me do, I fhall for the great Love and Refpect I now have, and always had for you, endeavour to do it, and if I die, I die contented, becaufe it is to pleafe you, from whom I have receiv'd fo many fingular Favours.* Having faid this, he left the Mayor, without giving him Time to reply, and went walking about, confidering with him felf how he might fteal this Bed. At laft, a Thought came into his Head, which he believ'd would do his Bufinefs. You muft

muſt know then that a Doctor of Phyſick died
ſome Days before in *Colcheſter*, and was buried
there in St. *Mary*'s Church-Yard ; *Will* goes
in the Dead of the Night, and digging up the
Grave, takes out the dead Body by the Heels,
and taking him upon his Back, walk'd gently
on towards the Mayor's Houſe unobſerv'd, and
mounting up a Ladder, which he had purpoſe-
ly contriv'd to ſtand at one Corner, very
fairly began to untyle that Part of the Houſe
over the Chamber where the Mayor lay. But
as this made ſome Noiſe, ſo it of Courſe
awaken'd the Mayor, who being a Widower
lay then alone, expecting at the ſame Time
the Event. Scarce was a Hole made in the
Roof of the Houſe, when *Will* let fall the
Doctor through, the Noiſe ſurpriz'd the May-
or to be ſure, and hearing no one ſtir, he riſes
out of his Bed, and by the help of a Candle,
that was burning in the Chimney, he plainly
diſcover'd, as he thought, betwixt Fright and
Fear, the Body of *Will* on the Floor, who he
imagin'd had broken his Neck by the Fall.
This gave the Mayor no ſmall uneaſineſs, and
he began to lament his Curioſity in the moſt
doleful Terms. *Unhappy Wretch that I am*
(ſays he) *what ſhall I do now ? What will the
World ſay of me when they ſhall know that I have
been the Occaſion of this Fellow's untimely Death ?
But well, it cannot be help'd now, I muſt e'en
convey him out as well as I can.* So calling to
one of his Men, in whom he could ſafely con-
fide, quoth he, *See here*, Tom, *what a ſtrange*
Tran-

Tranſaction has happen'd, by one that I thought little of, Will. Chance, *whom I have ſo often entertain'd at my Table, has attempted to break into my Houſe, to rob me, but in the Attempt has broke his Neck: Oh! horrid Ingratitude, to commit this Folly to his beſt of Friends; however, I have that Pity for his Misfortune, that to hide form the World upon what an unlawful Account he came by his Death, you, and I,* Tom, *will take the Pains privately to bury him; the Church-Yard is near at Hand, and 'tis now the dead Time of the Night, ſo that before Break of Day we can dig a ſhallow Grave, and throw him into it.* The Man in compliance to his Maſter's Pleaſure conſented, who alſo in a ſort of Surprize took the dead Corps for *Will. Chance*, becauſe he had put his Coat upon him; ſo wraping him up in an old Blanket, away they trug'd to the Church-Yard, where finding a Grave ready made to their Hands, they flung their Load into (tho' unknown to them) its proper Place. In the mean Time as the Mayor and his Man were Abroad, *Will. Chance* got into the Houſe, and carried off his Bed; which when they return'd back, put them into a worſe Fright than before, as ſuppoſing *Will's* Ghoſt had, in their Abſence, play'd the Thief, to be reveng'd on the ſudden Loſs of its earthly Tabernacle. But that which ſhortly after rais'd their Admiration more, was next Day, when *Will. Chance* came in *propria perſona* to demand the 5 Guineas of the Mayor, according to his

former

former Promife. At firft he would not believe his own Eyes, really taking him for a
Hobgoblin, 'till he felt he was Flefh and Blood,
and then being acquainted with *Will*'s whole
Stratagem, how he got his Bed, he accordingly
paid him 5 Guineas.

Shortly after this Adventure *Will. Chance*
committing fome petty Larcenies in *Colchefter*,
he was by a Bench of Juftices given to an
Officer to carry into *Flanders* for a Soldier,
and accordingly he was put on Board a Pacquet-Boat at *Harwich*, which lying ftill at
Anchor for a fair Wind, he in the Night took
the Opportunity of leaping over Board unperceiv'd, and fwiming a Shore, made his
Efcape : But not daring to return Home he
rov'd about the Country, Robbing now and
then upon the *Foot-Pad* for a Livelyhood ; and
once furprizing Sir *Jonathan Thornicroft*, Bart.
he unawares knock'd him off of his Horfe,
and rifled him of a Diamond Ring worth 120
Pounds, a Gold Watch worth 50 Pounds,
and 290 Guineas. A great Noife of this Robbery being made all over the Country, with
the Promife of a Reward of 100 Pounds for
any that did difcover this bold Robber ;
whereupon *Will.* putting himfelf into a
genteel Equipage, fled to a rich Uncle which
he had at *Theford* in the County of *Norfolk*,
to lie up there *Incognito*, 'till this Noife
and Hubbub was all over. His Uncle was
a very rich Grazier, who carefs'd and receiv'd him with all fignal Tokens of Re-
fpects,

spect, and Marks of Friendship, as could possibly be shown a near Relation ; nay, in such Sort that *Will.* (had not *Satan* blown up those infernal Sparks which were bred in the Bone) should not have found in his Heart to play him the Prank he afterwards did ; but where Covetousness acts for Empire, Vertue must give Place ; so far was it predominate in him, that forgeting all Humanity, he continues in the Resolution of Cheating him ; and after some Discourse counterchang'd, which smel'd of nothing else but Courtesy and Piety on his side, he fell to bargaining with him, and bought 20 Oxen, paying down 30 Pounds, and signing an Obligation for the rest, which he promis'd to pay within a Month or Two, and having taken leave of his Uncle, he hired one to drive the Oxen to *Norwich.* After 2 or 3 Months were expir'd, the old Gentleman not hearing from *Will,* turns him to his Writings, where he found the Nest, but the Birds flown, for *Will* had temper'd the Ink with Saltpetre, and other corrosive Ingredients, which eat through the Paper: This startled the old Man so, that he suddenly took Pen in Hand; and writ the following Lines.

Cousin,

S I N C E Fate will have it so, that I must stile you thus, it makes my Blood to boil, and renders me sensible of an inward Grief, to think how I am lock'd in Bonds of Affinity with one who is a Perpetrator of such hellish Practices,
and

and damnable Inventions, as I, to my smarting find you guilty in, notwithstanding your hypocritical Expressions when I saw you last; do you think that God directs the World blindfold? Or that your wicked Actions will go unrewarded? Leave off (I advise you) these unjust Courses; and if you desire either Grace, or Prosperity, make Expiation for your past Trespasses, by a sincere and unfeign'd Contrition; rendering to every Man his own, and to me that which you stand indebted; or otherwise rest confident, that I will not only have it by due Course of Law, but also bereave you of your Reputation, if you have any. This consider, and do as you tender your Welfare. I am

Edmund Chance.

Will, so soon as he had receiv'd this Letter, seem'd to be greatly concern'd at the Matter, and the better to maintain his Esteem with supporting Appearence against any future Suspicion, he cries Whore first, and summon'd his Uncle to appear at the Assizes at *Norwich,* having in the mean Time suborn'd a false Witness or Two, to give Evidence to a forg'd Paper, he had caus'd to be written, wherein his Uncle was found to confess himself indebted to the Father of *Will.* in the Sum of 600 Pounds, payable in case of his Decease, to this his unlucky Son; whereto the usual Hand and Mark of the Uncle was artificially Counterfeited, with a different Ink from the Body of the

Obliga-

Obligation, both temper'd with Soot, to seem a Writing of such standing as the Date would require. Besides this, he had also forg'd a certain Discharge, the Tenor whereof was thus,

I the underwritten do acknowledge and confess, to have received from the Hands of Edmund Chance, *my Uncle, twenty Oxen, valued according to bargain, between my said Uncle and my self, the Sum of two hundred Pounds, which I receive in Payment and Abatement of the Sum of six hundred Pounds, due to me from the said* Edmund Chance, *by Virtue of a Writing obligatory, for Monies lent and contracted by Merchandize. Which said sum of two hundred Pounds, shall be accountable as Part of Payment and Abatement, of the said Sum of six hundred Pounds, without Fraud, or cover. Sign'd at* Colchester, &c.

William Chance.

This Acquittance was cunningly seal'd up, and sent in a Letter to a Countryman that liv'd near *Colchester,* whom he had also hir'd to be an Assistant in the Matter ; and he according to the Order of *Will,* deliver'd it to his Uncle, in the Presence of the Court. *Will,* so soon as he saw him begin to open it, pray'd the Court to examine his Papers, which they did, and found the Discharge, that made so much for *Will,* that Judgment was pass'd in his Favour, and the Defendant constrain'd not only to renounce his Pretence, but also condemn'd

demn'd to pay the fuppos'd Remainder of the
Sum that was mention'd in the Obligation,
which (the Price of the Oxen deducted, and
the 30 Pounds he paid down) was 430 Pounds.

But not long after this Succefs in his Villany, a certain Goldfmith in *Norwich*, whom
he had cheated out of a Note of 50 Pounds,
took upon him to be reveng'd on him for it,
which he thus put in Practice. He had in his
Houfe a Servant-Maid, to whom he imparted
his Defign, and giving her Inftructions, he deliver'd her 2 Pair of Pendants, the one Pair
True, the other Falfe, but fo like each other
in Fafhion, that an ordinary Judgment could
not diftinguifh them. With thefe fhe pofts
her Way to *Will. Chance*, who now had Money enough, where coming to fpeak with him,
fhe proffer'd them to fale, telling him that fhe
was of good Parentage, notwithftanding her
then being in the State of a Servant, in which
Condition fhe had diligently ferv'd for feveral
Years together, and fo had got a fmall Sum of
Money, which fhe intended to difpofe of to
an advantageous End, only wanted about 10
Pounds more, which fhe pray'd him that he
would do her the Favour to lend her upon the
Pendants. *Will. Chance*, who had a reafonable
Judgment in Jewels, could not value them
lefs than 6 Times the Money, readily gave
her the Sum fhe ask'd upon them, on Condition fhe fhould pay 20 Shillings *per* Month
Intereft; and put his Mark to a Writing whereby he confefs'd to have receiv'd fuch Jewels
from

from her, which upon Payment of the Monies lent, he was oblig'd to make Reſtitution of. Whilſt he was thus buſy in ſigning the ſaid Note, the Wench clandeſtinely drew out the falſe Pendants, and convey'd the true Ones into her Handkerchief, which ſhe laid on the Table, as a neceſſary Inſtrument for a *Hocus Pocus* Trick in Time of need. For that Time they took their Leave of each other, and the Maid returns to her Maſter, and told him what had paſs'd, which pleas'd him extreamly well. Some Time after the Goldſmith and *Chance* accidently met one another, when calling to Mind, how he had lately been cheated by a Servant Wench (not knowing that it was a Contrivance of the Goldſmith, whom he thought at this Time to be Friends with him) ſet up his Wind-Pipes, and told the Story ; ſharply reprehending the Vices and ungodly Practices of this iron Age, and gloſs'd the whole Matter with ſo much Candour and Integrity, that the Goldſmith, if his Conſcience had not been aſleep, muſt needs have repented his deſign'd Revenge. Never were 2 better met, the one acting Innocency, and the other Puritan ; *Will.* often crying out, *Good-lack-a-Day, what will this wicked World come to at laſt ? well, is it poſſible! what a ſinful Age is this we live in !* and the like. After this Manner they ſpent their Way, 'till they arriv'd at the Goldſmith's Houſe, whither he had invited *Will.* to Dinner. They were no ſooner enter'd in a-Doors, but in comes the
Maid,

Maid, whom *Will,* fo foon as he faw, knew
to be the fame that had put a Trick upon him.
He was no longer able to with-hold his Fury,
but immediately taxes her with the Cheat,
and gave her a whole Volly of Whores and
Jades. But the Wench, who had no fmall
Meafure of Impudence, firſt made as if ſhe
was amaz'd, and afterwards began to act her
Part, telling him that he was a Cheat, and
that he ſhould not put her off fo, in faying
that the Pendants were Counterfeit, which
ſhe had brought him, for ſhe could bring ma-
nifeſt Proof to the contrary. Upon that ſhe
ran out in all haſte and call'd an Officer, who
arreſted him there in the Room. *Will* thus
furpriz'd, addreſſes himſelf to the Goldſmith,
and makes his Complaint, what hard Meafure
he had. But the Goldſmith inſtead of comforting him, threaten'd to fall upon his Bones;
faying, *You Rafcal! think you that I will juſtify
your Villany, or that your hypocritical Expreſſions
have wrought fo far upon me, as to have ſuch a
mean Conceit of this Gentlewoman, who is as
well fam'd for her Vertue, as thou art infamous
for thy Infamy. Theſe Jewels to my Knowledge
are not Falſe, but it is thy Naughtineſs would
perſuade me to it, for they have been twice fold
for more than 50 Pounds, and if thou wilt not
return them, we'll convert thy Bones into Dice.
So Officer take him away.* Accordingly *Will's*
hurried to a Spunging-Houfe, where he began
to look about if he could fee a Hole to make
his Eſcape, and at laſt efpy'd one, through
which

which he forc'd his swinging Carcase, though
that being far from the Ground on the outside,
he durst not jump off; but seeing a little
thatch'd House on the North-side of the Prison, he resolves to fly that Way, and off he
comes; but the Roof being a little too weak,
he fell quite through, and so upon a Bed, on
which lay a young Country Wench, and her
Paramour, without the Knowledge of her Father, or Mother. These Sinners were not a
little amaz'd, but thinking that some Judgment
was come upon them for their wicked Doings,
it being dark, one ran one Way, and the
other another Way, but whither, I protest,
I never yet could learn; however, *Will.* ran
away too, with his Tail between his Legs,
and made all the haste he could for *London.*

Now *Will. Chance* having soon exhausted all
his ill-got Money upon Drinking, Gaming,
and Whoring, he betakes himself to House-
breaking, for which he had been twice committed to *Newgate*, and try'd at the *Old-Baily*,
but had the good Luck to escape Hanging then,
because the Witnesses were defective in their
Evidence. This Success in his Roguery did
but still harden him in Wickedness, insomuch,
that there was not a Jayl throughout *London*,
for receiving Felons, but what he was more
than once a Tenant in. He was once condemn'd at *Hertford* Assizes for the Foot-Pad,
but his Time not yet being come to take his
Leave of the World by an untimely Death,
he was Repriev'd, and after an Imprisonment
of

of 2 Years and a half, he pleaded to a Pardon granted by Queen *ANNE*, and obtain'd his Liberty once more ; but not making good Ufe of his Freedom, and the Royal Mercy he receiv'd, he purfu'd his old Courfes, and went altogether upon the Foot-Pad, 'till he and another being apprehended for Robbing a Gentleman near *Paddington*, of a Silver-hilted Sword, and 42 Shillings in Money, they were committed to *Newgate*, where his Comrade making himself an Evidence, to fecure his own Neck ; when he came to take his Tryal at *Juftice Hall*, he was convicted and received Sentence of Death, which at firft he did not feem to value ; for whilft he was in the condemn'd Hold, he was very profligate, Swearing, Curfing, Drinking, Singing, and Dancing, to the great Hind'rance of other condemn'd Malefactors from their Devotion, but when the Dead-Warrant was brought the Night before his Death to the Lodge of *Newgate*, his Countenance chang'd at the fatal News, and he began to employ the few Minutes he was to live in ferious Meditations of his approaching End, which was on *Wednefday* the 21ft of *April* 1715, when he was Hang'd at *Ty-burn*, Aged 35 Years.

Colonel

Colonel JAMES TURNER, a Houſe-Breaker.

JAMES TURNER, was Born in the City of *Worceſter*, in the Year 1609, of very wealthy Parents, who put him Apprentice to a Goldſmith in *London*, where, when he had ſerv'd out his Time, they ſet him up with no leſs Stock than the Sum of 3000 Pounds, which ſoon got him a Wife, who was a Fortune of 2000 Pounds more, with which becoming a very thriving Man in the World, and taking great Delight in the military Art, he at laſt was made a Captain in the Train'd-Bands, arriv'd next to a Major's Poſt, next, to that of a Lieutenant-Colonel, and at laſt to be a Colonel.

But theſe high Poſts cauſing him to keep as high Company, and when he March'd out with his Regiment, being very expenſive in his Entertainments, inſomuch that his Extravagancy both in private and publick, very much drain'd his Pocket, ſo to keep up his Character and Grandeur, his Pride and Ambition, incited him to act ſome clandeſtine Matters, which his Station and great Buſineſs,

N   ſor

for some Time shrouded from the World; but yet they were not carried on with so much Secrecy, but that some of 'em came to be discover'd, as you shall hear by the Sequel of the following Narrations.

One Day Colonel *Turner* applying himself to an eminent Merchant of *London*, whose chief Traffick was in the *Streights*, and at *Greenland*, whither he sent every Year several Ships ; of this same Merchant he bought to the Value of 260 Pounds in Train-Oyl and Whalebone , besides 128 Pounds in Rice , which he promis'd to pay for upon Delivery; for which purpose he next Day repairs to the Merchant's House, with a Bag of Money, where the Goods were deliver'd, *Turner* tenders him the Money in Gold, amounting to 361 Guineas, wanting but 18 Pence, for which the Merchant signs an Acquittance. Now *Turner* in the mean Time had a Couple of Comrades of his not far off all the while, whom he had instructed what to do, and now seeing an Opportunity, they stept up to the Door, and one of 'em calling the Merchant aside, as if he had earnest Business to impart to him, held him up with an invented Story, while the other clandestinely takes up the Bag of Gold, and Acquittance, and steals away with his Consort. When *Turner* saw all effected, he walks demurely back again with the Merchant into the Compting-House, where seeing the Money, and Paper gone, began to rage and stamp like one mad, not knowing what
to

to do in the Case, but at laſt began to upbraid *Turner* with Theft. *Turner* highly incens'd at the Affront, began to give him ſcurvy Language, which was again retaliated; in ſhort, to high Words they came, and from Words to Blows, when the Merchant had the worſt of it, and *Turner* acquainting him of his Occupation, and Colonel's Poſt in the Train'd-Bands the Merchant cry'd *Peccavi*, and begg'd Pardon for affronting a Man of his Character:

A little after this Exploit, being at *Chicheſter*, and his covetous thieving Diſpoſition inciting him to rob a wealthy Merchant there, he found out 4 or 5 Rogues, whom he brib'd to be aſiſting to him in this Affair, who glad of the Opportunity, promiſ'd to behave themſelve after his Directions. One of them was to paſs for a Baronet, dreſt and attir'd in a genteel Habit to ſuit his Character, and the others were put in Liveries, and to follow him as his Footmen. In the mean Time *Turner* knowing a certain Merchant at *London*, with whom this *Chicheſter* Merchant had great Dealings, Forges the following Letter from him at *London* to this in the Country.

Mr. Atkins,

THE Inclination which I have towards your Perſon, for many conſiderable Cauſes and Reaſons, moves me to let you underſtand of a rich Opportunity I have in ſerving you, in a Bargain of ſuch Commodities as I am ſenſible you deal in, which may tend to your Advantage, if

N 2　　　　　　　*you*

you have any Conveniency of coming up to London, *and honour me with your Presence; I make no doubt but you will think the Journey worth your while, and consequently make an advantageous Bargain, which is the only Desire and Hope of,*

> *Sir,*
> *Your humble Servant,*

Thomas Charlwood.

Atkins, upon the Reading of this Letter, determines to set forward to *London,* and make use of such an Opportunity, especially because the same Person from whom this Letter was suppos'd to come, had formerly sent him advice about some other particular Affairs, which fell out very luckily, and according to this Resolution sets forward that Night.

In the mean Time the sham Baronet being inform'd he was set out on his Journey, goes with his pretended Footmen to the Merchant's Wife, *Turner* having assur'd him that she was a brisk open-hearted Dame, and therefore gave him Encouragement to use the more Freedom with her. When he had got access, and found her in every Thing agreeable with the Character *Turner* had given him, he began first to entertain her with soft and fair Discourse, and so gradually to take a larger Liberty, 'till he had got the Scope he aim'd at, and won her Consent to go to Bed with him. This the Footmen marking, among whom *Turner*

per-

perfonated one, they acted their Parts with
the Maids below, who fpar'd not for Wine
all the Time, 'till the Maids were both fo
drunk, that they were not fenfible what they
did, and at laft fell both afleep, the one under
the Kitchen-Table, and the other in the Cel-
ler before the Tap, with a great Stone-Bottle
in her Arms. When the Footmen faw that
the Coaft was clear, the Miftrefs above with
their Mafter, the Maids faft afleep, and the
Doors, by Order of Mrs. *Atkins* fecurely
bolted, began to hunt up and down the Houfe
for Keys, which after a little feeking they
found, and went to a Money-Cheft, in which
they met with 1600 Guineas, and about 100
Pounds in Silver. Having got the Money,
they ran out, leaving the Door open, and
knock'd at fome of the Neighbour's Doors,
praying them to have the Goodnefs to come
to Mrs. *Atkins,* who lay defperately Sick:
This done, they betook them to their Heels.
The Neighbours, who held it a piece of Civility to vifit Mrs. *Atkins* in fuch a Time, efpe-
cially, as fome of them knew that her Huf-
band was gone from Home, went in, and going into the Chamber where fhe was wont to
lie, ftood a little at the Door, whifpering together, and at laft open'd the Door very foftly,
to go in. The pretended Baronet, hearing
the Door open, drew back the Curtain, and
fees 3 or 4 Women marching foftly towards
the Bed-fide; upon which he jumps out of
Bed in his Waftecoat and Drawers, and with
his Coat on his Arms made all the haft he

could

could to get out, before any more of that kind of People came; leaving his Breeches behind him, in which was the Copy of the abovesaid Letter. *Turner*, who tickl'd mightily, to see this Issue of his Project, was not far from them, but looking out, saw a heap of Seamen's Wives at the Merchant's Door; whereupon he ran forthwith to see what was the Matter, and after a little Enquiry learnt how the Matter was. *Well* (quoth he) *such People ought to be punish'd without Mercy who violate their Husbands Beds; it were a Sin in the highest Nature to conceal it; and those who would keep such Things from the Knowledge of Justice, deserve as much themselves.* So away he went, and presently Mrs. *Atkins* finding she was Robb'd, the Neighbours secur'd her Gallant, who was kept in Custody 'till the Return of her Husband, which was within 3 or 4 Days, who finding what had happen'd, was very ill at Ease, wishing he had not taken that Journey, being now asham'd to shew his Head Abroad, and restless with his Wife at Home; however, he was resolv'd to be at ease with both of them, for he got divorc'd from his Wife, and the following Assizes he Hang'd her Gallant.

Now *Turner's* Pockets being well lin'd with Gold, for he secur'd all the Guineas to himself, and pop'd his Fellow-Labourers off only with the 100 Pounds in Silver, and then making the best of his Way towards *London*, he puts up at an Inn in *Darking*, the Hostess whereof
was

was a Widow : Here he call'd briskly for Wine,
and was attended after the beſt Manner, but
lighting into a Company of Sharpers, and
falling to Dice with them, he loſt all his Money in one Night. He was now ready to
Hang himſelf, to think he ſhould be ſo unfortunate as to loſe all his Gold at once ; however,
he continu'd here ſtill, running in Debt for
his Horſe and himſelf, for above 14 Days, pretending that he ſhould ſhortly have 200 Pounds
return'd to him from ſome of his Tenants at
Portſmouth, writing Letters Daily (as he pretended) for that Purpoſe, to clear the Houſe
before he went. Nevertheleſs, every Time
Turner roſe from Table, his Landlady look'd
for her Money, who ſeeing nothing come but
a few airy Caſtles, at laſt aſſum'd the Boldneſs
to ask him, when he thought to pay her.
Turner then told her, that the next Day he
ſhould receive ſome Money for a Bargain of
Wine, he had ſold to a Vintner at *Goſport,*
and upon the Receipt of that Money he would
pay her. Now the Landlady perceiving him
to deal in Wine, pray'd him to ſhew her the
Way to purify Claret , *Turner* gives her ſome
Inſtructions in Writing, which he proteſted
coſt him a great deal of Money in *France.*
He told her beſides, that he had a Way to
make one Pipe or Veſſel, yield two Sorts of
Wine ; as for Example, if it be a Hogſhead
of White-Wine, that it ſhould run both White
and Claret, from the ſame Veſſel, at two ſeveral Cocks, as diſtinct and different, both in

4 4 Taſte

Taste and Colour, as if it were two Sorts of
Wine. The Landlady prays him to teach her
that Art, saying, that she was a poor Woman,
and burthen'd with a Charge of Children, and
by her late Husband's Negligence brought so
much in Debt, as she was never able to pay.
Turner, at first seem'd to scruple, saying, it
was a Mystery that only another besides himself in all *England* knew; however, said he,
I shall tell you on Condition that you will
swear upon your Honesty never to reveal it.
This she promis'd to do, and told him that
she would reckon him the Centre of her Happiness ever after. Well, quoth *Turner*, then
at Night we will try it, at what Time you
shall send your Maid of an Errand, and we in the
mean While will all get Things in a Readiness.
The Evening being come, the Landlady sends
out the Maid on a skeveless Errand, which she
thought would cost her an Hour or Two at
east; in the mean Time *Turner* provides him-
elf with an Auger, to pierce the Cask, and a
Paper or Two of Powders, which must be
the Ingredients; so calling his Landlady into
the Cellar, falls to boring a Hole in the Cask;
and then another; which when he had done,
cries out, *Good lack a Day, what have I forgot !
the main Ingredient I have in my Chamber, which
is the first that I must use :* And so pray'd the
Landlady to stop the other Hole so long with
her other Thumb, which she did. *Turner*
seeing her so hard engag'd at stopping, marching up Stairs into his Chamber, takes his Portmantua,

mantua, and rummaging the House finds a Bag
of Money, which was left to the Care of the
Landlady by a Butcher, and so trips off. The
Landlady being thus employ'd waited a while
with Patience, 'till she grew weary, begins to
cry out, *Where are you, Sir, if you stay much
longer, the Maid will come.* But no Answer
was made, she then calls out again, a second
and a third Time, still receiving no Answer;
whereupon she began to smell a Cheat, and
fain would she go to see for him, but could
not leave the Cask; and in this Posture she
was fain to stay 'till her Maid came Home,
who wondering to see her Mistress fast to the
Cask, ask'd her, what was the Matter? *Prithee* Nan (says the old Woman) *set your Thumbs
to these two Holes, 'till I go above.* The Maid
relieves the Mistress, and the Mistress runs in
all haste up Stairs, to see for her Guest, but
entering his Room finds him not, and going
into another, sees her Linnen and other Goods,
all on a heap together, whereupon she cries
out with a lamentable Voice, *Thieves, Thieves,
I am undone, I am robb'd, I am undone, all I
have in the World is Stoln.* The Maid hearing
her say so, forgets herself, and in all haste
runs up also, to see if her new Petticoat and
Headcloaths, were not Stoln likewise. The
Woman runs up and down the House like one
distracted, the more when she mist the Butcher's
Money; and the Maid runs out in all haste to
call in the Neighbours, who understanding the
Business, got an able Fellow to pursue *Turner,*

N 5

who

who by that Time was far enough out of their reach.

About 3 Days afterwards, *Turner* having taken a Compass round the Country, arrives at *Blandford* in *Dorsetshire*, where he takes up his Lodgings at an eminent Inn, and met accidently with a young Parson, with whom sitting at Supper, insinuated himself so far into his Acquaintance, that they became mighty Familiar. Next Day the Parson prays *Turner* to accompany him into the Fair then kept there for Horses, to buy one, and to give him his Judgment about it. *Turner* accordingly went with him, and a Horse the Parson Bought for 25 Pounds, which was carried Home to the Inn, and set up in the Stable, and shortly after they return'd, and supp'd together. Next Morning the Parson asks *Turner* whether he would Breakfast with him, to which he easily assented, and when they had done, they paid the Reckoning, when the Parson Saddles his Gelding, and makes himself ready for a Journey. *Turner* seeing him lay on a heavy Portmantua behind him, thought it more than a venial Sin to lose such a considerable Booty, so told him he would bear him Company part of the Way, if he would be pleas'd to accept of it. The Parson was glad to have his Company; so *Turner* immediately goes to a Hackney Stable, where he, with the Recommendation of the Landlord, hires an old Jade that could hardly trail her Legs after her. This done, they both mount, and so soon as they were

were got out of Town, the Parson being proud of his new-bought Gelding, rides out to try him, and then prays *Turner* to difmount, and try him, which he did, and lets the Parfon ride fo long on his old Hackney. *Turner* now mounted on the Gelding, rides a good Way forwards, and honeftly returns again, and fo a fecond Time a little farther, returning likewife again. But the Parfon taking more Delight to fee another ride his Horfe than himfelf, prays him to ride off again, which he did, and then fo far, that he never faw him after.

But tho' he made a very good outfide Show to the World, as going hitherto unfufpected in the Neighbourhood, for being fuch a Villain as he was, yet at laft being not fatisfy'd with what Wealth he had gotten by unlawful Means, he was refolv'd to Rob one Mr. *Francis Tryon*, a great Merchant in *Lime-Street*, *London*; and in order thereto, one of his Accomplices in the Dufk of the Evening hiding himfelf in a Cellar, when Mr. *Tryon* went to Bed, which was very early, his Man, and Maid Servant, went to a Friend's Houfe to Supper, which favourable Opportunity ferv'd very well for *Turner*'s Purpofe, who being let in by his Comrade at the Street-Door, they went up into Mr. *Tryon*'s Bed-Chamber, who was a very antient Man, where ufing him very barbaroufly, and inhumanly, they gagg'd and bound him Hand and Foot, and then going into the Ware-Houfe, they took from thence in Diamonds, Jewels, Saphires, Rubies, Emeralds,

ralds, Ophirs, Pearls, and other precious Stones, to the Value of 4907 Pounds, several Pieces of Gold, to the Value of 16 Pounds, 4 Shillings, and 3 Pence, and 1023 Pounds in Silver Money, number'd in all 5946 Pounds, 4 Shillings, and 3 Pence ; a great Part of which being found in *Turner's* House, and other Places where he had planted it ; he, and his Wife, *Mary Turner*, and his Sons, *John, William,* and *Ely Turner*, were all apprehended and committed to *Newgate*, by Sir *Thomas Allen,* Knt. and Alderman, and try'd for the same at *Justice-Hall* in the *Old-Baily,* where he was convicted, and had pronounc'd against him the following Judgment, *That he should go to the Place from whence he came, and so to that Place of Execution which shall be appointed to him by Authority, there to he Hang'd by the Neck 'till he be dead ; and the Lord have Mercy on his Soul.* But his Wife, and 3 Sons, were acquitted. And accordingly, the abovesaid Colonel *James Turner,* was drawn in a Cart from *Newgate* to *Lime-Street-End* in *Leaden-Hall-Street,* on the 21st of *January,* 1662-3, and there Executed on a Gibbet erected for that Purpose, Aged 53 Years.

JACK

JACK SHEPPARD, a Houfe-Breaker, and Foot-Pad: WILLIAM BLEWET, EDWARD BUN-WORTH, alias FRAZER, EMANUEL DICKENSON, &c. *Foot-Pads, and Murderers: CHRISTOPHER LEONARD, and JOHN DYER, alias JACK the COBLER, Highwaymen.*

SEVERAL Biographers, or Writers of Lives, have pretended to give an Account of the Tranfactions of thofe moft celebrated, but yet infamous Villains, *Jack Sheppard, Will. Blewet, Frazer, Dickenfon,* &c. and have omitted Paffages, which are the moft material Ones that occur'd in all their villainous Tranf-actions, whilft they refided on this Side the Grave, which take as follows.

Jack Sheppard, who was not only conten-porary with *Blewet, Frazer,* &c. but alfo joyn'd in a ftrict League with 'em to run the Courfe of the greateft Villanies that could be perpetrated by Mankind; had acted with 'em in feveral Exploits of Street-Robberies; one

of

of which was in the open Day Time, thus; A Gentleman coming out of a Hackney-Chair, to go into the House of the Honourable 'Squire H——y, in *Ruffel Street* by *Bloomsbury-Square*; *Sheppard*, prefently Collars him, under Pretence he was an Officer, and had a Writ againft him. The Gentleman asking, *At whofe Suit ?* Up ftep'd *Blewet*, and *Frazer*, as Followers to *Sheppard*, faying, *You fhall foon know at whofe Suit.* So hurrying the Gentleman into a Coach, they paid the Chairmen their Fare, who dar'd not prefume to a Refcue, and carried their pretended Prifoner to *Weftburn-Green*, on one Side *Padington*, and there difcharg'd the Coachman, as pretending to be within two or three Fields of Home; they Robb'd the Gentleman of a Gold Watch, a Gold Snuff-Box, a Gold Tweezer-Cafe, a Silver Hilted Sword, and a Purfe of 80 Guineas; then binding him Hand and Foot, they there left him, faying, they would truft him upon Parole of Honour, to find Bail to the Action, againft they came back again, or elfe they muft be oblig'd to carry him to Jayl, becaufe the Time was that Day expir'd for Return of the Writ.

Not long after this roguifh Exploit, they committed the like again upon one Madam *Stephenfon*, a Widow Gentlewoman, of about 500 *l. per Annum.* She was going through *Lincoln's-Inn-Fields*, to pay a Vifit to Sir J—— L——m's Lady : As fhe was knocking at the Gate, *Jack Sheppard*, in Company of *Blewet*,

and

and *Frazer*, Arrests her in a *Fob-Action* of 200
Pounds, and hurries her in a Coach to a blind
Ale-House in *Kent-Street*. This was done about
9 in the Morning, putting the Gentlewoman
into a great Surprize, who said she ow'd not
a Farthing in the World, nor did know any
such Person as their Writ express'd. Quoth
they, *Madam, whether you know, or do not know
the Plaintiff, we cannot help that, but we know
very well who employ'd us; therefore, that must
be Try'd at Law betwixt you two. But in
Respect to her Sex and Honour, they would not
presently carry her to Jayl, as her Plaintiff
earnestly desir'd them, but would give her the
Liberty of an Hour or Two of sending for Bail,
which if she did not do, she must excuse them,
if then (tho' much against their Will) they
put her under a stricter Confinement.* The poor
Gentlewoman return'd 'em Thanks for their
Civility, and giving them a Guinea, desir'd
'em to be at the Charge of sending a Porter to
two Gentlemen whom she nam'd, to come
presently to her. With a great deal of Complaisance the pretended Bailiffs take the Guinea,
and sent a Porter to where she order'd, and
both the Gentlemen immediately coming with
the Porter, in order to be Securities for the
Gentlewoman, they desir'd to see the Plaintiff,
Quoth *Sheppard*, and *Blewet*, the Plaintiff was
such a damn'd rigorous Fellow, that tho' they
had sent to him half a dozen Times to acquaint
him, that they had the Gentlewoman in
Custody, whom he order'd to arrest, he sent
Word,

Word, he would not come near her, but at their Peril requir'd the Debt, good Bail, or a Jayl. The Gentlemen said, they would then go themselves to him; so *Sheppard* calling a Coachman, to whom he had before given his Cue, away went the two Gentlemen, Gentlewoman, and the sham Officers, to *Kennington-Common*, and where discharging the Coachman, and it being Night, they next discharg'd the Prisoner, by taking her Gold Watch, and Diamond Ring, and from her Friends, the two Gentlemen, a Couple of Watches, and from all three about 240 Guineas; which they said should be Security enough without a Bail-Bond, for the Lady's Appearance, which they would leave to her own Pleasure.

Ned Bunworth, alias *Frazer*, being once committed to *New Prison*, on Suspicion of Robbing the *Exchequer*, and there lay some Time, 'till having a opportunity, Mr. *Everett*, the Turn-Key of the said Prison, being oblig'd to be at *Westminster* upon some Business on a Tryal, he made his Escape, there being several others in the Prison concern'd with him in endeavouring to obtain their Liberties, as one *Higgs*, since Executed with him for the Murder of Mr. *Ball*, and *Thomas Love*, since Transported for the *Kid-Lay*, they being at that Time Prisoners with him. *Bunworth* also there became first acquainted with *Christopher Leonard*, with whom he committed several most notorious Robberies on the Highway, Pad, *&c. Bunworth*, and *Leonard*, being two

as

as brave, bold, nimble, and ftout Fellows, as
has been Executed for this many Years, never
fearing any Thing that they went about.

The abovefaid *Chriftopher Leonard,* now in
Newgate, formerly an Evidence againft *Richard Trantrum,* and others, fince Executed at
Tybourn, for breaking open a Throfter's Houfe
in *Spittle Fields,* and taking from him Things
to a confiderable Value; he being a young
Man, and making Intereft, obtain'd his Liberty, but fince falling into a wicked Gang, fuch
as *Bunworth, Blewet,* &c. and with 'em hath
committed feveral moft notorious Robberies,
Fellonies, and Burglaries.

As alfo one *John Dyer,* alias *Jack the Cobler,*
now in *Newgate,* who lies for Tranfportation,
he being an Evidence againft feveral who were
Executed at *Tybourn,* for being concern'd with
them in feveral Robberies on the Highway; the
faid *Dyer* being committed to *New-Prifon,*
there to remain 'till he had convicted his Comrades; but he with one *Hugh Kelly,* now in
Newgate, and *Thomas Love,* did contrive to
make their Efcape, by Way of Murder; they
having agreed to watch an opportunity; the
firft Contrivance they had, was to have follow'd *Everett,* who then was Turn-Key between the Gates, and there to have cut his
Throat, but if that fail'd, they was to have
boar'd their Way through the *Hole,* which
was the Place where they lay; but *Kelly* being fomewhat Timerous, and not quite fo
Blood-Thirfty, difcover'd the Plot, by means
to

to find fome Favour ; the Recorder being inform'd of thefe barbarous and bloody Thoughts,
order'd them to be fafe convey'd to *Newgate* ;
where they now both are, and lie to be Tranfported ; there being a Razor, a Chizel, and a
large Boore, found conceal'd in *Dyer*'s Bed,
which was in a Hammock where he lay :
Kelly being one of the Perfons that fwore
againft *Jonathan Wild*, his Brother *Thief*, and
Thief-Taker.

But now to come more particularly and
clofer to *Blewet*, and *Higgs*, two of the moft
audacious and notorious Villains, that were
ever known in all preceeding Ages, or ever
will be paralliz'd in any to come ; when they
had Murder'd *Ball*, for the Thieves have now
made a League among themfeives, to be kept
fo inviolable, that they will never let a *Thief-
Taker* rife to that Height for the Future as the
late *Jonathan Wild*, of naufeous and infamous
Memory ; they and their Accomplices, fled
by different Routs for *Holland*, *Higgs*, and
another went by the Way of *Margate*, in
the Ifle of *Thanet* in *Kent* ; but *Will. Blewet*, and
two more of the Murderers (for *Marjeram*, *Legee*, and *Frazer*, remain'd in *England*) took their
Rout by the Way of *Harwich*, in *Effex*. As thefe
laft were going to make their Afylum in a
foreign Country, to be fcreen'd (as they hop'd,
but contrary to their Expeftation) from Juftce,
they met with one *Henry Sandal*, a Hop-Merchant, upon the Road betwixt *Colchefter* and
Maningtree ; whom pulling from his Horfe,
and

and taking a Silver Watch, Value 6 Pounds, and 11 Guineas ; quoth *Blewet* to his Comrades, *This is such a trifling Matter the old Rogue has about him, that we must put him in a Sweat.* So the said *Blewet* pissing in his Hat, and forcing *Sandal* to drink it off upon Pain of Death, at the same Time holding a Pistol to his Breast, they then forc'd him to strip himself stark naked ; then drawing their Swords, as the Hop-Merchant danc'd, according to their Direction, they now and then, gave him a Prick to move brisker, and to shew Capers, 'till at last he was so much out of Breath, that he fell down upon the Ground, as if expiring his last, which he did the next Day, through this Fatigue, and the Wounds they gave him, which prov'd a little too deep.

After the committing of this tragical Villany, they made the best of their Way for *Harwich,* where a favourable Gale wafted them over to *Holland* ; and at *Rotterdam* he and *Higgs,* met again. Hence they went to *Delf,* and from thence to the *Hague* : Here *Blewet,* and *Higgs,* went to one Mr. *Huggerswaert,* a *Dutch* Mercer, and bespeaking as much Silk, Velvets, and Sattins, which came to about 250 Pounds, for (as they pretended) an *English* Lady, then at *Delf* ; the said Mercer came along with 'em with the Goods towards *Delf* ; but within half a Mile of the Town, taking their desir'd Booty from him, they flung him into a Dike, where he lost both his Goods, and Life together.

Shedding the Blood of a Man, *Blewet*, and *Higgs*, no more valu'd than drinking a Morning's Draught together. And so undaunted were they at committing this Murder, that they had the unparallell'd Impudence to go back to the Deceas'd's Widow, and telling her her Husband was paid for what Goods he had carried out with him, and that she must lend another Parcel, which they then pitch'd upon, and came to about 150 Pounds more; the poor Woman deliver'd them to her Journey-Man, to carry to her Husband; but it being then the Dusk of the Evening, when they came to the *Green-House* in the Wood, on that Side towards *Delf*, they there took the Goods from the Man, gagg'd and ty'd him Neck and Heels, and made the best of their Way for *Amsterdam*, the Capital City of *Holland*.

Being arriv'd here with all their Booty, which they sold to a *Jew* for 236 Pistoles, they soon consum'd their wickedly got Gains, and return'd again to *Rotterdam*, but in the Way thither, they committed several Robberies betwixt *Amsterdam*, and the *Hague*; betwixt the *Hague*, and *Delf*; and in their Journey betwixt *Delf*, and *Rotterdam*, meeting with the Lady *Van Dickenson*, in her Coach, attended with two Footmen, besides the Coachman, they had the most audacious Impudence and Insolence, to attack her Ladyship at Noon-Day, taking from her a Gold Watch, a Diamond Ring, and 90 Pistoles; and whilst *Higgs*,

stood

ftood Guard over the Coachman, and the two Footmen, with a Piftol in each Hand, *Will. Blewet*, went into the Coach, and Ravifh'd the Lady; after which they cut the Reins and Braces, of the Horfes, and then proceeded on their Journey to *Rotterdam*.

When they were at *Rotterdam*, their riotous Living gave great Sufpicion, and upon the King of *Great-Britain*'s Proclamation being arriv'd in *Holland*, for the Apprehending fuch and fuch Perfons, nam'd in it, Guilty of Murder and Robberies in *England*, *William Blewet*, the grand Rogue, *Emanuel Dickenfon*, and *Thomas Berry*, alias *Teague*; *John Higgs*, and *Thomas Wilkins*, made their Efcape, the Firft of which was took coming from *Portfmouth*, were apprehended upon Sufpicion, and Advice thereof being difpatch'd, Meffengers were forthwith fent over, who brought 'em all hither in Chains.

Of the five Villains, that had fled thither, for Sheltr, onley the aforefaid three were then brought over. However, they were fafely conducted to their Country, excepting *Teague*, in iron Boots, put into *Salva Cuftodia*, and being brought to their Tryal at *Kingfton* upon *Thames*, in the County of *Surry*, they were there condemn'd. But tho' they were under Sentence of Death, yet were they fo far from preparing for their latter End, that they fpent the fhort Time they had to remain upon Earth, in all Vicioufnefs; for *Ned Bunworth*, alias *Frazier*, was always damning and finking, becaufe before he died, he had not Murder'd fuch Perfons,

fons, whom he and *Blewet*, had prick'd down
for Death ; he own'd with a great deal of
Pleafure, the Shooting of the Earl of *Har-
borough*'s Chairman ; and tho' under Sentence
of Death, he would often fay to the Prifoners,
*I fhall be fweetening in the Air, while you little
Dwarfs in Iniquity, will be ftinking in your
Graves.* And that he muft agree with fome
Body to wipe his Shoes this Summer, or elfe
they would be too Greafy. *William Blewet*,
who had the Honour of being Factor to the
late *Jonathan Wild*, for difpofing of his ill-got
Goods in *Holland*, was as wicked as *Bunworth*.
Dickenfon, a *Dutchman*, would often fwear,
That he was oblig'd to come and Rob in England,
*becaufe his own Country was fo miferable a Place,
that it would not afford him Provifion to fubfift
on, Wood to hang him on, nor Earth to bury him
in.* *Berry*, the *Irifhman*, faid, *He was Born
and Bred, to Live and Die a Rogue.* *Higgs*,
alias *Hicks*, faid, *He was only forry, that he
could not have a Game of Shuffle-Board before
he dy'd.* And *John Legg*, faid, *That if he
was Hang'd, he fhould never be his own Man
again.*

But their appointed Time being come, that
the Government thought fit they were not
worthy to live any longer upon Earth, they
were upon *Wednefday* the Sixth of *April*,
1726, Executed at *Kingfton* upon *Thames* ;
and *Will. Blewet*, and *Ned Bunworth*, as being
the greateft and moft notorious Villains, were
Hang'd in Chains in St. *George's* Fields, by
Southwark, near the Place where the Murder
was

was committed, *Emanuel Dickenſon*, and *Thomas Berry*, on *Kennington-Common* (the Firſt of which two was by Order of the Government ſince took down) and *John Higgs*, and *John Legee*, on the Road-Side between *Kingſton* and *London* (both ſince Stole away) for a Terror and Example to others, of being Guilty of Robberies, and Murders.

F I N I S.

A

Compleat LIST

OF THE

Most remarkable Rogues,
Things, and chiefest
Occurrences, relating
to them.

A

Pag.

ARnold Powel, *decently Hang'd*,
28.
Allen, *a Highwayman,* *up to the*

O   *Head*

The CONTENTS.

Pag.

Head and Ears in Love with a Bona
Roba, 44.
Attestation of the Ordinary of New-
gate, 182.

B

Blewet's Murders in England and Hol-
land, 282. 283.
Blewet, hang'd in Chains in St.George's
Fields, by Southwark, 286.

C

Chamber-Pot bor'd through, to the great
Prejudice of the Woman's Bed and
Husband, 101.
Captain Shavaleir, who was kill'd by his
own Grenadiers in the West of Eng-
land, Robb'd, 132.
Countess of Zealand had three hundred
sixty five Children at one Birth, 148.
Chance Hang'd, 264.

Dick.

The CONTENTS.

Pag.

Dick Shepherd, *Sh---ts before the King of* France, 213.

E

Elegy on Jonathan Wild, 23.
Epitaph on Jonathan Wild, 25.
English *Highwaymen Rob in* France, 92.
Epitaph on Barton *the Highwayman,* 111.
Eleonor Sympson *Hang'd,* 124.
Earl of Pembroke *Robb'd,* 129.

F

Fair most strangly haunted by Pick-Pockets, 126

G

Glanister, *an old Fence,* 42.

O 2   Gentle-

The CONTENTS.

Pag.

Gentlemen and Ladies Robb'd in one of
the present King's Coaches, 80.
General Fairfax *Robb'd upon the High-*
way, 149.

H

Hymn to Tybourn, 11.
Highwaymen Rob Highwaymen, 87.
Highwaymen Gagg'd and Robb'd, 233.
Highwayman turns Benedictine *Fryer,*
Robs and Ravishes his Penitenti-
aries, 131

I

Jonathan Wild's *high Birth and Educa-*
tion, 2.
Jonathan Wild's *great Title in the*
Weekly-Journal, 5.
Jonathan Wild *Hang'd,* 18
Jane Sprackling *Married to* Jonathan
Wild, 3.

Justice

The CONTENTS.

Pag.

Juſtice Saunders *Robb'd by a Jilt he
pick'd up,* 1-18.
Juſtice Saunders *like to have been cut for
a Calf,* 120.
Impoſthumes ſtrangely Cur'd, 126.
Information of Thomas Lichfield, 181.
Jack Blewit *rid of two Plagues at once,
a bad Wife, and a ſtinking Jayl,* 226.
Jack *the* Tinman, *takes a Gentlewoman
by the Breech, as making his Eſcape
out of a Jayl through a Houſe of
Office,* 234.

K

King's *Coach Robb'd on the Highway,*
80.
King James *the Firſt, helps to take Robbers and Murderers,* 147.

L

Lady Robb'd of *her Jewels,* 196.

O 3

The CONTENTS.

Pag.

Lawrence, *and* Clare's *Speeches, before*
Hang'd, 203.

M

Minister Reads one of the Chapters of St.
Paul's *second Epistle to the* Corrin-
thians *wrong,* 106.
Major Strangwayes *press'd to Death in*
Newgate, 165.
Mayor *of* Colchester's *Bed Stole from
under him,* 153.

N

Note *of* Talbot, 179.
------ *his Letter to a Person of Quality,*
177.
Norket *Murder'd by her Husband,* Grand-
mother, *and Aunt,* 116.

Oliver

The CONTENTS.

O

Pag.

Oliver Cromwell *Robb'd,* 152.
Oliver Cromwell *Crown'd with the Close-Stool-Pan,* 153.

P

Parquot, *a* Frenchman, *Hang'd for Robbing in* England, 33.
Price, *at the Bell in the* Old-Baily, *Robb'd of two Silver Tankards,* 97.
Pembroke *rides with his Face to the Horse's Arse,* 148.

Q

Quilt Arnold, Jonathan Wild's *Clerk,* 14.
Question ask'd by the Watchmen in Gray's Inn Lane, 74.

Richard

The CONTENTS.

Pag.

Richard Jewkes, *Robb'd in a Bawdy-House,* 99.
Richard Keel, *and* Lowther, *Hang'd in Chains at* Holloway, 106.

S

Song of Chivy-Chace, *Sung by a Clerk of the Parish at Church, instead of a Psalm,* 167
Speech of Barton, *one of the* Blacks *of* Waltham, *lately Hang'd,* 113.
Sawney Beane, *Executed, with his Wife, eight Sons, Six Daughter, eighteen Grand-Sons, and fourteen Grand-Daughters,* 144.
Sham Letters, 180.
Sir Jonathan Thornicroft *Robb'd,* 256.
Shepherd *brings a Skeleton from the Gallows to his Master,* 209.
Strangwayes's *Letter to his Brother before press'd to Death,* 170.

Talbot's

The CONTENTS.

T

Pag.

Talbot's *Account of his being* dogg'd *and* *stabb'd,* 177.

Turner *a House-Breaker,* 265.

Turner's *sham Letter,* 267.

Turner *Hang'd at* Lyme-Street End, 276,

V.

Viscount Dundee *cunningly* Robb'd, 126.

W

Wild *Drunk at the Gallows,* 18.

Wright, *Perruke-Maker,* Hang'd *alive* *for not dealing honestly in* live *Hair,* 36.

Wooldridge, *a Broker of* Harp-Ally, *kill'd,* 52.

Wilson *thrusts his Cane through the* Picture *of* our Saviour's Crucifixion, *in*

The CONTENTS.

Pag.

in the Bodleian *Library at* Oxford,
　　　　　　　　　　　　　51.
Wilson's *bold Exploits on the Highway,*
　　　　　　　　　　85 86.
William, *and* John Hawkins, *Highwaymen,*　　　　　49. 65.

Y

*Yeoman of the Guard lets the King's
Lodgings be Robb'd, by way of Civility,*
　　　　　　　　　　　　　42.

Z

Zachary Howard *Hang'd,*　　155.
Zachary Clare, *a Baker's Son at* Hackney, *Hang'd.*　　　　　203.

This Day is Publish'd, by S AM. B RISCOE, *at the* Bell-Savage *on* Ludgate-Hill, *the following Books.*

I. THE Memoirs of the Rife and Fall, of the great Mr. *Law,* in *France*; during the Administration of the late Regent, and the prefent Duke of *Bourbon.* Written by a *Scotch* Gentleman, who was privy to all thefe Transactions. The third Edition. Price 1 *s.*

II. The *Merry Traveller*; or a *Trip upon ten Toes* from *Morefields* to *Bromley* in *Kent*: An Humourous Poem, on their pleafent Adventure thro' the Town, *Southwark,* and on the Road. By the Author of the *Cavalcade.* Price 1 *s.*

III. *Whipping Tom's New-Year's Gift*; or a Rod for a *Proud-Pady,* newly bundled up in five feeling Difcourfes, Serious and Comical, that touch the Fair-Sex to the Quick, on their immodeft Drefs, Behaviour at the Toylet, and lewd Tittle-Tattle over their poifonous Tea. In Profe and Verfe. By the Author of the firft Part. Price 1 *s.*

IV. *The Delights of the Bottle,* or the Humours of a Tavern : A merry Poem. By the Author of the *Cavalcade.* Price 1 *s.*

V. *De-*

BOOKS Printed for &c.

V. *Democritus*, or a Week's Trip round *London* and *Westminster*. Price 1 s.

VI. The Character of King *Charles* II. By the Duke of *Buckingham*. With a Conference between *George* late Duke, and a Jesuit, whom King *James* sent to convert him in his Sickness. Price 6 d.

VII. *George* late Duke of *Buckingham*'s Key to his Play of the *Rehearsal*. Price 6 d.

VIII. *The State of the Law*, or an Alphabetical List of Honest Attornies of Town and Country, the Places where they live, or to be found, in *London*. In two Parts. Price 1 s. 6 d.

IX. There will speedily be Publish'd; at the Desire of several Gentlemen; *The Appendix*, or third Part. Therefore if any honest Attornies, in Town or Country, will send his Name, it shall be inserted, if sent to *Sam. Briscoe*, at the *Bell-Savage* on *Ludgate-Hill*, paying the Postage.

X. Essay in Praise of Knavery. Price 1 s.

XI The Secret History of the *Free-Masons*, from their own M. S. Roll, writ above 200 Years. Price 1 s.